Risk-Based E-Business Testing

For a listing of recent titles in the *Artech House Computing Library,*
turn to the back of this book.

Risk-Based E-Business Testing

Paul Gerrard
Neil Thompson

Artech House
Boston • London
www.artechhouse.com

Library of Congress Cataloging-in-Publication Data
Gerrard, Paul.
    Risk-based e-business testing / Paul Gerrard, Neil Thompson.
      p.   cm. — (Artech House computing library)
    Includes bibliographical references and index.
    ISBN 1-58053-314-0 (alk. paper)
    1. Electronic commerce—Management.   2. Risk management.
  I. Thompson, Neil.   II. Title.   III. Artech House computing library.

HF5548.32 .G468   2002
658.8'4—dc21   2002074496

British Library Cataloguing in Publication Data
Gerrard, Paul
    Risk-based e-business testing. — (Artech House computing library)
    1. Computer systems—Testing   2. Risk management   3. Electronic
    commerce—Computer networks
    I. Title   II. Thompson, Neil
    005.1'4

    ISBN 1-58053-314-0

Cover design by Igor Valdman

Microsoft® screen shots reprinted by permission from Microsoft Corporation.

Netscape browser window © 2002 Netscape Communications Corporation. Used with permission. Netscape Communications has not authorized, sponsored, endorsed, or approved this publication and is not responsible for its content.

© 2002 ARTECH HOUSE, INC.
685 Canton Street
Norwood, MA 02062

International Standard Book Number: 1-58053-314-0
Library of Congress Catalog Card Number: 2002074496

10 9 8 7 6 5 4 3 2 1

To my family: Julia, Max, and Lizzie
—Paul

*To the memory of my father, who served the public with information
in the days before the Web and knew the meaning of quality*
—Neil

*To all those testers who do the best job they can,
but always think they should be doing more*
—Paul and Neil

Contents

Preface

There were two motivations for writing this book. First, I am continually trying to organize the flood of information that comes at me from all directions to make sense of it all. In the vain hope that there is always a better way to organize ideas, I find myself grouping ideas together and continually looking for patterns in the way these groups relate to each other. It's a bit like indexing, and it helps me to remember stuff. When I encounter a new problem and a solution is required, I can retrieve the relevant information quickly, even if I learned it years ago and never used it in the same way before. In deciding to write this book, I wanted to provide an organized collection of methods, techniques, and tools for testing e-business systems. The organization of these methods should make it easy for someone embarking on a new project to make some sensible decisions about what to do. I wanted the book to work for high-adrenaline, high-pressure, fast-paced projects, but also for more comfortable, well-resourced, highly organized projects (although all projects involve adrenaline, pressure, and a fast pace at the end).

The second motivation for writing this book was my dissatisfaction with the use of risk as a driver for testing. For as long as I can remember, testing experts and practitioners have talked about risk, risk-based testing, and how testing addresses risk. I tried to understand risk-based testing better, but when I looked for deeper insight into risk and testing, there seemed to be little hard information to go on. The usual mantra trotted out states that risks are bad; testing addresses risk, so we should test to find as many bugs as we can to mitigate that risk. When I speak to testers and ask what a risk is, I have usually gotten a description of various types of bugs. Now, I'm not saying there's anything wrong with the notion that risks can be types of potential bugs and that testers should focus on these in their testing. The main goal of a tester is to expose faults in software, and I've been preaching that to testing classes for 10 years now. This simple idea is fine when it comes to designing some test cases, but I don't think it is a useful strategy for planning the test effort in a large project or in a project with extreme time pressures or without requirements or, well, any project I can think of.

The discipline commonly called *risk management* defines risk subtly and less tangibly. I've read a few books on risk now, and the relationship between risk management and testing is a little tenuous too. Most risk-management methods treat risks at too high a level to be useful for testers. This is no surprise. How many types of bugs could you think of? Thousands before lunchtime, probably! There is a gap between what management thinks a risk is and what testers do. There is a second problem, however; testers can't use the risk-management discipline as their managers do. Risk management doesn't scale up to larger volumes. What does risk-based testing mean if there is such a disconnect between management and test practitioners? Risk-based testing sounds good, but what does it mean to a manager who is doing risk-based project management?

The risk-based test methodology set out in the initial chapters of this book attempts to use early risk analysis to connect the concerns and objectives of senior management with the test process and activities of the project's testers. The consequences of so doing are obvious; most of them are beneficial. If the test process is developed specifically to address the risks of concern to stakeholders and management, we get the following results:

- Management is better able to view the testing and so has more control over it.

- The budget for testing is likely to be more realistic.

- The testers have a clearer understanding of what they should be doing.

- The budget allocated to testing is determined by consensus, so everyone buys into the quantity of testing planned.

- The information-provision role of testers is promoted, but fault detection is as important as ever.

- The information provided by testers increases their influence on management decision making.

- Release decision making is better informed.

The risk-based methodology integrates nicely with an inventory of product risks, grouped by the specific test techniques that address them. The product risks detailed in Chapters 9 through 15 can be taken together and used as a candidate risk register to get a project risk analysis off the ground. By combining a methodology for creating a test process with a library of risks, each having associated test techniques, test managers have a ready-made handbook for building a master test plan that is comprehensive without being too prescriptive.

The risk-based test method is universal. Risks pervade all software projects, and risk taking is inevitable. This book attempts to help identify a project's relevant risks and focus the attention of testers onto the risks of most concern. Testing aims to mitigate risk by finding faults, but it also aims to reduce uncertainty about risk by providing better risk information to management, enabling management to better steer their projects away from hazards and make better decisions.

Audience

This book is aimed at test managers and people who test. It should be useful to developers and testers working on large, well-organized projects, as well as those working on projects so small (or chaotic) that no specific testing or test management role has been defined. The test techniques chapters should be informative to people who are new to e-business and the Internet and those who have specialized in one testing area. Project managers interested in implementing a risk-based approach to testing should find the early chapters on risk and the later chapters on making it happen of use. The book should also be of interest to students wishing to understand how test planning, design, and execution activities can be integrated with project risk management.

Structure

Part I Chapters 1 through 4 provide an introduction to risk-based testing and the relationship between risk management, risks, and the testing process. Testers are encouraged to use the language of risk to articulate their missions and negotiate test budgets with management and stakeholders. A methodology for creating a test process based on a consensus view of product risk is presented.

Part II Chapters 5 through 8 set out the types of failure that e-business systems are prone to and the threat those failures present to these systems. Of course, a test strategy needs to take into account many factors other than risks, and these other factors are described. The test types and techniques are organized into a test process framework, together with the other considerations relevant to formulating a test process.

Part III After a short introduction, Chapters 9 through 15 present 24 techniques for testing e-business systems. Each chapter summarizes the risks covered by the techniques, then presents the techniques in some detail, and ends with a list of tools and references for further reading. Chapter 16 covers postdeployment monitoring, and Chapter 17 provides a summary of the tool types that are useful to the e-business tester, together with some guidelines for their selection and use.

 Chapters 9 through 15 describe the e-business test techniques in more detail. The test techniques are grouped under the test type headings identified in Table 7.1, the Test Process Framework. There are two further chapters added: Chapter 16 covers postdeployment monitoring and Chapter 17 provides a summary of the tool types that are useful to the e-business tester with some guidelines for the use of proprietary tools. Appendix B provides some ideas for simple home-brew tools that might help in your functional testing.

 It should be noted for the majority of techniques described here, the description of the technique could not be comprehensive. Whole books have been written about security audit, performance evaluation, and object-oriented testing and usability, for example. This book aims to provide an overview of all of the broad categories of risk with enough detail to give test managers and testers sufficient information (including references to other books) to decide on the scope of testing and what pitfalls lay ahead. These chapters are intended to give you an insight into the essential characteristics of the test techniques, why you might select them for inclusion in your test strategy and how to structure them into an effective test process. Each chapter provides references for further reading on the techniques or tools that support them.

 On the subject of tools, most chapters provide examples of the use of tools or remote testing services. We are not promoting specific tools, but are using the tools that we have personal experience of to illustrate the typical way that such tools are used. Chapter 17 provides an overview of the types of tools and sources of tool information. One further point to note is that many tools have features that support multiple test types (as we have defined them). We suggest you mix and match tools to suit your specific concerns, work practices, development technologies, and budgets. We haven't yet found a perfect combination of tools and we doubt whether one exists, as all projects have their different needs. Where a tool takes a novel or innovative approach to a particular aspect of the testing task in hand, we may highlight it if it offers a particular benefit to testers.

The chapters may refer occasionally to a specific technology such as Active Server Pages, Java, or VBScript for example. There are many development products on the market and in the time taken to publish this book, no doubt there will be many more. We have not attempted to keep pace with such developments. Some technologies such as XML for example, open up new possibilities for business-to-business systems and their users. Wireless Application Protocol (WAP) phones, PDAs, and other mobile devices will soon make the Web all-pervasive. The risk implications of these technologies have not yet been fully established. The testing of these technologies requires more experience to be gained. Perhaps a revision to this book will include them someday. In the meantime, testers will have to innovate to address these emerging risks. It is hoped that the risk-based approach, the test process framework, and the outline test techniques described in this book will provide enough support and guidance for you to create your own test techniques for specific types of risks.

Each chapter begins with a summary of the risks that the chapter's test techniques address. For each test technique described in the chapter, the potential causes of the problems are discussed and the method described. If there are alternative methods or there are tools that have different approaches, these are described and illustrated where appropriate.

One of the challenges of e-Business testing is: where does subsystem (developer) testing stop and system level testing begin? Even though you might be a system or acceptance tester and not particularly interested in what developers do to test, we encourage you to look into the "more technical" techniques further. Allocation of responsibility for more and less technical techniques is a major consideration for your test strategy. You can only make these decisions by knowing what kinds of testing can be done and who is best placed to perform it. If you do not liaise with earlier testers or developers, you may find that some of your tests may duplicate tests performed by others. Even worse, you may find that if you assume others do some types of tests, they may not be done at all.

Each chapter ends with a listing of tools and references for further reading.

The risk listings that appear at the start of each of Chapters 9 through 15 are not ordered or prioritized, but are grouped by the test techniques that we proposed are most appropriate to addressing them. Some of the risks listed would have dramatically different consequences but we have not pre-judged any of the probability or consequence scores that you might assign in your own risk workshops. The groups of risks are in the same order as the test techniques are described in the chapters. Some risks could be addressed by more than one technique. For example, in Chapter 9, confusing text on Web pages could be checked using spell and grammar checking tools or as part of a usability assessment (Chapter 13). You must decide which technique(s) you use to address these specific tests. The risk and test objective tables are a guideline.

When the W-Model is described in Chapter 4, we suggest that any and all deliverables from the development activities could be tested. Require-ments, specifications, designs, and code itself can all be subjected to some form of review or inspection process.

We haven't included reviews as Web testing techniques because these techniques are not specific to Web-based systems or affected by the technol-ogy used to build them. Many of the risks associated with requirements, designs, and specifications can be addressed at least in part by review activi-ties. When considering the behavior-related failures that could occur, con-sider whether these failures could be traced back to failings in earlier documentation and whether a review could expose shortcomings in these documents. Of course, you will probably conduct unit, integration, and sys-tem tests on the built software but early reviews are effective at finding the most potentially expensive faults much earlier and cheaply than later dynamic testing. References [1, 2] provide a good introduction to inspec-tions and review techniques.

In Chapters 9 through 15, we describe test techniques that are either Web specific, or are influenced by the fact that Web technology is being used to build the software under test. In effect, all of the dynamic test techniques (and the static analysis of Web pages) are affected to greater or lesser degrees and because of this, they were described in the techniques chapters.

Part IV   Chapters 18 through 20 address some of the practicalities of "mak-ing it happen." Chapter 18 discusses the influence of different development methodologies and technologies on the test process. Chapter 19 presents insights into the test-planning and organizational challenges presented by e-business projects. Chapter 20 covers the particular difficulties of test execu-tion and making the release decision.

Appendixes Appendix A outlines the essential technical knowledge that e-business testers should have. Appendix B sets out some of the opportunities for building your own test tools and presents some examples of how they might be used.

Finally, a list of acronyms and abbreviations is included, followed by a comprehensive glossary of terms.

The Web Site

A Web site has been created at http://www.riskbasedtesting.com to accompany this book. The site not only promotes the book (you can order copies on-line, of course), but also contains downloadable material extracted from the book, including document templates and a candidate risk inventory. Please take the time to visit.

Needless to say, any errors in this book are my responsibility. If you find any, please e-mail me at paulg@evolutif.co.uk, and I will post errors and their corrections on the Web site.

References

[1]   Freedman, D. P., and G. M. Weinberg, *Handbook of Walkthroughs, Inspections and Technical Reviews*, NY: Dorset House Publishing, 1990.

[2]   Gilb, T., and D. Graham, *Software Inspection*, Wokingham, U.K.: Addison Wesley, 1993.

Acknowledgments

This is my first book. As soon as I decided to write it, I knew I needed help. It didn't take long to work out whom to ask. Neil Thompson is the smartest test manager I know. I was tasked with writing a test strategy for a major e-business project for Barclays Bank, PLC, in December 1999. Using the approach set out in this book, working with the staff of the bank and the system integrator, I documented a risk register with over 70 distinct risks. Working as a team, we formulated a test process in a single marathon meeting. I drafted a skeletal test strategy around this test process. Neil picked up where I left off; it was his task to complete the strategy and make it happen. By any measure, this was a big project: It had a large budget; it was technically and organizationally complex; politics occasionally came into play; and it was stressful. In the months that followed, Neil did make it happen. I am delighted to report that he saw the project through to its successful "go-live." I am also very grateful for his contribution to this book. Neil wrote Chapters 18 through 20 and has made contributions throughout the text.

I would like to thank my partners at Systeme Evolutif, Cindy Morelli, Paul Herzlich, and Zvi Herzenshtein, for their patience in letting me do my own thing for most of 2001. I start work again tomorrow—honest. I would also like to thank my colleague Sean Conley, who finds me interesting pieces of work to get involved in.

Neil and I would like to thank all of our clients, particularly Malcolm Brown, Bob Wilson, and our other colleagues at Barclays Bank.

Without our reviewers, this book would be a jumble of off-the-wall ideas. We extend our sincere gratitude to them all: Isabel Evans, Julie

Gardiner, Kath Harrison, Grenville Johns, Cem Kaner, Wayne Mallinson, Erik Petersen, Lloyd Roden, Steve Splaine, Lawrence Titterington, and Erik van Veenendaal.

The British Computer Society Specialist Interest Group in Software Testing (BCS SIGIST) is a continual source of inspiration because it allows us to meet testers on the front lines. I thank all of SIGIST's members and especially the committee's volunteers, who continue to promote the testing discipline with enthusiasm.

We also appreciate the international diversity and exceptional community spirit of the EuroSTAR conferences. Neil and I each presented papers at the first EuroSTAR in 1993. We have hardly missed this annual gathering since then.

I would like to thank Artech House, particularly Tim Pitts, who seemed to think this book was a good idea, and Ruth Harris, who has provided me with valuable advice and encouragement throughout the writing of it.

Neil would like to thank his parents and family, friends, teachers, and colleagues, who have helped (or at least tolerated) him over the years.

Finally, I would like to thank my wife, Julia, for transcribing the tapes of the seminars I ran in 2000 and 2001, upon which much of this material is based. More importantly, I thank her for the "program management" of me through the whole exercise.

Part I
The Risk-Based Testing Approach

1

Introduction to Risk-Based Testing

Most e-business projects entail high pressure and tight timescales coupled with risky project foundations; however, the initial madness of the dotcom phenomenon subsided within a couple of years. Many of the start-ups that embarked on new systems development, driven by marketing hype and advertising, have come and gone. The pressures on the developers and testers in these environments were extreme. Many of the pressures were simply driven by the need to deliver quickly.

Risky Project Foundations

Even though the frenzy has diminished, most e-business start-ups have limited venture capital and rapid burn rates before they acquire customers and revenue. Typically, products need to be launched, marketing activity ramped up, and subscription numbers increased rapidly to obtain the next round of venture capital. Where the founders of a company are looking to attract investment, or perhaps even sell out, they must also maximize the attractiveness of their assets. Management may prefer to enhance or expand its product offerings before they actually work. The pressure to deliver may override the pressure to get it right.

Where established businesses have embarked on e-business strategies, the pressures on developers and testers can be just as extreme. One of the main drivers of e-business projects in these environments is the threat posed by competitors who may already have made an impact with an e-commerce site. Marketers, seeing the competition pull ahead, need little encouragement to alarm senior management into making a move. Keeping up is rarely an option. A company must overtake its competitors in a single leap to stake its claim in the new market and gain recognition and market share before the battle is lost.

Reduced timescales are not the only problem; many projects are based on risky foundations. Although the fundamental architecture of the Web is stable and the infrastructure we call the Internet is robust enough for most purposes, e-business projects face several technical and organizational risks.

Small-scale developments can rely on proven technologies that have been used on many of the largest sites. Smaller-scale Web sites also use less mature technologies that will not be pushed to extremes. Most projects are aiming high, however; market potential is vast, and most companies seeking investors forecast huge volumes. Computer and network infrastructure has become a commodity, so many large-scale developments have critical dependencies on software sophistication to assure scalability, reliability, and resistance to failure. Most of the larger, successful Web sites started out using the simplest technology in the early days, but it seems that most new developments are based on bleeding-edge technologies.

New technological offerings appear on the market weekly. Vendors are more than willing to offer competitive prices to prospective customers if the sale will result in a marketable reference site. Therefore, market pressures push companies towards these technologies before they are fully proven.

Given the novelty of many of these technologies, you can be sure there are few developers (or testers) with the required skills to use them or with extensive experience of them in successful projects. The natural inclination of most developers is to press continually for marketable skills in new technologies, regardless of whether useful, usable, and reliable systems can be built efficiently using them. In the skills market, those in highest demand command the highest salaries. If a product vendor gets its marketing right, sales follow and the demand for new skills soars. With all new products, however, inexperienced developers tend to make basic mistakes; these mistakes are reduced as developers become more experienced. Projects staffed with more than a certain critical mass of experience tend not to suffer such basic problems.

The development culture is driven by the technical staff's need to stay ahead in the skills market. In stable environments where staff are experienced and competent, it seems inevitable that salaries increase more slowly and staff move on to acquire new skills. Given most companies' need to retain skilled staff (and managers' needs to stay ahead too), the use of technologies that are not yet mature and supported by the skills market will continue.

In summary, most e-business developers (and their ambitious managers) operate in an environment characterized by risky projects using new technologies with compressed timescales and staffed by inexperienced personnel. Intense business competition in an uncertain, fast-paced environment leads to aggressive marketing of novel software and hardware products and a shortage of proven skills.

Pressures on Testing and Quality Assurance

E-business project managers may be dealt ambitious project objectives, given the incumbent risks and constraints, of delivering systems that may be implemented rapidly and that will grow in scale and profitability faster than competition can react. A holistic view of e-business would include in its scope the entire software and hardware infrastructure, integrated legacy systems and third-party components, back office staff, media and Web marketing, and affiliate programs, as well as the reliable delivery of the products and services to be sold.

If you consider that most e-business projects aim to deliver some form of service to the marketplace, the scope of deliverables is very wide and the risks to success of the project even greater. Management may have to shoulder broader responsibilities than it is prepared for.

Can-do attitudes adopted by the management and development staff in e-business projects make thorough test planning harder to accomplish. A project manager who insists on extensive testing and quality assurance (QA) might be regarded as overly cautious. Given the confidence of the technical staff on a project and the vendors of the new products to be used, coupled with the spectacular success stories of clients using their technology, most project managers would naturally stifle their reservations about the ambitious nature of a particular venture. After all, this might be the manager's first e-business project, and he or she needs the experience to progress up the promotion ladder.

Most managers would choose to deliver a system on time rather than one that works perfectly. Why is this? Well, if they resource testing at the expense of development, the project may automatically fail to deliver enough functionality, regardless of its quality. If they squeeze test planning in the hope that "it'll be all right on the night" and that faults can be fixed quickly in production without any disasters, then maybe, just maybe, they'll get away with it.

Until organizations have experienced enough failures to change the development climate, most managers go with the flow. They plan optimistically, under-resource testing and QA, and hope for the best. They might consider the major risks to success and may even institute a regime of risk assessment, resolution, and monitoring; however, they are not likely to do so at a level of detail that will have any real impact on the behavior of developers and testers. Penalty clauses in supplier contracts may provide some reassurance, but if a project doesn't deliver or delivers late, no amount of compensation can restore lost e-business opportunities.

When companies embark on developments in new technologies, they start from scratch. Whereas a supplier brings its technology and consultants to a new project, responsibility for testing may be left to the customer to manage. Hardware and software environments, processes, techniques, tools, and, of course, skills all have to be acquired quickly. Inexperienced project managers, unused to building test teams and setting up test environments, often hire testers too late for them to gain enough knowledge to test a system adequately. Thus, there is probably too little time for them to mitigate adequately the risks inherent in the projects they join.

Given the novelty of application areas and technologies and the inexperience of managers and developers in most e-business projects, inevitably many e-business testers also lack the skills and experience to do their jobs effectively. Over time they will acquire the necessary skills, but what are they to do in the meantime?

The Tester's Manifesto

The testers of modern systems face considerable challenges. To focus the minds of those responsible, we have compiled a manifesto for testing. In projects involving risks (all of them, we think), testers need to provide visibility of the risks to management and propose reliable test methods for addressing them throughout the project. In this way, project managers will be better informed, and testers will have clearer test objectives. The tester's manifesto is:

1. *Assess software product risks.* Identify and assess, through consultation, the major product risks of concern and propose tests to address those risks.

2. *Estimate overall test effort.* Estimate, based on the nature and scope of the proposed tests and on experience, how expensive and time-consuming the testing will be.

3. *Gain consensus on the amount of testing.* Achieve, through consensus, the right coverage, balance, and emphasis of testing.

4. *Acquire budget to do enough testing.* Convince management to allocate enough of its budget to testing that will address the risks of concern.

5. *Plan, implement, and execute tests.* Specify and run tests that address the risks of greatest concern.

6. *Provide information for a risk-based decision on release.* Perhaps the most important task of all, is to provide information as the major deliverable of all testing.

This book sets out an approach for identifying and assessing product risks and provides methods and tools to address these risks systematically throughout the project life cycle.

Textbook Testing and the Real World

Some testing textbooks preach the value of testing as an absolute: Risks are bad, and testing mitigates risk, so you must use the most rigorous techniques, the most advanced tools, and the most stringent review practices you can afford. Failure to adopt such an approach is perceived as bad practice, or at least to be discouraged. Testers are incited to adopt the almost fundamentalist view that testing without requirements is impossible, project managers who cut testing budgets are incompetent, and testers must stick to their guns and constantly argue for bigger test budgets and more time.

Evangelizing test zealots are often isolated within their own projects. Everyone knows that systems can actually be built without documented requirements and that successful software products can be constructed without the use of formal inspections. It is possible to build systems without white-box testing and rigorous black-box test design based on perfect, stable requirements and acceptance criteria that cannot be compromised. Just look at the practices of the most (commercially) successful software companies. In the febrile gold rush towards e-business success, testers who preach perfection are likely to be crushed by their stampeding colleagues and managers.

Textbook approaches often leave no room or flexibility for dealing with real-world challenges. There is little allowance for poor or missing requirements; there can be no compromise on quality or time; and resources or technical infrastructure should not limit the test plan. Further, the benefits of early release (with known bugs) are rarely mentioned.

The problem with this ideal-world approach is that although textbooks can help with specific, technical issues, they do not usually provide enough guidance on strategy. They do not help much if you are under time pressure, and compromise is inevitable. We've met hundreds of testers personally, and we teach the textbook fundamentals of testing. We often ask testers if they always get the budget they require to do testing or whether, when the developers slip and testing starts late, the release date is moved back. In the vast majority of cases, the answer to both questions is a resounding no.

Typically, the story goes like this: The boss asks you for an estimate for the testing. You think about it for a while and derive an estimate based on your own experience. You are influenced by the fact that last time you weren't given enough time, and the project slipped, testing was squeezed, and some significant bugs slipped through into production. You tell your boss you need 8 testers for 10 weeks. What is the project manager's usual response? Something along the lines of "Thanks. I can give you four testers for six weeks."

Is that the way it works in your company? It seems that this is a common response from most project managers. Has your project manager ever asked you if you've got enough budget or if you need more? It happens, but not often. Only risk-averse managers that have been bitten on previous projects think that way.

Essentially, the pressures that make testers' lives hard are not new. Testers always gripe about being at the wrong end of the project, even about being underpaid and ignored. When was it different? Testers who adopt the textbook approach have always been under pressure; always been hassled; never gotten the budget requested; never been understood. It's so unfair!

Maybe testers get what they deserve though. They are always bemoaning their predicament and being negative. Management may not appreciate testers, but do testers ever explain what they do or what value they add in management language? Testers are quite capable of talking at length about how things can fail. They cite missing coverage, slippage, faults, incidents, using whatever test terminology is in use, but do they explain testing in terms that management will understand? Not as often as they should.

Why don't testers get the budget they need? Perhaps they don't explain very well what management gets for its testing budget. Does management understand what testers are trying to do? Does management get the assurance that testers are meant to provide? Doing lots of testing doesn't seem such a good thing if all a project manager gets for his money is lots of paperwork, delays, and hassle. Do testers ever explain to management in management's own language precisely what it gets for its money?

When development slips, testers might warn management that squeezing testing in response is a bad idea, but does this message get through? Testers wonder whether management can really be so stupid as to cut testing, but project managers might be thinking that testers always want more time, money, effort, and resources and that they are always complaining. They tell themselves that projects usually deliver something of value; no one dies or loses his or her job; and the users calm down after a few days, if we keep up with the fixes. We usually get there in the end, so let's squeeze the testing, and everything will be "all right on the night."

Testers always seem to be on the critical path of the project, yet they don't have enough influence. By the time it is admitted that the project has to slip, it's too late to fix everything by testing (no matter how good the test practices are). The bad decisions were made too long ago. Why weren't testers listened to earlier? Is it unfair, or do testers again get what they deserve?

Perhaps, at the start of the project, testers had little to say. Vague prophecies of disorder, failure, and doom do not win friends when the rest of the project is exuding confidence. Maybe, testers cannot articulate their concerns well enough to convince management that testing should not be squeezed. Welcome to the real world!

Testers have always struggled to gain influence with their management. The problems outlined above are not new. Testers have had to deal with such situations since software development began. When testers talk about failure in the language of risk, however, management might understand what the testers are talking about because even the managers have direct experience of things going wrong. Therefore, it's reasonably easy to explain to management that things can go wrong in language that the management understands.

Senior managers are users and consumers of the same technologies used by their internal staff and customers. This has never happened before. In this way, the Web has become the great leveler of expectations. Senior directors are Web users and have as much experience with using the Web as their software development staff. Perhaps now, if they use the language of risk, management will understand what their testers are saying to them.

The Risks of Early Release

Consider the typical software project with a fixed timescale for development, testing, and release into production. As the testers wait, the development team works under more and more pressure to deliver on time. Eventually, the first build is delivered into the test environment. Development has slipped and testing is starting 2 weeks late. Other than a lack of resources, what reasons might the developers have had for delivering late?

- The scope of development was underestimated; the system was bigger, more complicated, or more difficult than previously thought.

- The developers are inexperienced; the technologies are novel, and there were many more problems to solve than anticipated.

- The work proved to be error prone; the software proved to be faulty and difficult to correct.

- The requirements were not stable; developers had to rework much of the functionality affected by requirements drift.

Do any of these reasons for the slippage justify a reduction in testing? Common sense argues that if we've underestimated the project, we should do more testing. If the developers have been held up because they found many faults, then we can probably assume that early builds will be unreliable and that a week or two will pass before things settle down and we get some real testing done. Thus, testing will take longer. If the system was more complex than anticipated, then one would reason that it is a more difficult system to get right. Everything here points to more testing, not less, but the decision is made to stick to the original plan. The deadline does not move, and testing is squeezed.

This story has become all too familiar to testers over the years. The tester advises the project manager that he can now expect the worst: More serious problems will be found in testing; the testing will not be finished before the deadline; and the system will be released to users with known bugs. Once again, the tester must resign him- or herself to a traumatic, frustrating, and pressured end to another project. Does it need to end this way?

When the time comes to make the release decision, the essential question to be answered is, What is the risk of releasing now? Towards the closing stages of a project, do you have this impression that, as a tester, you know more about the product than anybody else does? Are you the best-informed person on the project because only you know what's going on and how close to (or far from) completion you really are? As the tester, you have an intimate knowledge of what works and what doesn't. All too often, this knowledge doesn't seem to filter up to senior management, at least not in time for it to be acted on. Risk-based testing is founded on the notion that late in a project the testers are the best-informed concerning the product's capabilities and flaws.

What Is Risk?

We are all born risk managers. Every time we cross a road, we take a risk. We may choose to cross the road at a signaled junction or crossing, where the traffic is brought to a halt occasionally, and we can cross in safety. If, however, we are at some distance from a safe crossing point or we are in a hurry and the detour would make us late for an appointment, we might take a risk crossing the open road. This is a decision we might all make when the traffic is light. If the road is busy, however, or the cars are traveling quickly, some would choose to walk the extra distance instead. As traffic speeds increase, more and more people would choose the safer option. Older, wiser, slower, sensible folk tend to take the safe option more than younger, foolish, faster, senseless folk.

Are Risks Wrong?

I have a son and a daughter. When they used to play on the climbing frames in the park a few years ago, they exhibited noticeably different behavior. My daughter would normally climb around the outside of the climbing frame or traverse the equipment by climbing through the center of the frame. She'd have a great time and be perfectly happy doing this. My son, on the other hand, would take great pleasure in climbing along the top, balancing on one leg, waving his arms around, nearly toppling, and shouting, "Look Mum! Look Dad! I'm about to fall! What do you think of this?" My wife couldn't bear it, and she'd panic, screaming hysterically, "Please come down!" I usually turned away and ignored him. Panicking just encouraged him.

I don't want to imply that boys and girls have different sensitivities to risk (although there may be something in this). The important point is that different people have different perceptions of risk. Clearly, my son's perception of risk is lower than the rest of the family's perception. He thrives on it, almost—it's great fun for him and agony for his parents. The question is, Is he wrong to take risks such as these? Is my son wrong to have a different perception of risk than his sister or his parents? Set aside the argument that it might be wrong to upset your parents. If the purpose of taking the risk is to entertain oneself and my son gets more fun out of risky play, I'm not so sure he is wrong. One could say that it is foolish to take risks that jeopardize your own safety for some purpose; one could also say it is wrong to take risks that jeopardize other people's safety or money (without their consent).

You might think horse racing is boring, but gambling on the result would make it more interesting. Once a year you might put a bet on the big race and enjoy that race, but only because you are risking a little money with the prospect of winning more. Some risk taking is fun because the risk is low and the potential rewards are high; other risk taking is inevitably for a tiny reward—we put our life at stake to cross a road to buy a carton of milk.

We can generalize and say that given the same circumstances, peoples' perceptions of risk can differ. It has been said that different people have their own "risk thermostats" and that their actions in the presence of risk are regulated by this mechanism. It should come as no surprise then that the perception of risk in a software project should vary across management, developers, and testers. It is not wrong for people to have differing perceptions of risk, but it might be wrong to ignore or suppress the information that would heighten (or reduce) the level of risk perceived by others.

In short, testers should make information about risks available to all stakeholders in a project so they are aware of the risks being taken. If the stakeholders decide to take those risks, the tester should not complain—he has done his job.

Is risk taking right or wrong? Is it right or wrong to deliver a system early before all the bugs are fixed? It depends on how informed the risk taking is, and that is the real point. Testers should get over any hang-ups about delivering early with known bugs if the decision to do so is based on sound data and assessment. Risk is perfectly natural: It wasn't invented with software; risk taking has been around as long as free will. Risk isn't right or wrong, risk just is.

The Definition of Risk

If a risk is something that could go wrong, then uncertainty is inherent in both the likelihood of the risk materializing and its potential impact. It is this uncertainty that causes us to be concerned about it. It is predictably ironic that there is no single, agreed-upon definition of risk in common use. We have seen several dictionary definitions including "the possibility of loss or injury" and "exposure to mischance." These definitions imply that a risk has two dimensions—an uncertain probability and a potential for loss or injury—which together determine its scale. In the software literature, views vary as to the meaning of risk, but this variety can help us to understand the depth of the concept. Risk is not like a simple technical term with a very specific meaning—the concept of risk influences all human behavior. It is no surprise that its all-pervasive nature has led to a plethora of definitions. Understanding risk can help us to understand the motivations of our projects' decision makers, which can help us help them to make better decisions, which in turn leads to our having greater influence over our projects.

Influences on Our Understanding of Risk

The works of several authors have influenced our thinking on risk. Peter Bernstein's book, *Against the Gods: The Remarkable Story of Risk* [1], presents a fascinating history of risk and tells the stories of the scientists and mathematicians who built up the theory of risk. It suggests that our ability to control risks (if we choose to) distinguishes present risk takers from those in the past.

Software Risk Management by Barry Boehm [2] provides a comprehensive toolkit for risk management. Boehm observes that good project managers are usually good at risk management. The most successful project managers might not have used formal risk management techniques, but they use the notion of risk exposure to influence their priorities and actions. His paper "Software Risk Management: Principles and Practices" [3] summarizes the established practice we call risk management.

In *Computer Related Risks* [4] Peter Neumann provides a comprehensive collection of failures reported to his Internet news group, comp.risks. The risk summaries in the book are sometimes entertaining, but the number and variety of problems that continue to occur in real systems make for somber reading.

Capers Jones's *Assessment and Control of Software Risks* [5] presents a catalog of 60 software risks classified like communicable diseases (a project disease is an unfortunate, but appropriate metaphor). Each risk is described in terms of its severity, frequency, root causes, cost impact, and potential methods of prevention, as well as other attributes.

In her book *Managing Risk* [6], Elaine Hall describes a process for managing risk systematically and presents a method for introducing and implementing risk management into an organization. She also introduces the different categories of project, process, and product risks, which serve as one of the bases for the risk-based test method presented in this book.

Safeware [7] by Nancy Leveson is a rich guide to approaches to risk in the high-integrity computer systems field. The methods used to ensure that systems are safe (that is free, or as free as possible) from accidents or losses are probably too expensive and time consuming for most e-business projects. At the same time, they represent the best tools and techniques for addressing the risks of failure from which we can choose. In this way, they represent the ultimate in best practice that all projects could aspire to.

Martyn Ould's *Managing Software Quality and Business Risk* [8] presents an approach to linking risk assessment and management to a quality achievement plan. In essence, the risk analysis has a large influence on the structure of the process model used to design, build, and test a system. We like the notion that a process model gives a risk-reducing structure to a project, and we have used this idea to focus testing wholly on risk reduction. Martyn defines a risk as "any threat to the achievement of one or more of the cardinal aims of a project," implying that risks are of the utmost importance to the sponsors of a project. (It is, after all, the sponsors who are paying for the project in the first place.) We will use this concept, combined with the notion of uncertainty, to set out our proposed definition of risk.

The Definition of Risk We Use in This Book

Every project has some cardinal objectives, some purpose or aim that the sponsors are prepared to pay for. They will willingly fund the development of systems to achieve these objectives. Typical objectives include increasing business, expanding into new markets, or decreasing costs. Most projects are started when a business case or feasibility study is approved. Typically, a project initiation document (PID) is prepared, which is the first real document in a project. The PID probably sets out the aims and objectives of the project and outlines costs, timescales, responsibilities, and so forth. The PID, or its equivalent, is the best source of information on the cardinal objectives of a system. These objectives are important, because these are what the sponsors believe they are paying for. Anything that threatens the achievement of these cardinal objectives is a risk.

Definition: A risk threatens one or more of a project's cardinal objectives and has an uncertain probability.

Let's explore this definition a little more. Nowadays, bridges are very, very safe—comparatively. The consequence of a bridge crashing down into ariver is catastrophic; it is the worst thing that can ever happen to that bridge. The risk of this occurring, however, is comparatively low because the probability is extremely low. Not everything that has a terrible consequence is very risky because we work hard to make the probability so low that it's almost negligible.

Risk exists only where there is uncertainty; that is, if a risk's probability is 0%, it's not a risk. The undesirable event will never happen, so there is no reason for concern. Suppose there is a hole in the road ahead of you. You can see it, you're walking towards it, and if you keep walking, you'll fall into it. If that undesirable event's probability is 100%, then it is inevitable, and it is not a risk. To avoid falling in, you would take a detour or stop walking—there is no uncertainty about that. In the same way, a known bug, detected through testing is not a risk: Tests provide some additional information and the particular microrisk associated with that bug has been eliminated [9]. Your perception of other related risks may grow, however, if you found a bug in code that previously you trusted.

Also, without a potential for loss, there is no risk. Unless I put money on a horse to win, I'm not going to enjoy a horse race because I won't care who wins—there's no gain, no loss, nothing to worry about. If an undesirable event is trivial, it is not a risk because no one cares whether it happens or not.

All our experience of software projects tells us that they are inherently risky. As almost every practitioner has directly experienced, the probability of success in a software project is less than 100%. These projects are inherently risky because there's great uncertainty as to whether we will achieve our desired end.

The word risk comes from the early Italian *risicare*, which means "to dare." In this sense, risk is a choice that we make, rather than inevitability. If we call someone daring, he or she would probably take this as a compliment because we usually admire people who are daring. But daring people take risks; we call them daring because we are more risk-averse than they are. One of our roles as testers is to inform our managers of the risks they are taking. If managers are ignorant of the risks they take, they are not daring; they are simply uninformed.

Of course, not every risk can be predicted ahead of time. As we proceed through the design, development, and testing, new threats to our objectives appear from perhaps unforeseen or unusual directions. As new risks are identified, testers should be prepared to adjust their test plans to account for them where appropriate. Other risks should be reported back to management, because perhaps they raise issues that only management could address.

Product Risk and Testing

There are three types of software risk:

1. *Project risk.* These risks relate to the project in its own context. Projects usually have external dependencies, such as the availability of skills, reliance on suppliers, constraints like fixed-price contracts, or fixed deadlines. External dependencies are project management responsibilities.

2. *Process risk.* These risks primarily relate to the project internally— its planning, monitoring, and control come under scrutiny. Typical risks here include the underestimation of the project's complexity or the level of effort or skills required. The internal management of a project, such as good planning, progress monitoring, and control, is a project management responsibility.

3. *Product risk.* These risks relate to the definition of product, the stability (or lack) of requirements, the complexity of the product, and the fault proneness of the technology, which could lead to a failure to meet requirements. Product risk is the testers' main area of concern.

How many risks did management identify in your last project? Most projects have between, say, 10 risks (for a small project) and maybe 50 risks (for a large program of projects). Typically, project managers need to manage around 20 risks, and risk reviews can be included in weekly progress meetings. From the point of view of project management, managing risks using the standard methods and tools works fine if you have 10 to 30 risks.

As testers, our focus is on product risk. If, however, we define product risk as the potential for a product to fail in some way, in how many different ways could products fail? Can it fail in 10 ways, or 20, or in 100,000? Of course, there is an almost infinite number of ways in which a product could actually fail. If you really had the time and imagination to work them out, maybe you could identify them all, but for practical purposes, there is no limit. Can risk management methods that can manage 20 risks be used to manage product risks on such a scale?

What tends to happen in real projects is that product risks are logged, but only at the very highest level. Typical product risks might be logged as meeting (or failing to meet) functional requirements, system performance objectives, or targets for reliability. This is as detailed as it gets because if you go into more detail, there is an explosion of variety in the failure modes. So the problem with traditional risk management is that it is very much geared to handling low volumes of risk.

The complexity of many risks is handled by giving each risk an owner, and the risk owner takes it from there. What a test manager needs is a method for managing product risks at a lower level, basing testing strategy, incident management, and progress reporting on those risks, and a means of identifying both the benefits available for delivery and the risk of releasing early during test execution.

Specification, design, and development methods may minimize the likelihood of failure in products, but software testing is the main tool for identifying modes of failure and increasing our knowledge of risks in software products that exist. Testing has a key role to play in addressing software product risks. Before we go much further, therefore, we need to define both products and testing in their broadest sense.

What Is a Product?

A *product* is a final or interim output from a project activity (i.e., any document, procedure, or software component generated by a project in the course of its execution). All projects generate many, many documents and other deliverables. Products are often separated into management and other, more technically oriented products. Alternative terms, such as *work-product* or *artifact*, are used, but we will stick to the term product in the rest of the book. There is a variety of possible products. Almost all products are of concern to testers.

- *Management products:* project initiation documents, project plans, quality plans, stage plans, resource plans, and so forth, which are mainly the concern of project management;

- *Documentation products:* specification-type documents, such as user requirements, designs, specifications, user documentation, procedures, and the like;

- *Software products:* custom built or bought-in components, subsystems, systems, interfaces, and so forth;

- *Infrastructure products:* hardware, computer and network operating systems (OSs), database management systems, middleware, and the like;

- *Testware products:* test strategies, plans, specifications, scripts, test data, incident reports, test summary reports, and so forth;
- *Other products:* conversion plans, training, user guides, and the like.

The quality of the technical products raises the concern that the faults in these products can cause failures in the final system. The purpose of testing is to detect these faults (so they can be eliminated) and reduce the risk of failure in production.

What Is Testing?

Over the years, quite a few definitions of testing have been promoted, and these have often been based on one or another single objective, such as finding faults. Myers in particular, promoted this single-minded objective in his influential book, *The Art of Software Testing* [10]. A later view from Bill Hetzel in his book, *The Complete Guide to Software Testing* [11], suggested that testing is a broader, continuous activity that takes place throughout the development process. Testing is a necessary information-gathering activity required to evaluate our (or others') work effectively. In our experience, testing has several distinct objectives, and as testing progresses through the life cycle, the emphasis on these objectives changes. We believe that there is no definition of testing in terms of a single test objective that can be complete.

A test is a controlled exercise with (potentially) several objectives. The objectives of a test might include one or more of the following:

- Detecting faults in the product under test so they can be removed;
- Demonstrating that the product under test meets its requirements;
- Gaining confidence that the product under test is ready for use (or reuse);
- Measuring one or more quality attributes (e.g., performance, usability, reliability, accuracy, security) of the product under test;
- Detecting faults in the baseline for the product under test;
- Providing data so that the processes used to build products can be improved;
- Providing data on the risk of release (and use) of the product under test;
- Providing data on the (potential) benefits of releasing the product under test.

Clearly, these objectives overlap. For example, if we find and eliminate faults and demonstrate that a product meets its requirements, we will probably also have enough data to assess the risk of releasing the product and have the confidence to do so. We will argue later that the ultimate objectives of a test strategy are the last two in the list: to provide enough information to judge whether the benefits of releasing a system outweigh the risks. This is the essential purpose of the risk-based approach to software testing.

What kinds of tests should we consider? Testing includes both *static* and *dynamic* tests. Static tests do not involve executing software and are mostly used early in the development life cycle. All human readable deliverables, including project plans, requirements, designs, specifications, code, test plans, and procedures, can be statically tested. Static tests find faults, and because they usually find faults early, they provide extremely good value for money. Static tests include reviews, inspections, and structured walkthroughs, but early test preparation can also be regarded as a static test activity as the process of test design finds faults in baseline documents.

Dynamic tests execute dynamic transactions of the software and are appropriate at all stages in which executable software components are available. The traditional component, link, system, large-scale integration, and acceptance tests are all dynamic tests. Many nonfunctional system tests, such as performance, volume, and stress tests, are also dynamic tests.

The test activities in a project are associated with all products and all stages of development. Every activity that involves an evaluation of a product we will call testing. Our test strategy focuses on the product risks of concern, and we construct our tests to pinpoint the particular product faults that can occur. Tests that focus on fault detection are more effective and efficient and are less likely to duplicate one another. This is the straightforward approach to test strategy that we advocate in this book.

References

[1]   Bernstein, P. L., *Against the Gods: The Remarkable Story of Risk*, New York: John Wiley & Sons, 1996.

[2]   Boehm, B. W., *Software Risk Management*, Los Alamitos, CA: CS Press, 1989.

[3]   Boehm, B. W., "Software Risk Management: Principles and Practices," *IEEE Software*, Vol. 8, No. 1, January 1991.

[4]   Neumann, P. G., *Computer-Related Risks*, Reading, MA: Addison-Wesley, 1995.

[5]   Jones, C., *Assessment and Control of Software Risks*, Englewood Cliffs, NJ: Yourdon Press, 1994.

[6]   Hall, E. M., *Managing Risk*, Reading, MA: Addison-Wesley, 1998.

[7]   Leveson, N. G., *Safeware*, Reading, MA: Addison-Wesley, 1995.

[8]   Ould, M., *Managing Software Quality and Business Risk*, Chichester, UK: John Wiley & Sons, 1999.

[9]   Thompson, N., "Zen and the Art of Object-Oriented Risk Management," *Proc. Euro-STAR Conf.*, Barcelona, Spain, November 8–12, 1999.

[10] Myers, G. J., *The Art of Software Testing*, New York: John Wiley & Sons, 1979.

[11] Hetzel, W. C., *The Complete Guide to Software Testing*, Wellesley, MA: QED, 1983.

2

Risk Management and Testing

Risk management is usually structured into a series of activities throughout a project. Martyn Ould's book, *Managing Software Quality and Business Risk* [1], sets out the following systematic, but simple, approach:

- *Risk identification:* Identify what could go wrong and take a view as to whether the risk is or is not significant and relevant to the project.
- *Risk analysis:* Consider the nature of the risk and assign scores for both probability and consequence. The product of these scores is called the *risk exposure.*
- *Risk response planning:* Take each risk in turn and decide how to deal with it. There are proactive and reactive risk response measures that can be taken.
- *Risk resolution and monitoring:* Implement risk responses and monitor them throughout the project. Adjust responses as circumstances change.

This approach is appropriate for risks in general, but as testers, we will naturally focus on the product risks of most concern. Risk response planning, resolution, and monitoring are generic risk management activities, and in the context of product testing, we perform the following activities after risk analysis:

- *Master test planning:* our risk response planning activity;
- *Test design, implementation, and execution:* our risk resolution activities;

- *Test execution management and monitoring:* our risk monitoring activities.

One point worth making relates to the number of possible product risks. In Chapter 1, we suggested that most risk management concentrates on high-level risks, of which a project would typically have, perhaps, between 15 and 30. As far as product risks are concerned, however, if we look at these in great detail, there could be thousands of possible failure modes to consider. How do we handle this? Essentially, we consider modes of failure at an intermediate level. It is easier to present examples of failure modes than it is to define this level. We would recommend that for any project, the number of failure modes under consideration should fall between 40 for a relatively simple project and 80 for a large complex project. Chapters 9 to 15 set out nearly 100 failure modes from which you might compile an appropriate candidate risk register for your project. At this level, we are aiming to identify the risks of most concern and the test types that are in scope for planning purposes. This is high-level test planning (or test strategy). When the time comes to designing individual tests, we might investigate failure modes in much more detail. This would be appropriate when error guessing or performing exploratory testing. This is test design (or test tactics).

It is unlikely that an early risk analysis will predict and document all product risks that testers will encounter when they get their hands on the product. As testing proceeds, the testers learn more about the product, and unanticipated problem areas come to light. This does not invalidate the early risk analysis. Rather, it is an inevitable consequence of doing testing in the first place—you can never reliably predict where the buggy areas will be before you test. Where new risks emerge, project management might decide to change the direction or emphasis of the testing. This simply reflects the impossibility of perfect planning and prediction, and the sensibile precaution of including contingency in your plans.

Before we take a closer look the four risk management activities defined by Ould, we will describe the most common process for risk identification and analysis: risk workshops.

Risk Workshops

Workshops are an effective way to conduct the risk identification and, later, analysis. In Chapter 4, we will discuss risk identification and analysis as early steps in the development of a master test plan (MTP). We normally conduct the early risk assessment in master test planning meetings.

It is essential that all of the project staff with views on risk be involved in risk identification and assessment. Anyone who has experienced failures in a system similar to the particular project under discussion has something to contribute to the risk workshop. These workshops and their resulting documentation make risks visible, generate ideas for resolution, and start the process of buy-in. Although it may be impractical to invite all relevant people to the initial risk identification meetings, they should at least be asked to review the list of candidate risks and to make suggestions for inclusion. When the time comes to perform the later risk analysis, nonattendees should be invited to indicate their private assessments for consideration in the workshop.

When we conduct risk workshops, we normally start by asking participants to summarize their concerns regarding the modes in which the final system might fail. These failure modes are generic descriptions of typical failures. Each failure mode identified becomes a candidate risk. Workshop participants should describe, briefly, their concerns about failure modes not yet logged on the candidate risk register. It will soon be apparent how much work will be required to complete the register. The mood of the meeting will emerge, and the chair should be prepared for some vigorous discussions, and perhaps disagreements, where views differ. If there is conflict, the differing views may reflect inconsistencies in the understanding of certain project issues or the perception of some of the identified risks, or both. Discussion, not conflict, is to be encouraged as the mistaken assumptions and other revelations that surface during these meetings are perhaps the most valuable outcomes of the risk analysis. When concerns are aired and risks identified, they can be managed, through either project management or the test activities subsequently planned and implemented. When testing is done late in a project, these mistaken assumptions spread across user, development, and project management and are only exposed when it is too late to recover from the looming disaster. A deep frustration experienced in many projects is that the concerns people had early on were never raised, discussed, and resolved. Small concerns escalate into major problems because the people who had those concerns assumed they were being addressed, when they were not. Many disasters can be avoided by the simple act of airing these concerns early.

Risk Identification

The most effective way to compile a register of risks is to convene a risk workshop. In some ways, the workshop is run as a brainstorming session, but the meeting itself should only take place after the participants have had time to think about the specific risks that concern them. This is where prepared lists of candidate risks come in handy. Many of the concerns that participants raise might already appear on this list of candidate risks.

For risk identification, the workshop has three main aims:

1. To add those candidate risks that participants feel are not already documented in the register;

2. To remove those candidate risks deemed not to be of concern;

3. To identify candidate risks in more detail where appropriate.

Checklists of common risks can trigger ideas for variations in the modes of system failure. Checklists are of course easy to use and can be maintained as experience of failures in your project testing is gained. Chapters 9 through 15 begin with comprehensive tables of risks, which can be used to set the agenda for a risk workshop in which each type of risk is considered and discussed in turn.

Generic risk lists and quality criteria also provide good triggers for people to speculate on potential failure modes. They are a great shortcut for deriving ideas for risks. Generic risks include areas of particular complexity, areas that were error-prone in the past and changes to existing code. Quality criteria include reliability, usability, performance, and so on. These represent the main functional and nonfunctional requirements areas that can trigger speculation as to novel modes of failure.

In his article "Heuristic Risk-Based Testing," James Bach [2] provides a useful list of both generic risks and quality criteria and an explanation for their use. Bach distinguishes between inside-out and outside-in risk analyses. Inside-out analysis focuses on the product as it currently does or will exist. You examine the product and ask what could go wrong. This type of analysis is obviously appropriate when there is a reasonably detailed specification or a product ready to be tested, and it is most useful in deciding testing tactics. Outside-in risk analysis is based on generic risks, such as the product's capability, usability, or performance. These generic risks help you to think about what might go wrong so that you can plan what testing is appropriate ahead of time. Cem Kaner's book, *Testing Computer Software* [3], has a comprehensive catalog of low-level software fault types that might also provide inspiration.

At the end of the workshop, the consolidated list of risks is agreed to and is ready to be analyzed. Not every risk identified will require attention, but project management can be reasonably confident all of the known risks of concern have at least been identified.

Risk Analysis

Risk analysis is concerned with the assignment of probability and consequence scores to each risk. In effect, the analysis stage aims to position every risk in a sequence whereby the most important risks (where exposure is at a maximum) will receive the most serious attention. It is possible that some risks will score so low that they do not warrant any attention at all. Even if that is the case, at least the risk has been identified, considered, and deemed unimportant consciously.

One of the underlying principles of risk management is that risks may be of concern initially because there is considerable uncertainty about potential problems—their probability and consequence may be high or low. The real concern is the uncertainty; we are not sure what the risk might be, and the doubt worries us. A prime objective of testing is to provide the following information (or evidence) in order to address this uncertainty:

- Testing may prove that the original concerns were justified because many faults were exposed.

- Testing may show that the concerns were less founded if few faults were detected.

Testing usually reduces the uncertainty that was the basis for the concern in the first place. This uncertainty can work in two ways, however. The probability of a failure might be reduced as faults are eliminated, but the fact that faults were found at all might increase the perception that the product is faulty and likely to fail because there are more faults yet to be found. Only when all the known faults are fixed and all tests are passed might this perceived risk of failure diminish.

Assessing Consequence

We need to assess the consequence (also known as the severity, loss, or impact) of the failure modes of concern. The most straightforward method for accomplishing this is to assign a numeric value to each consequence. Very broadly, we score the consequence of a risk on a scale of one to five, where one signifies the lowest consequence and five, the highest (see Table 2.1).

Table 2.1
Risk Consequence Scores

Consequence	Description	Score
Critical	Business objectives cannot be accomplished	5
High	Business objectives will be undermined	4
Moderate	Business objectives will be affected	3
Low	Business will be affected slightly	2
Negligible	There will be no noticeable effect	1

Although we have suggested numbers one through five as scores, you may choose to use fewer categories, such as high, medium, and low scoring three, two, and one, respectively. Some people prefer just to use the high, medium, and low scheme as it avoids prolonged argument about (somewhat arbitrary) numeric values; however, if you want to prioritize risks later, we suggest you adopt numeric scoring, as it is then possible to do arithmetic and prioritize more easily.

How does one actually assign scores for consequence? The guiding principle here is that the stakeholders (the users or user management) must take a view as to how severe the consequence would be were the failure under consideration to occur. The workshop participants should be encouraged to think in terms of its impact on cardinal business objectives and whether the failure renders one or more of them unachievable. They should also consider the failure's potential impact on business practices by asking themselves such questions as how it will impact the ability to take orders, collect revenue, or respond quickly to customer inquiries. The risk should be scored in accordance with its greatest impacts on any objective. Judgment must be exercised here. We recommend that if the projected failure makes any business objective impossible to achieve, it should be scored accordingly; regardless of the importance of the objective, the risk should be scored high if it blocks even the least important objective. For example, users might ask themselves, if the system has poor usability, or is slow to respond, how does that affect our ability to use the system to save time (and money)? If the usability is so bad that users refuse to use the system, how can we possibly achieve our objectives? That would be a critical consequence.

The consequence-scoring scheme might look familiar if you assign severity scores to incidents raised during system tests. With the risk scores we are speculating as follows: If a test failure of this type occurred during system testing, what severity would we assign to that incident? We are simply pre-empting the severity assessment of an incident, should it be raised in testing later.

Whichever scale you use, be sure to use the same scale for both risk analysis and later incident severity classification. If a software fault turns out to be negligible, it has no impact on the acceptability of the product. We are assuming (given the concern about the failure) that a serious fault will occur, and we retain this assumption until tests demonstrate that this mode of failure is unlikely. In effect we are treating the system as guilty until proven innocent. By looking at risks early on, we set the expectation at the earliest possible moment that the system does not work until proven otherwise. Testers would usually assume a product is faulty until all the prepared tests have been passed successfully—we are simply stating this explicitly before any tests have been run.

Assessing Probability

After assessing consequence, we estimate the probability that a selected mode of failure will occur. Again, we recommend the simple method of assigning a probability score of one to five to represent predictions of the likelihood of product failure. Table 2.2 provides a table of scores to use in assigning probabilities to risks.

Consider, for example, that one of the pieces of functionality under consideration is a calculation that is deemed quite important. How probable is it that this functionality will fail because it is faulty? The problem with this approach is that it is, of course, impossible to predict such a probability! How could you predict the probability that there is going to be a bug in some

Table 2.2
Risk Probability Scores

Probability (%)	Description	Score
81–100	Almost certainly, highly likely	5
61–80	Probable, likely, we believe	4
41–60	We doubt, improbable, better than even	3
21–40	Unlikely, probably not	2
1–20	Highly unlikely, chances are slight	1

software? Do you think that it is possible to assign a number to the probability, or do you think that it is pointless to guess?

Suppose your development team was writing a program to calculate an insurance premium. Insurance applications normally involve customers filling in very long, complex forms. To derive a final premium, most policy calculations require between 20 and 40 or more pieces of data and involve extremely complex processing rules. How confident would you be that your developers will get it right without testing? Given your past experience, although developers are generally competent, you might expect the odds to be about even that they will create a buggy program. Even though you might not feel confident in the precision of your estimate of the odds, you will almost certainly have an opinion to express. If you have little confidence in your assessment, you will tend to fear the worst; that is, if you feel you have insufficient information, you will tend to score the probability higher.

If you have reliable bug metrics from previous projects, you might use these to inform the probability scoring. Bug databases could be extremely useful here if they contained data on projects similar to your current project. Unfortunately, the usefulness of such metrics data is clouded by the differences between projects. Different technologies, application domain spaces, resources, methods, timescale pressures, criticalities, and project scales all vary and can make probability inferences inaccurate.

The most important thing, even in the absence of hard information, is for everyone at the workshop to express his or her opinion. If everyone agrees with an assessment of probability, be it high or low, perhaps that is the end of the matter; if there is a disagreement, however, then the workshop has exposed a fault line in the project. The differences in perception between the parties need to be explored. Your perception may be optimistic or pessimistic, but could it be disproved? Your uncertainty and probable lack of information, hence confidence in your assessment, make the case for obtaining more information. Score the probability of failure higher to promote the risk in the ranking process. You may have little confidence in your assessment, but you can only be proven right or wrong by testing. The uncertainty that gives rise to concern implies that you should assume the worst: It is more likely to fail. The resultant higher ranking of this risk implies that it is a candidate for doing more testing to gain more information and reduce the uncertainty.

It is sensible to suggest that all functionality will have bugs because we know that perfection cannot be guaranteed. It is not overly pessimistic to suggest that there is a nonzero probability of the developers leaving bugs in code. Developers should not therefore take offence if you predict that their code will have bugs; however, they might be sensitive to how you suggest this probability.

Let's look at how probability scoring might work in practice. Suppose, for example, the risk workshop participants are considering feature *X*. In the room are the project manager, the customer (who knows his business), the developer (who knows the technology and design), and the tester (you). You are assessing the probability of *X* failing. What might happen? The customer and the tester may regard the probability as high. The developer may regard the probability as low. How might the conversation flow? One possible scenario is as follows:

> *Developer:* I think it's a one, no problem.
>
> *Customer:* Five. I've been on the end of too many failures in the past. I'm sorry, but I can't accept anything lower.
>
> *Tester:* We know you haven't built this kind of software before; we also know that it is an extremely complex piece of functionality. So, isn't it reasonable to assume that the code is likely to have lots of bugs?
>
> *Developer:* Well, it is complex, and no, we haven't worked on this kind of functionality before, so you have a point. But, we will be focusing on doing more testing than usual.
>
> *Project manager:* Yes, that's probably true, but we want to assess the risk of failure before we decide to test or not. If we set aside any testing we might do, how likely is it that the code will have bugs in it?
>
> *Developer (grudgingly):* Okay, it's a four.

An alternative scenario might start the same way, but have a different outcome:

> *Developer:* I think it's a one, no problem.
>
> *Customer:* Five. I've been on the end of too many failures in the past. I'm sorry, but I can't accept anything lower.
>
> *Developer:* Well actually, you have a point, but in this case, we are reusing a component from the legacy *XYZ* application. We haven't had a problem with this component for years now and have reused it several times before. I'm sure we won't have a problem there. I think it's a one.
>
> *Tester:* That's understood, but I am still a little concerned because it has to be integrated into a new system, doesn't it? Can we make it a three then?

Developer: Yes, but in that case we should change the risk description to reflect component integration as the potential problem, rather than the component functionality.

What can you as a tester contribute to the discussion? In principle, you are there to facilitate and make sure that the kinds of problems you have experienced in the past are at least considered. If you are asked to predict the likelihood of failure, you can raise two issues. First, you might mention your experience in previous projects of this type and whether you found problems or not. If you have a sheaf of past incident reports and metrics at hand, these can make your case for you. Second, you might remind the people in the room that it is uncertainty that gives rise to concern and that until you have done some testing, you can make no authoritative judgment as you will have no evidence from which to determine that failure is or is not likely.

When asked to predict probability, you may say that common sense (based on real experience) tells you that it's high or low. Whether you are looking at functionality, performance, security, or any other area, however, if you have no evidence to guide you, you must say so. It may sound like a cop-out, but you might consider simply saying that you don't have enough information to comment! There is no point in speculating at random. If everyone is concerned about the consequence of a failure mode, but no one is confident about its probability, the conclusion should be that there is simply not enough information to decide. Testing might be able to provide that information to evaluate the risk more reliably.

Bear in mind that although users are able to assess the consequences of a failure, they are far less able to assess the probability of its causes. Users only have experience of failures in acceptance testing and in production. The testers and developers are probably best placed to discuss and agree upon the probability of faults occurring during development.

Do Risk Numbers Mean Anything?

It doesn't make sense to derive precise figures for probability. A perceived probability value of 3.616 out of 5 has no useful meaning. Precision isn't the point. The purpose of the scoring is to discuss, in the presence of the management and stakeholders, the perceived likelihood of things going wrong. The various views that emerge from the discussion (including the tester's possibly deliberate noncommittal contribution) are of most value. Stakeholder concerns are aired to technical staff and vice versa.

So, do the risk numbers themselves actually mean anything? Yes, in a sense, because we will use the numbers to rank risks (and testing tasks, too). Taken out of this context, however, the separate numbers for probability and impact are not directly useful. Again, the primary value of the risk analysis is the discussion it gives rise to. We are interested in smoothing out any disjoints in the project by hearing different factions' varying viewpoints, thereby viewing the risks in different lights. We are trying to detect and correct mistaken assumptions and misunderstandings. If developers don't think a particular failure is important, for example, they may be unlikely to spend much time trying to get a certain feature right. If the customer explains the significance of the feature in question, perhaps the developers will reconsider their approach. It is better to put developers straight early in the project, before things go awry. Testers are responsible for preventing, as well as detecting, faults. Disjointed perceptions count as faults, and the preventative activity of risk assessment can sometimes find the most serious faults of all.

In summary, early discussion about risk is likely to expose perceptions and behaviors that are amiss, as well as product faults, early in projects while it is still possible to recover.

Risk Exposure

Exposure is the essential measure of the scale of a risk, which we use to compare and rank risks. Exposure is calculated as the product of the probability and consequence of a risk. We suggest you use numeric scales for both probability and consequence so that the exposure calculation is straightforward. If you use scales of 1 to 5, the calculated exposure can therefore range between 1 for a low risk and 25 for the highest possible risk.

One feature of this calculation method is that the exposure for a failure type with either high probability or high consequence can still be deemed low. Risks with high probability, but low consequence, can have low exposure. Risks with high consequence, but low probability, can also have low exposure. The calculation of exposure gives us an overall number, which we will use to prioritize risks and steer preventative action.

Risk Response Planning

Ould's book [1] offers a straightforward categorization scheme for risk responses. There are preemptive and reactive risk-reduction measures. Preemptive measures aim to reduce the likelihood of a risk materializing, whereas reactive measures aim to reduce the impact of risk that has been realized. Preemptive risk reduction measures include the following:

- *Information buying:* We conduct investigation, study, analysis, prototyping exercises, or testing to learn more about the risk. For example, the evaluation of a prototype can be considered a test activity aimed at reducing our uncertainty. We can plan to test to buy information.

- *Process model:* We might, for instance, change the process we will use to build a new system. Typically, we implement a staged process to reduce risk progressively, and we normally define focused test stages and specific tests to reduce the risks of most concern.

- *Risk influencing:* We try to reduce the probability of a risk. For example, we might buy and use off-the-shelf components rather than build them ourselves.

- *Contractual transfer:* We sell the risk to someone better able to manage it. Rather than do certain work themselves, customers might outsource it and impose penalties on the supplier for late delivery or poor quality.

Reactive risk reduction measures aim to reduce the impact of the problem should it occur. These include the following:

- *Contingency plans:* We prepare for the materialization of the risk by having an alternative solution or a method of recovery from the problem. For example, we might order additional hardware should performance of a system turn out to be unacceptable when we deliver it into production.

- *Insurance:* We pay an insurer to take the loss should the problem materialize.

In general, reactive risk reduction measures are less satisfactory and are rarely the preferred option because prevention is usually less expensive than a cure.

Information Buying and Testing

Our concerns over the product to be built relate to the failures that might occur in production. These failures may be caused by faults that exist in requirements, specifications, or code. As testers, we seek out the faults that have the potential to cause failures. It is our uncertainty over the number, type, location, and severity of these faults in the various deliverables generated throughout a project that concerns us. Testing helps us to address these uncertainties by providing evidence of actual faults and evidence that certain faults are not present. It takes great skill to select the tiny sample of real tests that both finds faults and provides us with sufficient evidence to judge the risk of accepting a product.

Testing provides evidence by evaluating product deliverables in the following ways, among others:

- Prototyping and requirements animation for eliciting, improving, and evaluating requirements;
- Reviews (inspections, technical reviews, walkthroughs) of requirements, documents, specifications, designs, and code;
- Static analysis of code;
- White- and black-box dynamic testing of components, subsystems, systems, and multiple systems;
- Nonfunctional tests of performance, usability, security, and so forth.

It is sometimes overlooked that testing is a measurement activity. One of the major deliverables of testing is information that can be used by others to make decisions about the acceptability of the product. Of course, the traditional view of testers as software fault finders is still valid, but testers have another, wider role in projects—they are information providers. Testers expose faults by causing failures in tests, but failures (and identification of the faults that cause them) are only one aspect of the information that testers provide to their projects. The role of testers as information providers is a theme that will recur several times throughout the book.

Process Model and Testing

The purpose of structured test methodologies tailored to the development activities is to reduce risk by detecting faults in project deliverables as early as possible. The risks of failure give us an insight into the potential faults that cause us most concern and that we must pursue and eliminate. The process model we adopt is normally described in a test strategy. We describe in Chapter 4 how a test strategy is produced.

Risk Resolution and Monitoring

After planning risk responses, the next stage is to implement the risk-reduction measures. Normally, we allocate each risk to a risk owner who monitors and manages the risk over time. Risk reduction measures may not eliminate a risk, of course—risks rarely disappear completely. Therefore, we select risk response measures to reduce the residual risk to a commercially acceptable level.

As the project progresses, risks are monitored by their owners and current residual risks are assessed repeatedly to ensure they are within acceptable bounds. It is common for some risks to shrink and for others to grow in importance, forcing specific remedial actions or even a rethinking of the risk management approach.

Summary of Testing's Risk Management Role

Testing can reduce the risk of release. If we use a risk assessment to steer our test activity, the tester's aim becomes explicitly to design tests to detect faults so they can be fixed, thereby reducing the risk of a faulty product. Finding faults early, rather than late, in a project reduces the reworking necessary, costs, and amount of time lost. The dramatic increase in costs associated with finding faults late has been documented many times.

Fault detection reduces the residual risk of failures in live running, where costs increase very steeply. When a test finds a fault and it is corrected, the number of faults is reduced, and, consequently, the overall likelihood of failure is reduced. One could also look at it in this way: The microrisk due to that fault is eliminated. It must be remembered, however, that testing cannot find all faults, so there will always be latent faults on which testing has provided no direct information. If we focus on and find faults in critical features, undetected faults in these are less likely. The faults left in the noncritical features of the system are of lower consequence.

One final note: The process of risk analysis is itself risky. Robert Charette's article, "Risks with Risk Analysis" [4], sets out some sensible precautions. Risk analysis can both overestimate and underestimate risks, leading to less than perfect decision making. Risk analysis can also contribute to a culture of blame if taken too far. Along with the fact that there are other potential snags with risk analysis, you must understand that there is no such thing as an absolute risk that can be calculated after the project is over. Risk is by nature uncertain. As with the effectiveness of testing, the value of a risk analysis can only be determined with hindsight after the project is over.

References

[1]   Ould, M., *Managing Software Quality and Business Risk*, Chichester, UK: John Wiley & Sons, 1999.

[2]   Bach, J., "Heuristic Risk-Based Testing," http://www.satisfice.com.

[3]   Kaner, C., J. Falk, and H. Nguyen, *Testing Computer Software*, New York: John Wiley & Sons, 1999.

[4]   Charette, R. N., "Risks with Risk Analysis," *Communications of the ACM*, Vol. 34, Issue 6, June 1991.

3

Risk: A Better Language for Software Testing

A common difficulty for testers is that when they communicate in terms of test plans, incidents, faults, and so on, their managers do not get the big picture. One valuable by-product of risk-based testing is that test plans and test execution logs reference the test objectives derived from the original risk analysis, and this traceability is maintained throughout the test process [1]. You can identify the risks that have been addressed (tests passed) and the risks that are outstanding due to a lack of information (tests not run) or because we know they have not yet been addressed (tests failed). This way of relating test results to risks is particularly useful if you are squeezed. You can say that you have run some tests and found (and fixed) some bugs, so you are reasonably confident about the features that have been tested; therefore, some risks are cleared. The tests that are stalled because you are waiting for fixes, plus the tests blocked by those, plus the other tests you haven't yet run will indicate that certain other risks are still unmitigated. A decision to stop testing now is made with the clear knowledge of the outstanding risks of release.

So, risk-based testing talks to user management and project management in their own language. These are people who think very much in terms of risks and benefits. If testers address them in similar terms, management is more likely to listen to testers and make better decisions.

By looking at risks, testers act like the eyes of the project: They search out potential problems, some way ahead of where the project is now. Kaner, Bach, and Pettichord's book, *Lessons Learned in Software Testing* [2], uses the metaphor of headlights to describe the information-finding mission of testers.

By referencing tests to benefits of the project and, in particular, to the cardinal objectives, we can focus attention on the deliverables of most value to the project sponsors and spend our time testing the most important things. Further, as progress is made through the test plan, we can demonstrate through testing that the most valuable benefits are now available. Because the release decision is ultimately a judgment of whether the benefits to be gained outweigh the risks, tests will provide management with better data on which to base their decisions.

By using the language of risk to plan testing and report progress throughout test planning and execution, testers will be heard by management. Managers often listen to development team leaders, even when they talk in technical terms. The difference is that they present technology as exciting and beneficial. When testers talk in their own technical terms of the clerical details of tests, such as incident statistics, the message tends to be negative, and managers can become bored or irritated. Management may already think testers are slightly dull as a species, arguably because many managers don't really understand what testers do and what value they add. So, testers should raise their language to management's level. Note that we are not suggesting that testers avoid talking technically with developers or other technical staff. For example, the quality of incident reports is a key factor in getting faults corrected quickly and reliably. We are simply suggesting that, when talking to management, the testers talk in terms of risks addressed and outstanding, rather than tests, incidents, and faults.

Many testers think that towards the end of a project, they are the best-informed people on the project. Testers may not know so much about the technical details as designers and programmers, but they know what works and what does not work. They have, at least in a qualitative way, and even quantitatively (e.g., in terms of performance and sustainable user numbers), a very good idea of what the project is going to deliver. Managers will make bad decisions if they lack insight and data on the product's tested capabilities and shortcomings. Testers acquire that data in large quantities and should provide this information to management in a form it can handle, in a language it understands, and with added insight.

Difficult Questions for Testers

Some of the most fundamental questions that testers face are repeatedly dodged, or at best half-answered, on real-life projects. Testing done by the book often fails to address these questions because it sets out to do too much, and in the real world, we never have enough time and resources to do it all. The language of risk, however, helps to answer these four difficult questions:

1. How much testing is enough?
2. When (and why) should we stop testing?
3. When is the product good enough for release?
4. How good is our testing anyway?

These questions come up repeatedly in both public and private discussions within projects. Over the following sections, we try to answer these questions in the language of risk.

How Much Testing Is Enough (To Plan)?

Your project manager tells you, early in a project, "I need to schedule and resource the testing in good time. Can you please give me an estimate of how many people and how long you will need to do the system testing?" You sit down with the requirements, scan them, and get a feel for the complexity and scale of the system to be tested. You consult the architects, designers, and developers, who tell you what they think the particular difficulties with this project will be. You consult the users, who specified the requirements and who are users of existing systems. After a couple of days, you think you have an estimate pretty well pinned down. You can document your test environment and other needs a little later. The estimate is the most important thing for now. You go and talk to the boss, and the following scenario unfolds:

> "I need six testers for eight weeks."
>
> The project manager thinks for a moment and consults his draft schedule and resource plan. "You can have four testers for six weeks and that's all."
>
> You object and say, "But it'll take longer than six weeks! It'll cost more than you've allocated to test this system. The system is bigger than last time. It's more complicated. It's certainly too risky for us to skimp on the testing this time. That's just not enough."
>
> But the manager is adamant, muttering something about other dependencies, higher authorities, and so forth. What, you wonder, was the point of doing an estimate if the manager knew what the budget

must be all along? What relevance does an arbitrary budget have to the job in hand? Why doesn't management ever take testing seriously? The developers always get the time they ask for, don't they? It doesn't seem fair.

Is this a familiar scenario? Has it ever been possible to do enough testing in these circumstances? Just how much testing is enough? Was your estimate based on a known quantity of testing that you deemed to be sufficient? If your boss sets a budget that you feel is too low, what makes you think it should take longer? Why is the boss's idea of enough less than yours?

Even if testers have all of the information required to determine the right amount of testing, it might not be used to make the actual decision. If management values developers more than testers and listens to developers more, it's frustrating for the testers who have wasted time and effort coming up with estimates.

Typically, the tester's reaction is to say, it's going to take longer than 6 weeks; I can't possibly achieve what I need to do in that time; it's bigger and more complicated than you think. Are we not just playing some silly game here? Why are they asking for an estimate when the decision has already been made? In the minds of project managers, however, testers always want more time and resources than are available, and they are never happy with the budget allocated to testing. If, as a tester, you know the project manager will always knock your estimates down, it's tempting to increase your estimates to compensate, but joining in such a cynical distortion is not likely to increase the credibility of testing. So, let us look more closely at the question.

Is it even fair to ask how long testing will take? For most systems the time required for test execution is indeterminate. You don't know how many faults are in the software; you don't know their severity; you don't know how long they will take to fix. You might just as well ask the developers how many bugs they are going to put in. It's a good question to ask. You could say, "Tell me how many bugs you are going to put in, and I'll tell you what I need to detect them." But, where does this leave us?

We know there's no upper limit to how much testing we could do. An infinite number of tests could be planned and executed. If you imagine that the grains of sand on a beach represent the number of tests that could be run, then the tests we have time to implement might be represented by a single pinch. The essence of testing is to select this pinch of sand from the most appropriate grains on the beach. Testing is a sampling activity, and you can only ever do a microscopically small sample of testing. So, test planning must be about selecting the best sample of tests that we can run in the time available.

If we persist with this analogy, is there any point in trying to define the right amount of testing? Because there's no upper limit, there's no easy way to draw a line at the right amount. So, if management arbitrarily limits the testing time or resource available, we don't need to be upset or disheartened. Perhaps the risks of early release are actually worth taking; there might be a net benefit in shipping early, although testers are not typically conditioned to think this way.

It all boils down to this: Testing is always time constrained, and complaining doesn't help. We should have a more rational response based on our understanding of risk. A good tester should identify the risks of concern to a project and propose some activities (tests) that can help to measure or reduce those risks. When the testing is squeezed into a fixed time or budget, we can prioritize those proposed test activities in order of risk and include those tests that fit into the constraints imposed.

In most projects the risks of shipping early are not known, so release decisions are made on the assumption that all will come out right in the end: You got through it last time; maybe you'll be lucky again. In your projects, who knows the risks and benefits of early release? How do you decide when to go live?

One of the key responsibilities of a tester is to ensure that project management is aware of the risks being taken and to document them. Only if they are visible can management recognize the risks they take by squeezing testing. The mechanism is to present the risks, the tests that address those risks, and the risks that management will take by cutting back on testing. Rather than always moaning about needing more time, testers should take management ideas for both addressing risks and taking advantage of benefits. Management should recognize the value of this and that there will be a trade-off. This is more rational than saying, "We always halve the testers' budgets."

In summary, there's no kind of formula for the right amount of testing. In most environments, the level of testing can only be determined by consensus between project management, customer sponsors, developers, technical specialists, and testers. Tests are deemed in scope if they address the risks of concern. Tests can be descoped if they address risks that are deemed too low to worry about, if the test is too costly, or if a test is not the best way to address a particular risk. If no one can see the value of doing a test, it's probably not worth doing. The proper level of testing should be determined by consensus with the tester facilitating and contributing information to the consensus process.

When Should We Stop Testing?

Typically, test plans include acceptance or exit criteria that define a set of targets, such as the following, to be met by a given test stage:

- All tests planned have been run.
- All incidents raised have been resolved.
- All faults found have been fixed and retested.
- All regression tests run without failure.

In your projects, do you ever actually meet acceptance criteria such as these? Typically, time runs out before all tests have been run without failure, some incidents remain open, certain faults still need to be fixed, and retests and regression tests are left incomplete. When decision time comes, have you ever heard the management team ask, Is this really a high severity fault? Compromises are nearly always made: Known faults remain in the system as it is shipped. These faults were deemed acceptable, perhaps on the understanding that fixes would be implemented within some agreed-upon period after release. So, if in most projects the acceptance criteria are compromised in these ways, are the criteria useful at all?

Some testers preach perfection: All bugs are bad; all bugs could be found by testing; therefore, we must select the strictest test techniques and apply them. Objective, inflexible acceptance criteria are sensible guides to ensuring things are done properly. It's very easy for self-appointed experts to preach perfection, but in the real world, it never works like that. When you run out of time, the question becomes, What are the risks of releasing now?

There is a balance to be struck, and this involves comparing the benefits to be gained with the risks. Testers should be able to identify the benefits of release because they know what tests have been run and passed, and these are the evidence that certain benefits are now available. The tests that have failed provide evidence that certain features do not yet work, and so some risks have not yet been addressed.

If tests can be traced back to some risks, you can report at any time the status of those risks. If our test documentation matches tests to risks, we can demonstrate coverage of the risks. In this way, we can trace which risks have not yet been addressed. Normally we talk in terms of coverage of the functional requirements. The risk-based alternative is that we construct tests that cover the risks, and we measure risk coverage using the same standard documentation types as normal. As well as clustering our tests around documented features to say they are covered, we allocate those same tests to risks so we can report risk coverage too.

Suppose we have adopted the risk-based approach, and we encounter the classic squeeze: We run out of time before testing is complete. We must answer two inevitable questions:

1. What are the risks of stopping testing now?
2. What are the benefits of releasing now?

If we have recorded the risks to be addressed by each test, we can identify those risks that have been covered and those that remain outstanding. If we can relate tests to benefits, we can identify the benefits that are ready to be delivered. In most cases, the risks that are addressed aren't the main issue. We need to understand the benefits to be delivered and the residual risks. An imbalance in favor of the benefits allows us to make a positive release decision.

When Is the Product Good Enough?

The *good-enough* approach provides a framework for the release decision. James Bach introduced this idea in 1997 [3], and it has caused some division in the consulting community. On one hand, some experts think it's a cop-out, that it compromises too far, is too simplistic to be useful, promotes shoddy work, and so on. On the other hand, its supporters promote it as reflecting what we do in real life when a less-than-perfect solution is inevitable. The good-enough approach is helpful to understanding the risk-based test approach. It is a good framework for release decision making in projects where risks are being taken.

Were you ever asked as a tester whether a system was good enough to ship? When the time comes to make the big decision, how will you answer that question? If you say, "Well, it's just not ready," the project manager thinks, Testers always say that; they're never happy, and you are dismissed as a pessimist. Suppose you say, "Well, it looks ready to me." Will your project manager put a piece of paper under your nose, asking you to sign it? If you sign, are you taking on someone else's responsibility?

So, what is "good enough" and how does defining it help with the release decision? To understand this, we will start with a look beyond the good-enough approach towards best practices. Many consultants advocate best practices in books and at conferences. They ask leading questions like,

Would you like to improve your processes? Could anyone possibly say no? The consultants' proposition is usually reinforced by such mantras as the following:

- Product perfection can only be achieved through continuous process improvement.

- All bugs are bad; all bugs can be found; so, you must do more rigorous testing, using the most stringent approaches and techniques available.

- Documentation is always worthwhile.

- You can't manage what you can't count.

While they have some value, these mantras can break down under close scrutiny. There is no guarantee that process improvements will result in perfect products. Documentation frequently fails to get the right information to the right readers at the right time. The main purpose of such mantras is to help consultants sell their services. We coined the term *process hypochondriacs* a few years ago to describe those who cannot resist these suggestions and see them as guaranteed cures. A medical hypochondriac becomes aware of a new drug on the market for a particular disease or condition and thinks, I've got symptoms like that, so that drug sounds like what I need! A process hypochondriac reads a survey in one of the technical magazines that says 73% of companies don't do method X, then feels that he or she must have the problem of not doing method X and calls the consultant whose contact details are conveniently listed at the bottom of the page. Yet, who is to say that the 73% that aren't doing method X have a specific problem to solve by that method, or that the problem is always the same problem? Consultants selling services exploit such compulsive behavior.

The good-enough approach is a reaction to this compulsive formalism, as it is called. It's not reasonable to aim for zero defects (at least in software): Your users and customers never expect perfection, so why pretend to yourself and to them that you're aiming for it? The zero-defect attitude just doesn't help. Your customers and users live in the real world—why don't you? Compromise is inevitable, you always know it's coming, and the challenge ahead is to make a decision based on imperfect information. As a tester, don't get upset if your estimates are cut down or your test execution phase is squeezed. Guilt and fear should not be inevitable just because a project is constrained by a lack of budgetary or other resources and has more than zero defects remaining.

In the context of a system (or increment or enhancement) to be released, good enough is achieved when all of the following apply:

- It has sufficient benefits.
- It has no critical problems.
- Its benefits sufficiently outweigh its noncritical problems.
- In the present situation, and all things considered, delaying its release to improve it further would cause more harm than good.

This definition means that there is already enough of this product (this system, increment, or enhancement) working for us to take it into production, use it, get value, and get the benefit. "It has no critical problems" means that there are no severe faults that make it unusable or unacceptable. At this moment, all things considered, investing more time or money into perfecting it would probably cost more than shipping early with the known problems. This framework allows us to release an imperfect product on time because the benefits may be worth it.

Testing fits into determining whether a product is good enough by addressing the following questions.

- *Have sufficient benefits been delivered?* The tests that we execute must at least demonstrate that the features providing the benefits are delivered completely, so we must have evidence of this.
- *Are there any critical problems?* The incident reports that record failures in software provide the evidence of at least the critical problems (and as many other problems as possible). There should be no critical problems for a product to be deemed good enough.
- *Is our testing adequate to support this decision?* Have we provided sufficient evidence to say these risks are addressed and the benefits are available for release?

Who Decides?

It is not a tester's responsibility to decide whether the product is good enough. An analogy that might help here is to view the tester as an expert witness in a court of law. The main players in this familiar scene are as follows:

- The accused (the system under test);
- The judge (the project manager);

- The jury (the stakeholders);
- Expert witness (the tester).

In our simple analogy, we will disregard the lawyer's role and assume that the prosecution and defense are equally good at extracting evidence from witnesses and challenging facts and arguments. We will focus on the expert witness's role. These are people brought into a court of law to present and explain complex evidence in a form that laypeople (the jury) can understand. The expert witness must be objective and detached. If asked whether the evidence points to guilt or innocence, the expert explains what inferences can be made based on the evidence, but refuses to judge. In the same way, the software tester might simply state that based on evidence certain features work, and certain features do not, and that certain risks have been addressed, while other risks remain. It is for others to judge whether this makes a system acceptable.

The tester is there to provide information for the stakeholders to make a decision. After all, testers do not create software or software faults; testers do not take the risks of accepting a system into production. Testers present to their management and peers an informed and independent point of view. When asked to judge whether a product is good enough, the tester might say that on the evidence obtained, these benefits are available, but these risks still exist.

If as a tester you are actually asked to make the decision, what should you do? The answer is that you must help the stakeholders make the decision, but not make it for them. In some instances, the risks you anticipated 6 months ago, which in your opinion would make the system unacceptable, might still exist. If those were agreed upon with the stakeholders at that time, the system cannot now be acceptable, unless they relax their perceptions of the risk. The judgment on outstanding risks must be as follows:

- There is enough test evidence now to judge that certain risks have been addressed.
- There is evidence that some features do not work (the feared risk has materialized).
- Some risks (doubts) remain because of lack of evidence (tests have not been run, or no tests are planned).

This might seem less than ideal as a judgement, but in the e-business world, it is preferable to unrealistic, ideal-world acceptance criteria, such as those discussed earlier. You may still be forced to give an opinion on the readiness of a system, but we believe that by taking a principled position as an expert witness (and taking it as early in the project as possible), you might raise your credibility with management. Management might then give you the right responsibilities on future projects.

The Classic Squeeze on Testing

The well-known squeeze on testing occurs when the developers deliver late, but the go-live deadline remains fixed. The acceptance criteria might be used to determine what happens next, but all too often it is obvious that these criteria cannot be met in time. The pressure to release might be so great that the acceptance criteria are set aside. There may be some attempt to downgrade the severe bugs, perhaps. Acceptance criteria are an uncomfortable reminder of the idealistic attitude of the early stages of the project and do not make the decision to release any easier to make.

The risks that were apparent at the start of testing have been visible throughout. When testing is squeezed, some risks may have been addressed, some benefits may be available, and testers may have revealed new risks to be addressed, but the outstanding risk is apparent to all involved. If the decision to release is actually made, the stakeholders have explicitly chosen to accept a product before they have evidence that all risks are addressed and that all benefits are available. This should not cause the tester any problems. The stakeholders have judged that they had enough information to make that decision.

In fact, the information required to make the release decision is available on the first day of test execution; the balance of evidence simply weighs heavily against release. A positive (though perhaps surprising) principle for risk-based testers is therefore that the time available for test execution has no bearing on your ability to do good testing.

How Good Is Your Testing?

How good is your testing? How would you know? Suppose your boss asks you that question half way through the test execution phase. How would you respond? Do you remember that final day of testing on your last project, when you knew you would go live the following day? You hadn't completed all the tests, but management made the decision (with some trepidation) to go live anyway. Were you certain that your testing was good enough? How could you have known? When the system went live, did users experience problems or was the implementation process smooth? You did a lousy job or a great job, depending on the answer to that last question. The challenging question is this, however: Wouldn't you have liked to know how good your testing was during the testing? Tricky.

What do we mean by good testing? The most common definition is based the number of faults found. If you've found most (if not all) of the important faults during testing, and users found few in production, your testing is good. A metric often quoted is the fault detection percentage (FDP), which is defined as the proportion of all the faults known that were actually found by testing. FDP = $T/(T + P)$ is expressed as a percentage, where T = faults found by testing, P = faults found in production, and $T + P$ = the total known faults (so far). FDP is a calculable metric after a project is finished and the users have had some time to find the residual faults on a system (perhaps a few months). In the midst of testing, however, FDP is incalculable, as you don't know how many faults remain to be found in production.

Experts who promote metrics like FDP also say that you can never find all faults; you can never be perfect; you can never detect the last fault. Good testing is finding a high proportion of faults, but the ultimate target of zero faults is impossible to achieve. Implicitly, your test effectiveness or ability as a tester is measured on this FDP scale—a scale that cannot be calibrated while you are doing your job. FDP is an interesting metric after a system has bedded in. It can be useful for future process improvements, but it can't instill confidence that the testers are doing a good job now; therefore, this metric is not useful during the activity it is meant to support. We need another way of calculating test effectiveness.

Formal coverage measures, against code or requirements, provide a measure of thoroughness, but coverage is only an indirect measure of the quantity of tests evenly distributed according to some arbitrary model. Coverage provides a quantitative assessment of the completeness of testing measured against arbitrary targets. There is some evidence that one of the simplest black-box testing techniques, boundary value analysis (BVA), is more effective than other more expensive techniques [4], but this a difficult, under-researched area. There is no practical limit on the rigor and cost of white-box methods, for example, so can a coverage measure reflect the quality of testing? The answer is no because the measure itself is arbitrary. Ultimately, coverage is a one-dimensional measure of the quantity and thoroughness of testing, not its quality.

A Definition of Good Testing

Because testing is ultimately intended to address risks and provide evidence that risks have or have not been addressed, we propose the following alternative definition of good (or good-enough) testing:

- It provides sufficient evidence of the benefits delivered.
- It provides sufficient evidence of the current risk of release.
- It accomplishes these tasks at an acceptable cost and in an acceptable time frame.

Using this definition, if project management commits to identifying and assessing product risks early on, the performance of the testers can be assessed without reference to having enough time or to bug counts. Even if granted less than adequate time for doing "thorough" testing, the quality of the testing can be assessed very simply, before the project ends: Good testing provides knowledge of the status of benefits and the risk of release.

This definition of good testing implies that the knowledge of risks is a prerequisite to doing any testing. The measure of test quality is the value of the information provided by testers. Even on the first day of test execution, although they haven't run any tests, good testers should be able to report on the current risk of release. The stakeholders take the risks, enjoy the benefits, and pay the bills. Good testing provides sufficient information on the risks and benefits throughout a project for stakeholders to decide how much testing is enough and to make a balanced release decision. Good testing provides sufficient information in a timely manner at a reasonable cost.

The testing is good if the stakeholders deem the following to be true:

- The testers have identified all of the significant risks.
- The tests planned address the documented risk.
- The tests executed provide the stakeholders with enough information to be confident that the risks have been addressed and the benefits are available for release.

This sounds admirably simple, but how could a metric be derived from this? The problem with this way of evaluating testing is that it is both qualitative and subjective. Compared, however, with selecting an arbitrary coverage measure, getting the stakeholders to judge the adequacy of the testing seems reasonable. The reason we test is to address the stakeholders' perceived risk, and only they can judge whether the testing has achieved this goal.

References

[1]   Thompson, N., "Zen and the Art of Object-Oriented Risk Management," *Proc. 7th EuroSTAR Conference*, Barcelona, Spain, November 8–12, 1999.

[2]   Kaner, C., J. Bach, and B. Pettichord, *Lessons Learned in Software Testing*, New York, John Wiley & Sons, 2002.

[3]   Bach, J., "Good Enough Quality: Beyond the Buzzword," *IEEE Computer*, Vol. 30, No. 8, 1997, pp. 96–98.

[4]   Reid, S., "Module Testing Techniques—Which Are the Most Effective?" *Proc. 5th EuroSTAR Conference*, Edinburgh, Scotland, November 24–28, 1997.

4

Risk-Based Test Strategy

At the end of Chapter 1, we set out eight objectives that are appropriate for testing and suggested there was some overlap between them. Here, we have consolidated the eight into four, and we propose that an overall project test process is a structured set of test activities designed to address these four key objectives:

1. To detect faults in software products (documentation and software) so that they can be corrected;

2. To demonstrate and build confidence that stated (and unstated) requirements have been met;

3. To provide evidence that the business benefits required from systems are available;

4. To provide data on the risk of release (and use) of the system under test.

These objectives imply that we must have intimate knowledge of why software faults occur, that we have a good understanding of the requirements and potential benefits of a system, and that we have knowledge of the perceived risks of implementing such a system.

What is a risk-based test strategy? Let us consider the four test objectives above in some more detail. We can restate each of these objectives in terms of risk:

1. We can regard unfound faults in documentation or software as microrisks because each one, being unknown to us, has the potential to cause failures, and this uncertainty gives rise to our perceived risk.

2. We test to eliminate the uncertainty that requirements have not been met. If we find faults, these can be fixed and removed. If we do not find faults, our confidence increases (our uncertainty decreases).

3. We test to eliminate the uncertainty that benefits may not be attained. Tests provide evidence that these benefits are available and the system has value if released to users.

4. We test to address and collect information about all of the risks above.

This means that we can summarize the objectives of all testing with the following definition: Testing aims to measure and reduce software product risk. Using this definition, the risk-based approach to test strategy is simple:

1. We identify software product risks of concern.

2. We design test activities that specifically address those risks (our test objectives).

3. We structure these test activities into an optimal test process.

4. We plan and design tests to achieve our test objectives.

5. We execute those tests and provide information to allow stakeholders to make a release decision based on available benefits and residual risks.

This is the practical implementation of the testers' manifesto defined in Chapter 1.

From Risks to Test Objectives

Risks describe potential outcomes that are undesirable. Risks represent the failures we believe could (but hope won't) occur. Essentially, it is the uncertainty that concerns us, but testing can help us overcome anxiety about potential failure. If we see many examples of our system working, processing typical (and untypical) business transactions in a near-production environment, our concerns about failure in production will diminish.

What kind of failures should we consider? We are concerned about calculations that don't compute correctly, Web pages that don't integrate, systems that make incorrect decisions or that make the correct decision at the wrong time, and so on. We can imagine most of these failures (or modes of failures) as high-level or generic bug categories. We can speculate that any bug occurring in testing and falling into one of these categories will render the system unacceptable, and we would assign it a high severity.

We use risk analysis to direct our attention to the most important concerns. Risks represent failure modes or high-level bug categories. So, to direct the testing we transform the definition of a risk into an objective for testing. The test objective becomes a guideline for the construction of detailed tests that shed light on the existence (or nonexistence) of bugs of a certain type. Why does this help testers?

1. If we focus on risks, we know that faults relating to the selected mode of failure are bound to be important.

2. If we focus on particular bug types, we will probably be more effective at finding those kinds of bugs.

3. If testers provide evidence that certain failure modes do not occur in a range of test scenarios, we will become more confident that the system will work in production.

So, how do we create a test objective from a risk? If the risk represents a failure that we don't want to happen, the test objective can be derived directly from the language used to describe the mode of failure. In fact a test objective typically reverses the language used to describe the risk. If a risk is that *X* might happen, then the test objective might be worded "to demonstrate that *X* does not happen." Often, it's as simple as that.

We use the word "demonstrate" rather than the word "prove," which might imply that we are able to prove with absolute mathematical certainty that a system works. Most testers know that this is impossible for systems of significant size, so we ought not to raise expectations. Yet, is the word "demonstrate" too weak? Well, it's probably the best choice under the circumstances because it represents exactly what we will do in terms of providing evidence upon which others will base a decision. After all, we can only run a tiny fraction of all the theoretically possible tests (with infinite resources), so we really are only doing a demonstration of a small number of tests.

Most testers know that their main goal in creating any test is to expose a fault. The risk-based test objective (to demonstrate that something works) does not contradict this view. To demonstrate that a feature performs a calculation correctly, we would of course subject the feature under test to boundary tests, extreme values, invalid data, exceptional conditions, repeated tests, and so on. We would plan and perform whatever tests we believed had a chance of causing the feature to fail in some way. If we expose faults and these are fixed and retested (and possibly regression tested), we are left with a collection of tests designed to detect faults, where some of them did detect faults, but do so no longer. In other words, we are left with evidence that a given feature works correctly under a wide range of circumstances, and our test objective is therefore met. There is no conflict between a strategic risk-based test objective and the tester's tactical goal of detecting faults.

Table 4.1 presents a few examples of how we might derive test objectives from risks. The big question now is, How many sample tests are enough to address a risk? We need to introduce test coverage measures into the process.

Risks, Test Objectives, and Coverage

The examples provided in Table 4.1 show that articulating a test objective by examining the description of a risk is fairly straightforward. At the same time, the examples show what the tester has to do, but give no indication of the quantity of testing to be done in any of the three cases. What is missing is a notion of coverage. The question is, How much testing is required to

Table 4.1
Deriving Test Objectives from Risks

ID	Risk	Test Objective
1	The Web site fails to function correctly on the user's client OS and browser configuration.	To demonstrate that the application functions correctly on selected combinations of OSs and browser version combinations.
2	Bank-statement details presented in the client browser do not match records in the back-end legacy banking systems.	To demonstrate that statement details presented in the client browser reconcile with back-end legacy systems.
3	Vulnerabilities that hackers could exploit exist in the Web site's networking infrastructure.	To demonstrate through audit, scanning, and ethical hacking that there are no security vulnerabilities in the Web site's networking infrastructure.

provide enough information to stakeholders to demonstrate that a risk has been addressed?

Let's look at behavioral testing first. There are excellent textbooks [1, 2] and a test standard, British Standard BS 7925-2 [3], that describe test design techniques. There are very well-documented coverage measures that relate to both functional (black-box) and structural (white- or glass-box) test design techniques. There are relationships between many techniques. For example, the BVA technique will generate more tests than the equivalence partitioning (EP) technique. In fact, BVA subsumes EP because it generates all of the tests that would be generated by EP, plus a few more, in most circumstances. As BVA is a stronger technique, we might use it where concerns about failure are higher. EP might be more appropriate where the concerns are lower. We have sometimes suggested to our clients that BVA is appropriate for functional system testing and that EP is appropriate for user acceptance testing. Many functional test techniques (e.g., decision tables, state transition testing, syntax testing) do not fit into such an ordered hierarchy, however. These (and other) techniques have specific areas of applicability. The tester should explain how they are used, as well as their potential depth and the consequent cost of using them, to the stakeholders.

Most structural test techniques are based on the path testing model, and there is a more inclusive ordered hierarchy of such techniques. Statement testing, branch testing, modified condition decision testing, and branch condition combination testing are increasingly thorough (and expensive). Of these techniques, statement testing is the weakest and branch condition combination testing, which subsumes all of the others, is the strongest. Although these techniques are increasingly expensive, there is little data available that compares their cost-effectiveness. BS 7925-2 [3] presents comprehensive definitions and a discussion of all of these techniques. The prepublication version of this standards material is also available free of charge at http://www.testingstandards.co.uk.

Some test techniques are less formal or not yet mature enough to have defined coverage levels. In the examples quoted in Table 4.1, the coverage targets for configuration testing and ethical hacking as means of detecting security flaws are likely to be subjective.

Where the test budget is limited, the tester should indicate how much coverage (in one form or another) could be achieved in the time available and ask the stakeholders whether that is acceptable. In the case where there is no budget stated, the tester might have to propose coverage targets of increasing thoroughness (and cost). The stakeholders must then take a view as to which of these coverage targets will be adequate. There are many techniques, discussed in Chapters 9 through 15, that do not have formally defined coverage measures. Where it is possible to conduct such tests with varying thoroughness, the testers and stakeholders need to agree how much coverage is enough.

The W-Model Extends the V-Model of Testing

Figure 4.1 presents the V-model of testing, in which the dynamic test stages on the right-hand side of the model use the documentation identified on the left-hand side as baselines for testing. The V-model further promotes the notion of early test preparation, which finds faults in baselines and is also an effective way of detecting faults early (see Figure 4.2). This approach is fine in principle, and the early test preparation approach is always effective. There are two problems, however, with the V-model as it is normally presented.

First, in our experience there is rarely a perfect, one-to-one relationship between the documents on the left-hand side and the test activities on the right. For example, functional specifications don't usually provide enough information for a system test. System tests must often take into account some aspects of the business requirements, as well as physical design issues, for example. System testing usually draws on several sources of requirements information to be thoroughly planned.

Second, and more importantly, the V-model has little to say about static testing at all. It treats testing as a back-door activity on the right-hand side of the model. There is no mention of the potentially greater value and effectiveness of static tests, such as reviews, inspections, static code analysis,

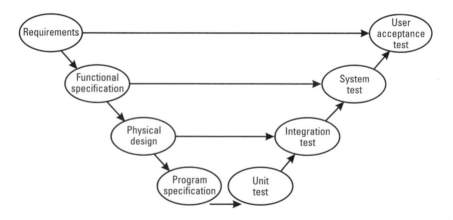

Figure 4.1 The V-model of testing.

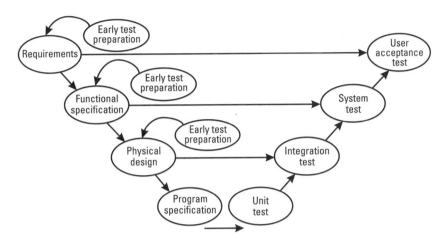

Figure 4.2 The V-model with early test preparation.

and so on. This is a major omission, and the V-model does not support the broader view of testing as a constantly prominent activity throughout the development life cycle.

Paul Herzlich introduced the W-model approach in 1993 [4]. The W-model (Figure 4.3) attempts to address shortcomings in the V-model. Rather than focusing on specific dynamic test stages, as the V-model does, the W-model focuses on the development products themselves. Essentially, every development activity that produces a work product is shadowed by a

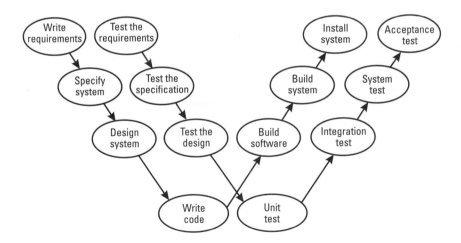

Figure 4.3 The W-model of testing.

test activity, the specific purpose of which is to determine whether the objectives of a development activity have been met and the deliverable meets its requirements. In its most generic form, the W-model presents a standard development life cycle with every development stage mirrored by a test activity. On the left-hand side, typically, the deliverables of a development activity (for example, "write requirements") are accompanied by test activities ("test the requirements") and so on. If your organization has a different set of development stages, then the W-model is easily adjusted to your situation. The important thing is this: The W-model of testing focuses specifically on the product risks of concern at the point where testing can be most effective.

If we focus on the static test techniques presented in Figure 4.4, we see that there is a wide range of techniques available for evaluating the products of the left-hand side. Inspections, reviews, walkthroughs, static analysis, requirements animation, and early test case preparation can all be used.

If we consider the dynamic test techniques presented in Figure 4.5, we see that there is also a wide range of techniques available for evaluating executable software and systems. The traditional unit, integration, system, and acceptance tests can make use of the functional test design and measurement techniques, as well as the nonfunctional test techniques, which are all available to address specific test objectives.

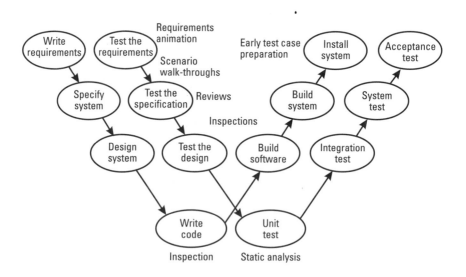

Figure 4.4 The W-model and static test techniques.

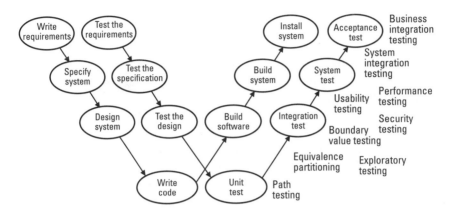

Figure 4.5 The W-model and dynamic test techniques.

The W-model removes the rather artificial constraint of having the same number of dynamic test stages as development stages. If there are five development stages concerned with the definition, design, and construction of code in your project, it might be sensible to have only three stages of dynamic testing. Component, system, and acceptance testing might fit your normal way of working. The test objectives for the whole project would be distributed across three stages, not five. There may be practical reasons for doing this and the decision is based on an evaluation of product risks and how best to address them. The W-model does not enforce a project symmetry that does not (or cannot) exist in reality. The W-model does not impose any rule that later dynamic tests must be based on documents created in specific stages (although earlier documentation products are nearly always used as baselines for dynamic testing). More recently, the Unified Modeling Language (UML) described in Booch, Rumbaugh, and Jacobsen's book [5] and the methodologies based on it, namely the Unified Software Development Process and the Rational Unified Process [6, 7], have emerged in importance. In projects using these methods, requirements and designs might be documented in multiple models so system testing might be based on several of these models (spread over several documents).

We will use the W-model in test strategy as follows: Having identified the risks of concern, we specify the products that need to be tested. Next, we select test techniques (static reviews or dynamic test stages) to be used on those products to address the risks. We then schedule test activities as close as practicable to the development activity that generated the products to be tested.

Master Test Planning

Our test process is normally defined in an MTP, or master test plan. The MTP is an overarching document setting out the context of the testing, the process to be used, the software product risks to be addressed, and the definition of the stages of testing to address them. In the MTP process, the direction and focus of testing, and, therefore, the content of the MTP document, are determined by consensus. Typically, the testers plan and organize the MTP development effort and facilitate the meetings required to reach the necessary level of mutual understanding and agreement. The stakeholders, customers, project management, users, and technical staff must all be consulted to ensure that all areas of concern are addressed and that decisions are supported by both business and technical knowledge. This consensus approach is essential to setting reasonable and clear expectations to, in turn, ensure buy-in and support of the plan when the going gets tough later.

We are strong advocates of workshop sessions to help projects build up a skeleton MTP quickly. These sessions are the best way to get project staff to raise their concerns and discuss their needs in terms of assurance that a system works and is acceptable. The workshop format also is an ideal place for brainstorming risks and, when the time comes, for analyzing them, as well as for exposing misunderstandings and conflicting perceptions or assumptions.

The following sections describe a comprehensive method for conducting a risk analysis and preparing a skeletal test process for inclusion in an MTP. You can streamline the method by nominating the risks in scope without the scoring if you want to.

Failure Mode and Effects Analysis

First, we need to introduce a technique called failure mode and effects analysis (FMEA), which is a method for identifying potential problems before they occur and using an analysis of their potential effects to decide what to do to prevent them. FMEA is one of many techniques used in the high-integrity software industry to analyze software risks and take proactive measures to reduce or eliminate them. The heritage of FMEA is in manufacturing and mechanical engineering, and FMEA is useful in many other domains, but its use in software projects is well established. McDermott, Mikulak, and Beauregard's *The Basics of FMEA* [8] is an excellent little book that introduces the technique and its application. Nancy Leveson's *Safeware* [9] provides a description of FMEA in the context of safety analyses and other techniques in general. FMEA is but one technique among many that come under the broad heading of hazard analyses.

The Risk-Based Test Process Method

The method for preparing a risk-based test process presented here is based on the first three activities of the generic risk management process described in Chapter 2. After risk identification and analysis, the response-planning stage is based on the FMEA technique and the remaining two tasks complete the test process for inclusion in an MTP.

The preparation of the risk-based test process has five stages:

1. Risk identification;
2. Risk analysis;
3. Risk response;
4. Test scoping;
5. Test process definition.

The technique described here is an adaptation of FMEA specific to our purpose: to develop a test process for a project. The key working document of the method is the test process worksheet (TPW), which is simply an inventory of failure modes (the risks) with additional columns for scoring and prioritization, assignment of test objectives, efforts, costs, and so on. Because it is a single table, the TPW is easily managed in a spreadsheet or database, with one row for each failure mode identified. Each failure mode has its own profile with perhaps 15 attributes defined in the columns of Table 4.2. The rightmost columns present how the failure-mode attributes are used in the five stages of test process development. The meanings of the entries in these columns are as follows:

C—attribute is created;

U—attribute is updated;

F—attribute is finalized.

Columns 13, 14, and 15, etc., relate to the proposed stages in the test process. Each project will have its own test stages (such as unit, integration, system, and acceptance) defined in accordance with its test strategy. The TPW is the working document that focuses attention on software product

Table 4.2
Failure Mode Attributes—Column Descriptions

Column Number	Column Heading	Column Description	Identification	Analysis	Response	Scoping	Process
1	Failure mode (the risk)	Provide a brief description of the mode of failure	C	U		F	
2	Benefits threatened	Identify which cardinal objective or business benefit(s) is threatened	C	U		F	
3	Probability	What is the likelihood of the system being prone to this mode of failure?		F			
4	Consequence	What is the consequence of this mode of failure?		F			
5	Exposure	Product of Columns 3 and 4		F			
6	Test effectiveness	How confident are the testers that they can address this risk?			F		
7	Test priority number	Product of Columns 3, 4, and 6			F		
8	Test objective(s)	What test objective will be used to address this risk?			C	U	F
9	Test technique	What method or technique is to be used in testing?			C	U	F
10	Dependencies	What do the testers assume or depend on?			C	U	F
11	Effort	How much effort is required to do this testing?			C	U	F
12	Timescale	How much elapsed time is required to do this testing?			C	U	F
13	Test stage A	Which person or group will perform this test activity?			C	U	F
14	Test stage B	Which person or group will perform this test activity?			C	U	F
15	Test stage C, etc.	Which person or group will perform this test activity?			C	U	F

risks, the risk analyses, and how testing will (or will not) address those risks. The completed TPW is an agreed-on test approach that can be inserted directly into an MTP, and the activities, responsibilities, dependencies, estimates, and timescales can be used in an overall project schedule. Figure 4.6 sets out the five stages of the method. Against each stage, the key activities are listed. The five stages are described in detail below; numbers in parentheses refer to the column headings in Table 4.2.

Stage 1: Risk Identification (Columns 1, 2)

An inventory of potential failure modes is prepared. These are derived from existing checklists of failure modes (most commonly) and generic risk lists that can be used to seed the discussions in a risk workshop. Developers, users, technical support staff, and the testers are probably best placed to generate the initial list of failure modes. At this stage, the probabilities and consequences are not considered. Failure modes that are obvious duplicates should be discarded. Some complex failure modes might be better split into multiple failure modes to simplify later analysis. This first stage is used only to

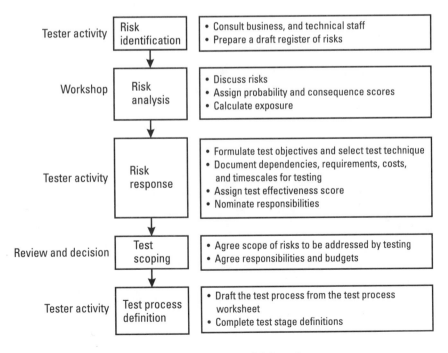

Figure 4.6 The five-stage method for preparing a risk-based test process.

generate the starting list of failure modes that represent the software product risks under consideration. The stages that follow will rationalize the list of risks.

The tester should compile the inventory of risks from practitioners' input, schedule the risk workshop, and copy the risk inventory to the attendees. Each risk is allocated a unique identifier.

Stage 2: Risk Analysis (Columns 1–5)

At this stage, the risk workshop is convened. This should involve technically qualified representatives from the business, development, technical support, and testing communities. The workshop should involve some more senior managers who are able to see the bigger picture. Ideally the project manager, development manager, and business manager should be present.

Each risk (1) is considered and its probability (3) and consequence (4) assessed. A consensus on each should be reached. Some guidelines for resolving discrepancies in perceived probability or risk are presented in the next section. The risk exposure (5) is calculated when the scores are agreed on. Table 4.3 is an example of a partial TPW showing these columns.

Stage 3: Risk Response (Columns 6–15, etc.)

When the candidate risks have been agreed on and the workshop is over, the tester takes each risk in turn and considers whether it is testable. If it is, the tester constructs a test objective (8), using the description of the failure mode. If possible, the tester then specifies a test activity or technique (9) that should meet the test objective. Typical techniques include requirements or design reviews, inspections or static analysis of code or components, or integration, system, or acceptance tests. Other risks will require technology-specific or specialized techniques, such as link checking or HTML validation, for example. Many risks relate to nonfunctional requirements, so usability, performance, or security tests might be appropriate. Chapters 9 through 15 provide guidance on failure modes and the specific techniques for testing them. Table 4.4 presents the risk analysis with the test effectiveness score applied.

The test effectiveness score (6) is a number between one and five that relates to how confident the tester is that a risk could be addressed through testing. A score of one would imply testing is not the way to address this risk or an appropriate test objective would prove to be unachievable. A score of five would imply high confidence that testing will find faults and provide

Table 4.3
Sample Risk Analysis Columns of the TPW

ID	Risk (1)	Probability (3)	Consequence (4)	Exposure (5)
	Client Platform			
04	Invalid or incorrect HTML may exist on pages without being reported by browsers or visible to developers or testers.	4	4	16
05	HTML used may work on one browser, but on others.	4	4	16
06	Users with client machines set up to use foreign character sets may experience unusual effects on their browsers. Foreign characters may be rejected by the database.	3	4	12
	Component Functionality			
13	Spelling mistakes on Web pages may irritate users and damage our credibility.	5	4	20
	Integration			
19	Links to on- or off-site pages that do not work make the site unusable.	4	4	16
20	Integration faults in the infrastructure may cause the full or partial failure of the application.	4	5	20
	Infrastructure			
60	Changes to existing infrastructure may be faulty and cause the new application to fail.	4	4	16
61	Changes to existing infrastructure may be faulty and cause existing applications to fail.	4	5	20

Table 4.4
Risk Analysis and Test Effectiveness Scores

ID	Risk (1)	Probability (3)	Consequence (4)	Exposure (5)	Test Effectiveness (6)	Test Priority Number (7)
	Client Platform					
04	Invalid or incorrect HTML may exist on pages without being reported by browsers or visible to developers or testers.	4	4	16	5	80
05	HTML used may work on one browser, but not others.	4	4	16	4	64
06	Users with client machines set up to use foreign character sets may experience unusual effects on their browsers. Foreign characters may be rejected by the database.	3	4	12	4	48
	Component Functionality					
13	Spelling mistakes on Web pages may irritate users and damage our credibility.	5	4	20	5	100
	Integration					
19	Links to on- or off-site pages that do not work make the site unusable.	4	4	16	5	80
20	Integration faults in the infrastructure may cause full or partial failure of the application.	4	5	20	4	80
	Infrastructure					
60	Changes to existing infrastructure may be faulty and cause the new application to fail.	4	4	16	4	64
61	Changes to existing infrastructure may be faulty and cause existing applications to fail.	4	5	20	4	80

evidence that the risk has been addressed. Where the score implies confidence, be very careful to identify and describe fully any assumptions and dependencies (10). Typically, these involve the availability of skills, tools, and test environments. You can also prepare an estimate of the effort (11) and elapsed time (12) required to plan, prepare, and execute these tests. Some tests will be separate, stand-alone exercises, and it is reasonable to estimate these separately. Where you know that a test will definitely be merged with other test activities, prepare a single estimate for all tasks that would be performed together and indicate which tasks are included. Put the total estimate for these tests against the first task in the group. If you add all of the estimates in Column 11, the total will be the overall cost of testing. Don't attempt to be absolutely precise in the estimate. These estimates are for comparative purposes and potentially for setting the budget for later testing.

The test priority number (TPN) (7) is the product of the probability, consequence, and test effectiveness scores; it is an indicator of how prominently this risk and test objective ought to figure in test plans. It is possible that some high-exposure risks score low TPNs because the tester is not confident that testing can address these risks. Other, relatively low-exposure risks might score well because it is easy to conduct the tests that address them.

The tester should nominate the person or group that will perform the testing for each objective in one of the test stages (13–15, etc.). The column headings you might use could be Reviews, Unit Test, Integration Test, System Test, and so on. The test stages used should be agreed on with the project manager beforehand. The project manager might wish to be in on the allocation of test activities to test stages and the assignment of responsibilities, so invite him or her to get involved first. At this point, these allocations are for discussion with the parties nominated to do the work, and although many test activities will be easy to assign, some later tests, for example, large-scale integration testing, might require both development and user involvement to execute because of their scale or technical complexity.

Table 4.5 shows an example of test objectives being assigned to test stages. In this partial listing, the development team will conduct the tests for test objectives 4–6, 13, and 19 during unit testing. The infrastructure team will conduct the tests for test objectives 20, 60, and 61 during the infrastructure test stage.

Stage 4: Test Scoping (Columns 1, 2, 8–15, etc.)

Scoping the test process is the review activity that requires the involvement of all of stakeholders and staff with technical knowledge. At this point, the

Table 4.5
Test Objectives Assigned to Test Stages and Teams

ID	Test Objective (8)	Infrastructure Test (13)	Unit Test (14)	System Test (15)	UA Test (16)
	Client Platform				
04	Verify that browser HTML syntax is correct.		Development team		
05	Verify that HTML is compatible across supported browsers.		Development team		
06	Confirm that selected local character sets are compatible with the database and do not affect usability of the browser interface.		Development team		
	Component Functionality				
13	Verify HTML page content spelling.		Development team		
	Integration				
19	Verify that all links to on- and off-site pages work and that there are no orphaned links.		Development team		
20	Demonstrate that infrastructure components integrate correctly.	Infrastructure team			
	Infrastructure				
60	Demonstrate that enhancements to existing infrastructure meet requirements.	Infrastructure team			
61	Regression test existing infrastructure to ensure existing functionality is not affected.	Infrastructure team			

major decisions about what is in and out of scope for testing are made; it is therefore essential that the staff in the meeting have the authority to make these decisions on behalf of the business, the project management, and technical support. There are two ways of reviewing the TPW.

The first and simplest method is to read each row in turn, considering the risk and its exposure score, followed by the test effectiveness score and estimates of costs, effort, and dependencies. A decision to include (or exclude) each test objective in the test process is based on the merit of each case. When the whole TPW has been assessed, the cost of the testing is calculated. If this exceeds the projected test budget, then a reassessment of the least important test objectives should be undertaken, which may require some discussion to resolve.

The second method is to use a report produced by the tester that ranks all risks in order of TPN with the running total of costs. If an approximate budget for testing has already been set, the workshop assumes that all high TPN risks above a certain threshold, where the budget is not exceeded, are in scope. The risks that are out of scope (below the threshold) are then considered in turn. Any anomalies, such as where someone believes a descoped test objective should be in scope, are discussed. Potential outcomes include dropping the test objective from the test plan, including the test objective at the expense of another test objective deemed less important, or increasing the budget to incorporate this test objective in the plan.

As a test objective is deemed to be in scope, the person or group nominated to perform the testing for that test objective should confirm acceptance of the responsibility or reject it, suggesting an alternative responsibility. In most cases, the responsibility is obvious, but some test objectives may fall between two stages or groups. Some test objectives may need to be jointly owned (e.g., by the system supplier and customer) in some circumstances. The responsible group(s) should check that the assumptions and dependencies identified for the test objective are correct.

Stage 5: Test Process Definition (Columns 8–15, etc.)

At this point, the scope of the testing has been agreed on, with test objectives, responsibilities, and stages in the overall project plan decided. It is now possible to compile the test objectives, assumptions, dependencies, and estimates for each test stage and publish a definition for each stage in the test process. The stage-by-stage test process can now be documented and issued in a draft MTP. The information required to complete the MTP can now be derived from the test stage definitions. Table 4.6 shows an example unit test stage definition, which assigns the test objectives nominated in Table 4.5 to unit testing.

Table 4.6
Sample Unit Test Stage Definition for a Web Application

Test Stage:	Unit Testing
Description:	Testing done on low-level components bought in or developed by the supplier, who will perform the testing
Object Under Test:	Web components in isolation and middleware subsystem
Test Objectives:	

Client Platform

04	Verify that browser HTML syntax is correct
05	Verify that HTML is compatible across supported browsers
06	Confirm that selected local character sets are compatible with the database and do not affect usability of the browser interface

Component Functionality

13	Verify HTML page content spelling and that HTML meets visual requirements

Integration

19	Verify that all links to on- and off-site pages work correctly and that there are no orphaned links

Baseline:	Physical design documents (work products from the macro design stage)
Entry Criteria:	Component code has been reviewed and signed off on
Exit Criteria:	All tests run successfully
	All incidents raised have been retested and signed off on
	All acceptance criteria have been met in full
Environment:	Development environment
Planning:	Joe Planner, supplier team
Preparation:	Developer, supplier
Execution:	Developer, supplier
Management:	Bill Smith, supplier
Sign Off:	Nancy Director, supplier, and Peter Auditor, customer team

Method Guidance

So far, we've provided an overview of the method. Here are some guidelines for making the process work smoothly.

Aren't the Risk Numbers Meaningless?

Taken out of context, the probability, consequence, and test effectiveness numbers are meaningless. Their purpose is partly to provide a means of prioritizing risks and test objectives for consideration for inclusion in test plans. The number should be used only as a rough guide along those lines.

More importantly, the numbers force the participants to think about how likely and how serious these risks are and how easy or difficult it will be to meet the test objectives. Disagreement among participants as to the numbers to be assigned indicates that there are different perceptions or mistaken assumptions around the table, and further discussion is in order. For example, the developers might regard a piece of functionality as so simple it cannot represent high risk. The users, however, might think that failure of this same functionality is completely unacceptable under any circumstance. The discussion that follows should force developers to rethink their stance and take that risk more seriously. On the other hand, customers might fear a particular failure mode and regard it as highly probable. The developers may have to explain the thinking behind reuse of a particularly reliable component and assure the users that it will be less likely to fail. The value of the numeric risk assessment is that it is a catalyst for these discussions. The numbers should not be used outside the context of the MTP process.

What If Participants Can't Agree?

It is likely that for some risks, consensus on the scores for probability or consequence will be difficult to achieve. It is inevitable that users, developers, and management have different perceptions of risk, so that initial views are bound to differ. Problems arise when participants at the table cannot accept differing viewpoints and assessment scores. Before the risk assessment workshops take place, the participants should come to an agreement as to how such disputes will be resolved. The most commonly used methods are as follows:

- *Assume the worst.* Given entrenched views, take the higher value for probability or consequence. This is more likely to promote the risk into the test plan, but better to include a risk that can be dropped later, than not include the risk at all.
- *Senior participant decides.* Where a dispute arises, the senior member (or chair) of the workshop takes a view and makes the final decision.
- *Consult the expert.* There is disagreement and uncertainty because the person with most knowledge does not attend the meeting. Consider taking time out to obtain the expert's views before making a final decision.

- *Compare with other risks.* It is often easier to compare a risk that is difficult to rank with other similar risks. Although scoring is hard, a risk may fall in between or be comparable to other risks. Use this to select values.

- *Take a vote.* Put the prospective scores to a vote. This assumes that all the participants are equally informed and also have equal influence. The chair has the deciding vote, but if there is doubt that a sensible outcome will arise, perhaps you should discuss it further.

- *Discuss it further.* Talk it through further. Maybe this risk should be put to one side while other risks are considered. There may be serious underlying concerns exposed by more discussion. Perceptions can be difficult to dislodge and it may take time to discuss the evidence for and against entrenched or misinformed views. You may have a better understanding of the bigger picture later.

Perceptions of risk are still perceptions. People differ in their view of risk, and that is perfectly natural. Wide disagreement, however, may be due to mistaken assumptions, prejudices, or incomplete evidence. Discussion, persuasion, reasoned argument, and hard evidence might all be needed to find the underlying cause of the risk and concerns and to achieve consensus. One of the major benefits of the workshop format is that these fault lines in projects can be exposed and resolved.

What If a Test Objective Is Unachievable?

If you can't do the job yourself, should you score the test effectiveness low? Suppose, for example, that poor performance emerges as a major risk. Performance testing is now a well-established discipline, but we know that it requires specialized skills, expensive tools, production-scale test environments, and time. If you lack the required skills, should you automatically score the test effectiveness low? You might feel that it would be dangerous to suggest otherwise. After all, you might get the job of doing the performance test! Because you lack confidence, it might seem appropriate to suggest a very low level of test effectiveness.

It might be more appropriate, however, to score the effectiveness high, but only if you have access to the required skills, either through internal training, the hiring of external consultants, or outsourcing the test entirely. Certain practicalities may lead you to choose one option over another, but you should describe the pros and cons of the alternate courses of action (even though performing the task yourself is not one of them). Outsourcing might be a common practice, but there might also be a freeze on such activities due to recent bad experiences. Whichever path you take, be prepared to justify the score you assign. If you do choose to be confident, make sure you state your assumptions and dependencies clearly. Costs, effort, timescales, and dependencies on other internal staff should all be mentioned. If you are tasked with doing the test, you will have at least set the expectations for your requirements.

One final option is to score the test effectiveness low, at the same time suggesting that you are not qualified to make such an assessment. A sensible suggestion might be to hire a consultant to study this risk further and make an appropriate recommendation. If there is a concern over security vulnerabilities and hacking, this may be your only option. After all, few testers have direct experience of ethical hacking and security assessment. Taking this route is not a cop-out—you are simply saying that this specialized testing task is outside your area of expertise.

If you have no confidence that anyone could achieve this test objective, just say so. The risk may not be prone to testing at all. In this case, the risk will most likely be referred to senior management to resolve in some other way.

What If the Testing Will Cost Too Much?

Performance testing can be a very expensive activity. If you calculate that the cost of achieving a test objective is much higher than you know the project can afford, what do you do? You could score the test effectiveness low, on the basis that you know the costs are too high so the required tests will never be done properly, if at all, but we don't recommend this route. When the time comes, management will ask why the serious performance risk is not ranked very high. If you say it is possible to conduct performance testing, but that you assumed the project wouldn't pay, management may think you were presumptuous. A better approach would be to score the test effectiveness high and document all of your assumptions carefully, then allow management to choose whether to take the risk or pay the price. This is a decision to be made by management, not you. You never know, this time they might just fund the test.

Shouldn't We Automatically Include Simple Tests?

Some tests are very easy or inexpensive to perform. They may address risks that are perceived to be quite low, but, under normal circumstances, it would be foolish to ignore or reject them. Examples might be Web page link checking or assessing the size of Web pages so they download quickly over low-bandwidth dial-up connections. In this case, the tester should promote these tests into the plan anyway and make such a recommendation to the project.

Don't Forget Generic Test Objectives

The risks and test objectives listed at the start of each of Chapters 9 to 15 are specific to the test types described in each chapter; however, there are test objectives that relate to broader issues, such as contractual obligations, meeting requirements, the acceptability of a system to its users, and so on. Other generic objectives might demonstrate that all or specified functional or nonfunctional requirements are met. These could relate to performance objectives or usability levels, perhaps. Nonnegotiable test objectives might relate to mandatory rules imposed by an industry regulatory authority, and so on.

Table 4.7 shows some generic test objectives that could be included in the definition of your test stages.

The risk-based test objectives we will encounter in Chapters 9 through 15 are included for use as a template for your test process. The full

Table 4.7
Generic Test Objectives

ID	Test Objective	Typical Test Stage
G1	Demonstrate component meets requirements	Component testing
G2	Demonstrate component is ready for reuse in larger subsystem	Component testing
G3	Demonstrate integrated components are correctly assembled or combined and collaborate	Integration testing
G4	Demonstrate system meets functional requirements	Functional system testing
G5	Demonstrate system meets nonfunctional requirements	Nonfunctional system testing
G6	Demonstrate system meets industry regulation requirements	System or acceptance testing
G7	Demonstrate supplier meets contractual obligations	(Contract) acceptance testing
G8	Validate that system meets business or user requirements	(User) acceptance testing
G9	Demonstrate system, processes, and people meet business requirements	(User) acceptance testing

complement of objectives for a test stage would normally include some generic test objectives; therefore, if appropriate, append these to the risk-based test objectives for each test stage.

Risks and Exploratory Testing

At this point it is worth mentioning exploratory testing (ET), a term coined by Cem Kaner in his book *Testing Computer Software* [10]. ET attempts to systematize a testing approach that puts exploration and discovery at the heart of the test process. Where there is uncertainty as to what tests to do next, ET leads you to speculate what the next test should be. The outcomes of the tests you just ran are used to trigger ideas for subsequent tests. James Bach is a prominent advocate of the technique (although he would emphasize it is not the same thing as a test design technique), and there are brief articles describing the approach on his Web site [11, 12].

When is ET used? This technique is most obviously applicable when it is not clear what tests might be run next. This problem might arise right from the start, when you are handed a risk-based test objective. If you are asked to test a system that is poorly documented and not well understood, the exploratory approach provides a framework for discovering what a product does, identifying areas of concern, and homing in on faults that might cause the most concern. If all the preplanned tests have been run, and there is time to explore, ET might expose faults in areas already proven to be error prone. When there is a holdup because you are waiting for a new build to arrive, ET provides a productive way to spend otherwise slack time between test cycles.

It goes almost without saying that most testers enjoy doing ET. It frees them from having to think in an abstract and artificial way about test design and documentation and allows them to follow their intuition and exploit the knowledge gained by running tests immediately. Preplanned, fully documented tests do not allow the same freedom and suppress the initiative of good testers. Nor do they normally allow variation or extra tests to be conducted on the fly. As a result, many excellent tests may never be run. It should be said that ETs should still be documented, but this occurs after they are run.

In which risk areas could you use ET? One obvious area would be context testing (Chapter 11), where the tester might speculate on ways of breaking the context of Web transactions. All of the functional tests could benefit from some ET activity. Penetration tests (Chapter 14) are another obvious area where the exploratory approach is often used in the testers' attempts to crack or subvert the countermeasures implemented by system administrators. The ET approach probably maps very well to that used by attackers in their pursuit of system vulnerabilities. Bear in mind that the ET approach is universally applicable and need not be constrained to the areas mentioned above. All of the risk areas described in later chapters would benefit to varying degrees from this approach.

It would be convenient if all of the risks made themselves visible at the start of the project. Of course, this never happens—some risks are hidden from us until we actually start to test the product. One of the major benefits of ET is that when new risks emerge from the execution of tests (preplanned or otherwise), you can use this technique to investigate these risk areas further. They might turn out to be more important than many of the risks envisaged at the start of the project. When formulating test plans, you should always make allowance for some exploratory testing to take advantage of the benefits it offers.

Risk- and Benefit–Based Test Reporting

One of the key advantages of risk-based testing is that it can provide comprehensive information to help management decide whether a system is ready for release. The key to providing this information is to reference every test to a test objective; in this way, every test pass or failure can be referenced back to a risk. When all of the tests that refer to a specific risk have been passed, we may deem the risk cleared: Enough evidence has been produced that the risk has been addressed. A second advantage of risk-based testing is that every risk has been assessed based on its impact on the project's cardinal objectives (the benefits). We can transform the list of risks and their impact on the objectives into a set of dependencies for each objective. Each objective is dependent on (or blocked by) a set of risks. When all the tests for all the risks are passed, the objective can be met (the benefit can be obtained).

Let's look at how these two ideas can be used to provide both risk-based and benefits-based test reporting and help management make better release decisions. These forms of reporting are most easily presented in a graphical format. Risk-based and benefits-based test reporting are wholly dependent on having performed a risk analysis and based the test process and subsequent tests on that risk analysis.

Suppose we have done a risk analysis and all tests for all test stages are related to risks. We can obviously say at the start of system test execution that none of the test objectives has been met. Therefore, we can presume that all of the risks to be addressed by this stage of testing still exist. That is, all known product risks are outstanding. With this assumption, we are saying that the system is guilty until proven innocent, or, in other words, the system is entirely unacceptable. This is obvious, perhaps, but why is this important?

On the first day of testing we can say, "We have run zero tests. Here are the outstanding risks of release." As we progress through the test plan, one by one, risks are cleared as all the tests that address each risk are passed. Halfway through the test plan, the tester can say, "We have run some tests. These risks have been addressed (we have evidence). Here are the outstanding risks of release." Suppose testing continues, but the testers run out of time before the test plan is completed. The go-live date approaches, and management wants to judge whether the system is acceptable. Although the testing has not been finished, the tester can still say, "We have run some tests. These risks have been addressed (we have evidence). Here are the outstanding risks of release." The tester can present exactly the same message throughout each test stage, except the proportion of risks addressed to those outstanding increases over time.

How does this help? Throughout the test execution phase, management always has enough information to make the release decision. Either management will decide to release with known risks or choose not to release until the known risks (the outstanding risks that are unacceptable) are addressed. A risk-based testing approach means that cutting testing short does not preclude making a rational decision; it just makes the decision to release less likely.

How might you report risk-based test execution progress? Figure 4.7 shows a diagram representing progress through the test plan in the form of risks addressed over time. Along the vertical axis, we have the known risks of

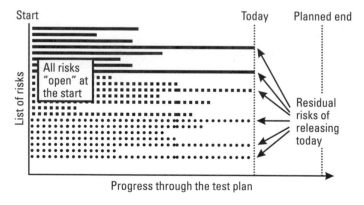

Figure 4.7 Risk-based reporting.

release to be addressed by the testing. On the first day of testing all risks are outstanding. As the test progresses along the horizontal axis, risks are eliminated as more and more tests are completed successfully. At any time during the testing, you can see the current risk of release (e.g., today, there are six risks remaining). If the risks represented by the solid line are critical risks, then it is clear that the system is still not yet acceptable. The tests not yet executed or not yet passed that block acceptance are clearly the high priority tests.

If we identified many risks in our project, and in a large, complex project you might identify between 60 and 80 risks, these risks are likely to be addressed across all the development and test stages. So, the horizontal scale might include all stages of testing, not just system or acceptance testing. As the project proceeds, the risks that the developers address through unit and integration testing are as visible as those in acceptance. The value of reporting against all risks in this way is that the developers and system and acceptance testers all see clearly the risks for which they are responsible. Management, too, has visibility of the risks and can see risks being closed as test evidence is produced. If test evidence is not produced, risks will remain open. If you have problems in your organization with developers doing testing badly or not at all, this form of reporting might encourage them to test (or test better) and produce the required information for management.

In many projects, the development activities are defined in terms of coding tasks. Sometimes the tasks are described as "code and test module X." Well, we know what developers really like to do, don't we? Coding gets 90% of the effort and testing is squeezed yet again. To avoid this, we always recommend that code and test activities in project plans be defined as separate tasks (sometimes planned and performed by different people), especially at the component level. For critical components, we can document the test objectives derived directly from the risk assessment in component test plans. We can reference those risks on test reports sent to senior management. If managers pay attention to these risks, developers might pay more attention to component testing.

Consider what might happen if, during a test stage, a regression test detects a fault. Because the test fails, the risk that this test partially addresses becomes open again. The risk-based test report may show risks being closed and then reopened because regression faults are occurring. The report provides a clear indication that things are going wrong—bug fixes or enhancements are causing problems. The report brings these anomalies directly to the attention of management.

Figure 4.8 presents a matrix of risks that block the cardinal objectives and benefits of the project. Reading along the top row of the matrix, Risk 1 is

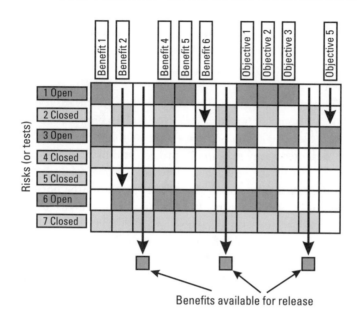

Figure 4.8 Benefits-based test reporting.

open, blocking Benefits 1, 4, and 5, as well as Objectives 1, 2, and 3. Risk 2 did block Benefits 2, 4, and 7 and Objectives 2 and 4. Risk 7 was closed today after all the relevant tests were passed. When Risk 7 was closed, Benefits 3 and 7 and Objective 4 were unblocked and "fell through." You can imagine this diagram as a little like the KerPlunk™ game, where marbles in a cylinder are held up by needles that pass horizontally through holes in the cylinder. As needles are withdrawn, marbles fall through. This is what we aim to do in testing: to focus on the tests that address the risks that block benefits and cardinal objectives. If a benefit is blocked, we can see straight-away which risks block it and, therefore, which tests we need to prioritize to unblock it.

Stakeholders are most interested in the benefits that are available and the objectives that can be achieved. Benefits-based test reports present this information clearly. Project management is most interested in the risks that block the benefits and objectives. This test reporting technique focuses atten-tion on the blocking risks so that the project manager can push harder to get the tests that matter through.

One final point: If testers present both risk-based and benefits-based test reports, the pressure on testers is simply to execute the outstanding tests that provide information on risk. The pressure on developers is to fix the faults that block the tests and the risks of most concern. Testers need not worry so much about justifying doing more testing, completing the test plan, or downgrading high severity incidents to get through the acceptance criteria. The case for completing testing is always self-evident and depends on whether enough test evidence has been produced to satisfy the stakeholders' need to deem the risks of most concern closed. The information required by stakeholders to make a release decision with confidence might only be completely available when testing is completed. Otherwise, they have to take the known risks of release.

How good is our testing? Our testing is good if we present good test evidence. Rather than the number of faults we find, our performance as testers is judged on how clear the test evidence we produce is. If we can provide evidence to stakeholders that enables them to make a decision at an acceptable cost and we can squeeze this effort into the time we are given, we are doing a good testing job. This is a different way of thinking about testing. The definition of good testing changes from one based on faults found to one based on the quality of information provided.

Most managers like the risk-based approach to testing because it gives them more visibility of the test process. Risk-based testing gives management a big incentive to let you take a few days early in the project to conduct the risk assessment. All testers have been arguing that we should be involved in projects earlier. If managers want to see risk-based test reporting, they must let testers get involved earlier. This must be a good thing for us as testers and our projects.

References

[1]   Myers, G. J., *The Art of Software Testing*, New York: John Wiley & Sons, 1979.

[2]   Beizer, B., *Software Test Techniques*, New York: Van Nostrand Reinhold, 1990.

[3]   British Standards Institute (BSI), *BS 7925-2:1998 Standard for Software Component Testing*, London: BSI, 1998.

[4]   Herzlich, P., "The Politics of Testing," *Proc. 1st EuroSTAR Conf.*, London, United Kingdom, October 25–28, 1993.

[5]   Booch, G., J. Rumbaugh, and I. Jacobsen, *The Unified Modeling Language User Guide*, Boston, MA: Addison-Wesley, 1999.

[6]   Booch, G., J. Rumbaugh, and I. Jacobsen, *The Unified Software Development Process*, Boston, MA: Addison-Wesley, 1999.

[7] Kruchten, P., *The Rational Unified Process—An Introduction*, Boston, MA: Addison-Wesley, 2000.

[8] McDermott, R. E., R. J. Mikulak, and M. R. Beauregard, *The Basics of FMEA*, Portland, OR: Productivity, Inc., 1996.

[9] Leveson, N. G., *Safeware*, Reading, MA: Addison-Wesley, 1995.

[10] Kaner C., J. Faulk, and H. Q. Nguyen, *Testing Computer Software*, New York: John Wiley & Sons, 1993.

[11] Bach J., "What Is Exploratory Testing? And How It Differs from Scripted Testing," http://www.satisfice.com/articles/what_is_et.htm, 2002.

[12] Bach J., "Exploratory Testing and the Planning Myth," http://www.satisfice.com/articles/et_myth.htm, 2002.

Part II
Risk-Based E-Business Testing

5

E-Business and the Consequences of Failure

Chapters 1 through 4 introduced the concept of risk-based testing and a method for designing a test process based on a consensus view of risk. The method is generic and, in principle, could be used in any software application area. In this chapter, we will introduce the concept of e-business and the issues surrounding the risk taking associated with e-business system developments. Chapters 6 through 8 cover the types of failure we see in Web-based systems and discuss issues of test strategy and some of the considerations for the test process.

E-Business, E-Commerce, and Everything E

Before we go any further, let's get some definitions clear. The e-phenomenon is immature, and vendors are generating new e-definitions fast and furiously. We summarize here the definitions presented at http://www.whatis.com, which is at least an independent authority.

- E-business *(electronic business):* a term derived from such terms as e-mail and e-commerce and referring to the conducting of business on the Internet, including not only buying and selling, but servicing customers and collaborating with business partners.

- *E-commerce (electronic commerce):* the buying and selling of goods and services on the Internet, especially the World Wide Web.

- *Intranet:* a private network contained within an enterprise. Typically, an intranet includes connections through one or more gateway computers to the outside Internet. The main purpose of an intranet is to share company information and computing resources among employees. An intranet can also be used to facilitate working in groups and for teleconferences.

- *Extranet:* a private network that uses the Internet to share part of a business's information or operations securely with suppliers, vendors, partners, customers, or other businesses. An extranet can be viewed as part of a company's intranet that has been extended to users outside the company. It has also been described as a state of mind, in which the Internet is perceived as a way to do business with other companies, as well as to sell products to customers.

E-business is a much broader term than e-commerce and includes such "e" variations as e-tailing and e-markets, as well as portals, and electronic exchanges. One could say that e-business is simply the use of Web technology to conduct any kind of business on the Web. Any information technology (IT) system that uses Web technology might now be called e-business. The Internet, intranets, and extranets represent the three (similar) ways in which e-business Web sites can be deployed.

A Typical Web Experience

Some time ago, I had to go to Brussels for a conference. I had never bought a flight on the Web, and I thought that it was about time I explored the airline Web sites and booked a flight on-line. When I browsed the popular airline Web sites, only a few airlines had sites that could be used to book flights. I wanted a flight from London, Heathrow to Brussels, and tried several sites before finding the one that seemed most likely to satisfy my need.

I browsed the site after a little difficulty navigating past the flashy "brochureware" pages and found the page on which to search for a flight. I entered the departure and destination airports, dates, and required time ranges. The site refused to give me a schedule of flights because I didn't get the names of the airports exactly right. I tried again. A list of flights duly appeared, and after a little effort, I worked out how to select the itinerary I preferred. To do this, I had to refine the ranges of departure times of the outbound and return journeys. At last, I had an itinerary I liked. The price was right and I was ready to go—or so I thought.

I clicked on the Book This Flight button and was presented with lots of information on how to become a member of the airline's frequent flyer program. I wasn't interested, so I continued. I was then presented with a page asking me to login as a frequent flyer or as an on-line customer, but I don't have an account. So, next, I clicked on the (barely visible) Register link. I tried to use my name as a login id—it was rejected of course, but no hints or suggestions for names that would work were suggested. I invented a silly name (that I'll never use again) and a suitable password.

It had taken me 10 minutes to get to this point, when I noticed at the top of each page, in a shade of blue almost indistinguishable from the background, some text saying, "Please do not press the back button." I wondered why not; I also wondered why I had chosen this Web site to book a flight.

At last, after a long delay, a form appeared. I counted 33 fields to be completed. I laboriously filled in the form and clicked on the continue button. After an even longer delay, the same screen reappeared with message at the top saying I had made a mistake and should look for the highlighted field. The highlighted field is a message in red that appears halfway down the page. I hadn't clicked the New Credit Card radio button. Curiously, there was one radio button in the radio button group—surely, a checkbox would have been better. At this point, I started to look for trouble and noticed that the three phone numbers I could provide (home, business, and mobile) had one, two, and three fields allocated respectively. Why on earth were there three telephone number formats?

Enough—I fixed the field entries, clicked continue, and was presented with a new form redisplaying the information for me to confirm. I clicked continue and saw a new page inviting me to complete the booking. I continued again, and during the longest delay up to that point, I speculated as to what awaited me next. It felt like minutes had passed, when I was finally presented with the message we all dread:

The page cannot be found.

The page you are looking for might have been removed, had its name changed, or is temporarily unavailable.

HTTP 404 - File not found

It took me more than 20 minutes to reach this point. Now what? I didn't know whether I had a flight booked or whether I had been charged for it. I didn't press the back button, of course. I called up the airline's telephone-sales number, asked what was wrong with the Web site, and got the response, "Our Web what?" Eventually, I spoke to a supervisor who confirmed that I had neither booked nor paid for a flight. Can a company that can't build and run a Web site be trusted to fly an airplane? I decide to get a flight somewhere else.

These were common problems with Web sites a year or two ago. Most people's reaction to such experiences is to vote with their feet. They leave the site, never to return, and in some cases, never to do business with their brick-and-mortar sites either. This experience was typical in 1999; the situation has improved somewhat since then. Sites established in 1999 (that are still going) have matured and are much more reliable and usable. Now, however, new Web sites are being generated faster than ever, and it seems that many of the mistakes made by the early adopters are being repeated as if there were no past experience to benefit from.

Web Site Failures and Their Consequences

A recent report from the Boston Consulting Group, "Winning the Online Consumer: The Challenge of Raised Expectations" [1], highlighted many complaints regarding Web site failures and their consequences for e-businesses:

- Almost 70% of on-line consumers reported that Web sites take too long to download, and more than half said that a site crashed before they could complete a purchase.

- 20% of consumers had difficulty getting sites to accept their credit cards.

- 11% of consumers had at some point ordered goods on-line and paid for them, but had never received them.

- 60% of on-line consumers said that they would change their on-line behavior as a result of a failed purchase attempt.

The nature of these behavioral changes is significant and worth emphasizing.

- 2% stopped shopping on-line.

- 2% stopped purchasing on-line.

- 41% stopped shopping on that particular Web site.

- 30% stopped purchasing from that particular Web site.
- 9% stopped shopping at that particular company's off-line stores.

These statistics make for sobering reading. Not only could a poor e-business site fail to gain more business; it could affect the business done by brick-and-mortar stores. These survey results show that satisfied customers shop more, spend more, and buy more frequently for a broader range of goods. Satisfied customers spend 57% more than dissatisfied ones. A satisfied customer is more likely to recommend the site to others. Unsatisfied customers will warn their friends and colleagues to avoid poor sites. Providing good service on a reliable, usable Web site is the best way to retain satisfied, loyal customers and acquire new ones.

E-Business Maturity and Risk

Peter Morath of American Management Systems (AMS) discusses a set of maturity levels for e-businesses in his book *Success @ E-Business* [2]. Figure 5.1 shows the following four levels of maturity defined in the AMS model:

- *Level 1:* Static sites that provide information or on-line brochures and the like.

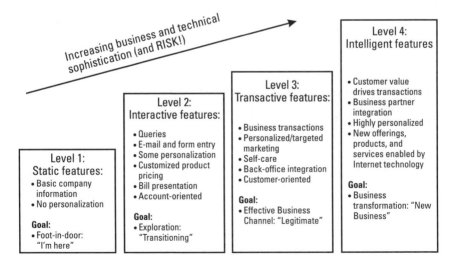

Figure 5.1 The e-business maturity model.

- *Level 2:* Interactive sites that have facilities for capturing customer feedback with some personalization and customized quotes, for example.

- *Level 3:* Transactive sites that allow customers to buy on-line, where customer data is proactively used for marketing, back-end legacy systems are integrated, and some degree of automated customer relationship management is possible.

- *Level 4:* Intelligent interactions with the site are driven by customer demand, services are seamlessly linked with business partners, the buying experience is highly personalized, and the e-business offers new products and services based on the new technology.

Few organizations have reached Level 4 yet, but the best-known, largest sites are probably there now. The more mature your e-business, the more sophisticated and complex your systems become. Dependency on technology increases dramatically and the consequences of failure rise just as fast. If your information-only Web site fails, who cares? If your Web site is your only source of revenue because you are a fully mature e-business and all of your business is geared around electronic distribution and sales, you probably don't have a manual fallback. If your system fails, you are in big trouble, so failure is unacceptable. It is obvious that the more mature your e-business, the more seriously you should take the risk of failure. On your next e-business project consider where your organization is on the maturity scale—it might give you insight into how seriously potential failures will be taken.

Web Time and Other Challenges to Testers

It might be regarded as hype, but there is no denying it: In some environments, "Web time passes five to seven times as fast." Bruce Judson's book *Hyperwars* [3], Evans and Wurster's *Blown to Bits* [4], and Peter Morath's *Success @ E-Business* [2] all provide lucid descriptions of the marketing dynamics that drive e-business. One marketing phenomena Judson quotes is the so-called law of twos. How many industries do you know of that are dominated by two big players? Coke and Pepsi, Hertz and Avis, and Procter & Gamble and Unilever are three pairs of competitors that dominate their markets. Those markets reached this point of maturity after many years of squeezing out or absorbing the smaller competition. One can argue that the

Internet is simply an accelerator of this process for e-business. The dominant market player got there first, the second player is the first player's competition, and everyone else is nowhere. On the Web, getting to market first has distinct advantages. Of course, capturing market share is foremost, but the first player to market gains the experience of operating in the market first. The risk of failure might be lower, because there is no competition. Taken to its extreme, the risk of coming second is that you might never catch up with the leader, but you might be caught up with by subsequent entrants into the marketplace. This is why the marketers place such emphasis on speed to market.

Other features of the Web-time phenomenon include the following:

- There are significant technology changes happening all the time. The products you are using today may not have existed 6 months ago. The developers using these products are inexperienced.

- In some organizations, the e-business projects may be owned and managed by nonexpert computer users. Software development is out; Web publishing is in.

- Those working in start-up environments experience this phenomenon particularly acutely. The sprint to market dominates every other objective. Many precedents suggest that in an immature market, getting to market first may mean that you will dominate the market. In this kind of environment, does quality come second?

- There are obvious cultural, practical, technical, and scheduling obstacles to implementing thorough QA and testing practices.

Testers are used to working on time-pressured projects, without requirements, using unfamiliar technology in cultures that prefer to code first and plan second, but testers have rarely encountered all of these difficulties simultaneously. Clearly, Web time poses significant challenges to testers, and we must accommodate these issues in our approach to e-business testing.

Although the technology has been around a few years now, the Web architecture has a "soft underbelly." Users easily expose the workings of the client front-end: They can examine source code and interfere with the workings of application code. The universality (and openness) of the Internet infrastructure makes it easier for attackers to exploit vulnerabilities. The ease of integration of collaborating partners highlights the need for greater reliability of partnering systems: The risks associated with more ambitious, complex systems are greater.

Risky Projects and Testing

In fast-paced software projects, risk taking is inevitable, so testers must become risk experts. They must identify failure modes and translate these into consequences for the sponsors of the project. "If X fails (which is likely if we don't test), then the consequence to you, as sponsor, is Y." In this way, testers, management, and sponsors can reconcile the risks being taken with the testing time and effort.

The pervasiveness of the Web may be coming to the tester's rescue. Everyone has experienced problems with Web sites. As a tester, no matter whom you talk to, be it the CIO, the CEO, or the finance director, he or she has experienced similar problems. Discussing the risk of failure is now easier because even senior management understand the types of failure that can occur and their consequences. This is a welcome boost for testers.

References

[1]   The Boston Consulting Group, "Winning the Online Consumer: The Challenge of Raised Expectations," http://www.bcg.com, 2002.

[2]   Morath, P., *Success @ E-Business*, Maidenhead, UK: McGraw-Hill, 2000.

[3]   Judson, B., *Hyperwars,* London: HarperCollins, 1999.

[4]   Evans, P. and T. S. Wurster, *Blown to Bits*, Boston, MA: Harvard Business School Press, 2000.

6

Types of Web Site Failures

To help us understand the nature of the risks facing e-business projects, here are a few examples of problems reported recently on both sides of the Atlantic:

- A book publisher found that its system sent out books with blank mailing labels because the address information was not carried through to the dispatch department although customer credit cards were being debited.

- Many Web sites advertise prices that include postage and packing. There are several reports of sites that assumed customers would be based in their home country. Anyone on the planet can access these sites, however, and place an order to be delivered to the other side of the world.

- A recruitment consultancy invited applicants to post their résumés on its Web site, but didn't provide facilities to manage them. They received thousands of résumés, but ended up trashing them.

- An airline advertised cheap tickets on its Web site, but didn't remove the pages when the promotion ended. Customers continued to demand cheap tickets. One successfully sued the airline when refused the special deal.

- A health food wholesaler offered trade prices on their Web site, but failed to direct retail customers to their local outlet. How many folks want 100 boxes of dried apricots?

- In the United Kingdom, an e-retailer advertised 21-inch TV sets at £2.99 rather than £299. Before the retailer corrected the problem, orders for thousands of the TV sets were taken.

- A British computer expert gained access to the bank account details of millions of Americans from his home during a routine check on his U.S. bank account. The Web site allowed him to "walk" straight into Internet bank accounts at institutions across the United States. Once in, he was free to carry out a wide range of financial transactions, including transferring funds, changing PIN numbers, and paying bills.

If these were isolated incidents, we might not be so concerned, but it is clear that the Web site failures that make the news are a small proportion of the failures that happen every day. The vast majority of Web site failures do not make the news. Every day, all Web users experience failures of one kind or another, whether it is poor performance or usability, lack of trust, or the Web pages not working. Given the very large number of ways in which a Web site can fail, we need to organize the various modes of failure and then use that organization to guide the discussion of e-business risk. From this, we will construct our strategy for testing.

Web Site As Retail Store

It is a convenient analogy to compare a Web site to a retail store. Just like a High Street store, anyone can come in to browse or buy. The store is open to all, including sales prospects, returning customers, minors, foreigners, hackers, crooks, and terrorists, as well as people who work for your competitors. In a real store, when someone walks into your shop, you might know instantly whether a person is a credible customer; on the Web, however, you have no way of knowing whether the person who just placed an order is a 9-year-old, a hacker, a crook, or a legitimate customer.

Your customers will remember good service and use your store regularly. As in a shop, if the buying experience is good, the payment process is quick, and customers get a good deal too, they will come back. They will not come back if the service is poor. If you go to a shop and the front door is locked, you will not hesitate and go elsewhere. If service is slow, you might abandon the purchase. (If you were in a store wishing to buy something, and only a single checkout was open, and there was a queue of people with full shopping baskets, you might walk out). Unless you are tied to one supplier (e.g., your bank), you will not hesitate to visit alternative sites. Because of the bad experience with the airline Web site, described in Chapter 5, I won't be flying with that airline for some time.

If a Web site does not behave the way that people expect, most will begin to distrust it. People prefer to deal face-to-face because we rely on personal contact to build trust. If a Web site fails, even marginally, the little trust a consumer has may be destroyed. The inertia that makes changing a supplier less convenient in the real world hardly exists on the Web. In the street, you might put up with poor service if the alternate store is a 15-minute walk away. If you found a vendor's Web site through a search engine, alternative vendors are just a click away.

When a Web site is difficult to use, most users lose patience much more quickly than you would think. Slow responses, confusing screens, cumbersome forms, unclear options, and a lack of useful feedback make Web sites hard to use. As Web master of http://www.evolutif.co.uk, I take care to look at the weekly statistics we get from our ISP. One of the surprising things that I discovered quickly was that approximately 75% of the visits to our Web site last less than two minutes. It appears that users do not study Web sites for long. They connect, scan pages very quickly, get what they want, and leave. Anything that tests their patience will make users leave sooner.

No Second Chances

One of the most disturbing findings of the research into Web site failures is that the majority of customers won't give you a second chance if they experience a failure on your Web site. Lack of confidence in your site, combined with the ease of going to another (competitive) site, makes this inevitable. The retail store analogy is useful because you can relate Web site risks to most peoples' everyday experiences. Web site visitors won't come back if the following occur:

- The door is locked (your servers are down);
- It is difficult to find the product required (the product catalog is out of date, incomplete, or inaccurate);
- They get easily lost in the store (the site is difficult to navigate);
- Service is slow or there is a queue at the checkout (performance is poor);
- They feel that they can't trust the staff (the site feels insecure because its behavior is counterintuitive).

The message to e-business companies is clear: Improve the reliability and usability of your Web site and give the customer a comfortable, fast, efficient, and secure buying experience.

Many of the Risks Are Outside Your Control

One of the biggest concerns to most e-businesses is that many Web site–related risks are outside their control. There is little you can do to reduce these threats, so the best you can do is be prepared for them. Some threats affect your users' experience while others may cause your on-line service to fail completely.

Unlimited Potential Users

Hundreds of millions of Web users could visit your Web site to browse or buy your products. Your servers may be perfectly able to support 1,000 visitors per hour, but what might happen if your marketing campaign is exceptionally successful? You have no control over how many users try to visit your site. After a TV ad is broadcast, most viewers with an interest in your site will visit you within the next few hours while they remember your Web address. Within 8 hours, most of those people inclined to do so will have paid you a visit. Could your technical infrastructure support 5,000 users, 10,000, or 10 million? After 8 hours, most will have forgotten all about your site, and the traffic on your site will return to what it was before. You cannot predict how users will attack your site. (Users don't set out to attack your site, but you may feel that your server is under attack when usage peaks.)

Many Potential Points of Failure

The availability of your Web service is not entirely under your control. A user attempting to access your service has to have a working client PC, OS, browser, dial-up connection, and ISP service. The Internet itself has to be up and running. On your end, your ISP, servers, and network infrastructure all must operate smoothly. Depending on your technical architecture, you might have between 20 and 40 specific points of failure in the layers of technology that your customers use to reach you. Many Web sites are hosted on servers operated and maintained by ISPs. Can you rely on these companies to provide the level of support you get from your internal data centers? Ensuring availability and reliability is quite a challenge for large, complex sites because there are so many points of failure.

You Have No Control over Client Platforms

Most users of the Web have traditional hardware, such as PCs, Macintoshes, or Unix workstations. An increasing number of Internet users, however, are acquiring Web-enabled devices that have different user interfaces from the traditional PC-based browser. WebTV, WAP phones, and PDAs are all being promoted as alternatives to existing browser-based devices. Cars, refrigerators, Internet kiosks, and many other Internet-capable devices will be marketed in the next few years. Did I say refrigerators? There is now at least one Internet-capable refrigerator on the market. When you take a beer out of the fridge, you scan the label into a sensor on the fridge. When the stock of beer is low, the fridge remembers to add beer to your next shopping order (I like this technology). Web-enabled devices will be pervasive in a few years' time. Will your current Web developments accommodate these future platforms? Screen size and resolution are obvious concerns, for instance, because all of these devices have different mechanisms for delivery.

You have no control over your users' hardware or software. Some may be using state-of-the-art 2-GHz machines with 512 MB RAM and the most recent OS and browser; others may be using 8-year-old 486s running DOS with a text-only browser. Will the later user's browser support the plug-ins and other bells and whistles your Web site requires?

You Have No Control over Client Configuration

As with the new Internet-ready devices that have different screen sizes and resolutions, your Web site may have to accommodate unusual user configurations, such as very large or very small screens and varying font sizes.

Visitors to your Web site may have any OS of any version and in any condition. If you have children who share your home PC, you know all about the problems caused by curious kids installing games, deleting files, and fiddling with control panels. A few years ago, while I was away from home for a few days, my son (who was 9 at the time) installed lots of game demos from free magazine-cover CDs onto my Windows 95 PC. When I returned, the machine was completely unusable. My dear son had installed game after game until he filled up the hard drive. He knew enough to understand that you put stuff into the wastebasket to get rid of it. He also knew you had to empty the wastebasket to really get rid of it. This he did without a care in the world. Unfortunately, he dumped most of the C-drive into the wastebasket as well. I decided to buy a new PC for myself and secure it with Windows NT. How many shared home PCs are tinkered with by kids and adults alike and are in a poor state? Will your site work with systems set to use 8-bit color, very high resolutions, large fonts, and so on?

Which Browsers Do You Support?

Most people use either Microsoft Internet Explorer (IE) or Netscape Navigator (Netscape), with the majority using the Microsoft product. But how popular is each of the browser types? How popular is each version of each browser? Web server logs capture much useful information, including a tag identifying the browser used to access the site. Internet.com is a very popular collection of sites that publishes statistics on its visitors. Table 6.1 presents recent statistics for browser types used by visitors to BrowserWatch.com (http://browserwatch.internet.com).

It is clear, at least according to BrowserWatch.com, that Microsoft IE dominates. Other browser types account for only a small percentage of users. These statistics relate to one site only, however; statistics for our site are different, and the statistics for yours will also be unique. Your site may have a different user profile. Different browsers might dominate the statistics if you offer a site for consumers versus academics versus Unix programmers.

BrowserWatch.com lists 106 browsers of which 66 operate on Windows platforms alone. These browsers vary dramatically in their functionality, sophistication, and level of adherence to HTML standards. Differences also exist between versions of each browser built for the same OS platform

Table 6.1
Top 10 Browser Types Visiting BrowserWatch.com

Browser	Count	Percentage (%)
Microsoft IE	54,139	59.1
Netscape	17,129	18.7
Opera	12,112	13.2
Powermarks	1,302	1.42
Konqueror	591	0.64
Lynx	512	0.55
Ibrowse	466	0.50
BunnySlippers	394	0.43
AvantGo	261	0.28
Indy Library	222	0.24

and between versions of the same browser running on different OS platforms. Although most users have mainstream browsers, you should consider the less popular browsers, too. If your Web site has a particular problem with one type of browser, it is almost inevitable that at least some of your users will be affected. Some browsers are likely to be quite old and not support the latest HTML standard, Java Virtual Machine, or plug-ins for example. Is this a concern?

Your Users May Not Have the Required Plug-Ins

Does your application demand that users have plug-ins? Whether a plug-in is popular or not, there are bound to be users who do not have it installed. If your site depends on a plug-in or an up-to-date version of Java Virtual Machine to operate correctly, bear in mind that not all users appreciate being asked to download required software. Some may refuse (most browsers have configuration settings that allow or disable such downloads and installations). In this case, will your application still work? How will your user know this? What happens if the download is refused or it fails to install?

Have you ever been to a Web site and seen a dialogue box appear, which says something along the lines of, "Do you want to download plug-in *X* (217K)?" Many users will refuse to accept unsolicited downloads. There is a particular plug-in that I rejected for some months because the plug-in installation process asked me to insert a Windows NT installation CD. I was working from home and the install disks were at the office; I could not do this, so the installation of the plug-in would always fail. Are the developers building your Web site assuming that certain plug-ins exist on your customers' machines? Are the developers assuming that the users who don't have the plug-in will download it without question?

The Context of Web Transactions Is a Risk Area

The HTTP protocol is stateless. This means that under normal conditions, every request to a Web server is treated as an independent, autonomous, anonymous transaction. The server cannot link series of messages from a single client machine without some further information. The usual methods for "maintaining context" are cookies and hidden fields on HTML forms. Cookies can be rejected or time out. Web transactions can be interrupted by loss of the network connection, a visit to another Web domain, or use of the browser back, forward, and refresh buttons. Users may also be interrupted and unable to complete transactions before their connections time out. Can the user reconnect and complete the transactions by using the browser back or refresh buttons? They may certainly try.

Users are very familiar with loss of connection, the back and refresh buttons, and opening new windows to display the same Web page. These may be difficult scenarios for developers to accommodate in their application coding, but the behavior of the system under such conditions must be safe for both the users and your e-business.

Cookies Can Be a Problem

Cookies are a common method for holding Web site–specific data on the client machine. Cookies are typically small amounts of data written to the client machine's hard drive to hold personalized data or data to be carried through Web pages as they are navigated. Mainstream browsers can be configured to warn the user when these are being requested by the Web sites visited. Some users will allow and ignore them, some will want to be reminded when they are invoked, and some will reject them. Will your application work if cookies are rejected?

Computers and login accounts can be shared. As cookies are normally assigned to either a computer or a specific account, will cookies that are intended to be dedicated to individuals also be shared? Could one user impersonate another by sharing a machine and the cookies residing on it?

Network Connections

If your Web site provides business-to-business services, it is likely that your customers access the Web via a high-speed local network, and the customer's site may have a direct connection to the Internet. In this case, the download speed of Web pages, even large ones, may never be a problem. Business users may be working from home, however, and many ordinary households use a dial-up connection and modem. The relatively low bandwidth of modems dramatically slows the pace of page downloads, particularly those containing large images. The perceived slow speed of the Web is usually due to over-large images that have not been optimized. This is a serious consideration: Slow Web sites are unpopular, and many people lose patience and leave them prematurely.

If your users access the Web using a 56K modem, then regardless of how fast your Web site is, they cannot download data any faster than 56,000 bps. A picture on your Web site that is 56 KB in size will therefore take around 10 seconds to download. If you have two images of that size, these will take perhaps 20 seconds to download, a length of time that is probably unacceptable to most people. In general, the entire size of an HTML Web page, including all its images, should not exceed around 50 KB to keep the download speed for dial-up users under 10 seconds.

Firewalls May Get in the Way

There are some situations where the configuration of a customer's firewall can cause your site to be unusable or inaccessible. Whether the customer's network administrator banned your site, or the settings of your Web server conflict with the remote firewalls, your site may be unusable or inaccessible.

Anyone Can Visit

Like a real shop, your Web site is open to the public. Users can be experts or hackers, but they are always unknown to you. Anyone on the Web is a potential customer, but you don't see him or her, and he or she doesn't see you. Some may be minors. How could you tell if a 10-year-old were placing an order with a parent's credit card? How would you know that you were selling alcohol to minors? A 9-year-old walking into a car showroom looking to buy a sports car is likely to stand out. I have a photograph of my son using my old Apple Mac in 1991 when he was only 18 months old. He was a competent computer user at age two. He's 12 now, and has 10 years of experience using computers. He can navigate the Web with ease. He can use search engines. He can buy products on-line. He can certainly get into trouble, because vendors do not know who is using a credit card to buy their goods or services.

You cannot easily protect yourself, because of this mutual invisibility between a visitor and a Web site owner. If you look at your internal company users, they are a very select group of people because they have probably been interviewed two or three times, they are dependent on the company to be paid, and they probably have a vested interest in the company as well. They are more likely to understand how you do business and less likely to abuse the company's intranet. People in the outside world are completely unknown to you and are probably unknowable.

Usability Is Now a Prime Concern

Your site is unlikely to be documented. Your users are almost certainly untrained. If the site is hard to use, they'll go elsewhere. What is your experience of Web sites? If you have found one difficult to navigate, confusing, unpleasant to look at, time consuming, or slow on more than one occasion, you may have just given up. Maybe you didn't even reach the functionality that was designed to help you place an order or find information. The user experiences good or appalling usability at the front door of the Web site, so usability is now a make-or-break issue for your e-business development.

Localization

Once your Web site is up and running, anyone on the planet who has the technology can visit and use your site. If you are offering an international service or delivery, this is a fabulous opportunity. People in foreign countries, however, prefer to use their own language. Many will not appreciate obscure address formats. They may wish to pay in local currencies. They may have their own local tax arrangements.

Address formats are a big deal on some sites. The United States uses zip codes, the United Kingdom uses postcodes, France uses departments, and so forth. It is particularly irritating to be asked to select a U.S. state (which is mandatory) when you live in another country (where shall I live today? Err...Texas!).

Character sets vary dramatically for different languages. Will your database accept all of these foreign language character sets? If you think this will not be a problem because you only market to local customers, think again. Why shouldn't a customer access your Web site while working as an expatriate in a Middle Eastern country, using a PC set up to use an Arabic character set? Will your back-end systems and databases accept these funny characters?

The Sequence of Points of Failure in a Web Service

As a user types in the URL of your Web site, and his or her browser requests the home page, the first of many failure points must be negotiated. If you imagine tracing a path through the user's hardware to your Web application software and back-end databases, you can speculate on the potential failure points that must be successfully negotiated before the user can achieve his or her objective, be it buying a book or obtaining the balance on a bank account. It is interesting to see the approximate order in which these failure points could be encountered, any of which would make the Web service unusable. We have grouped these failure points into four main types, which you can imagine exist in an almost chronological sequence.

1. *Site availability:* The Web site itself is unavailable. Why?
   - The Internet backbone is down.
   - Your ISP has had a failure.
   - Your Web server hardware is down.
   - Your Web server software has failed.

2. *Content availability:* The site is up, but its content is unavailable. Why?
   - The Web server is not configured to access the Web site content.
   - A page links to a nonexistent Web page or Common Gateway Interface (CGI) script.
   - A page links to a nonexistent embedded object (image, applet, frame page).
   - The linked page, CGI script, or object is secured, and the Web server is not authorized to access it.
   - The linked page, CGI script, or object has not been installed on the Web server.

3. *Response time:* The user experiences slow response times. Why?
   - A page or objects on it are so large it cannot be downloaded quickly.
   - Server hardware components have been underspecified.
   - Production transaction volumes have been underestimated and are being exceeded.
   - Hardware and software components are poorly tuned or unoptimized.
   - Application or infrastructure software components are inefficient.

4. *Usability:* Users find the site difficult or impossible to use. Why?
   - The pages are unpleasant to look at.
   - The site is poorly structured, difficult to navigate, or confusing.
   - The site does not obey the most common Web conventions.
   - The system transactions have been badly designed and sequenced.

You can imagine as you traverse the layers of the technical architecture and site design that site availability is the first challenge, content availability the second, response time the third, and usability the fourth, and so on. The list of failure points above is not meant to be comprehensive (security and trust-oriented problems are not mentioned, for example; nor is application functionality). It is intended to indicate an approximate layering of the types of faults that could occur.

When you are discussing the modes of failure with your business stakeholders and asking whether a particular failure mode is significant, you might consider putting the failure mode into one of the above categories to give nontechnical staff a context in which to consider the relevance of that failure mode. Given that any of the failure modes above make a system unusable, these categories might help you to make the case that testing for each failure mode is worthwhile.

7

E-Business Test Strategy

This chapter sets out some of the strategic issues to consider while planning e-business testing. Much of the testing for an e-business system requires technical knowledge to plan and execute, and we suggest that all testers need a minimal technical skill set to operate effectively. The test process may be the core of any test plan, but the scope of testing in each test stage and for the whole project needs to be determined as early as possible. In Chapters 9 through 15 we present 24 techniques for testing the functional and nonfunctional attributes of your Web applications. Here, we present a framework for constructing the test process from the risks analysis and those 24 test techniques.

Specialized Knowledge and E-Business Testing Techniques

Testers need more than a minimal technical knowledge to plan, specify, execute, and analyze tests of Internet-based systems. The technical details of how the Web works are easy to obtain—there are now hundreds of books covering HTML, CGI, Java, Active Server Pages (ASP), and all of the many other concepts, terms, and technologies. The knowledge seems easy to acquire, but where does an e-business tester's knowledge start? The more difficult question is, where does it end?

The topics listed in Appendix A comprise a minimum set of terms and concepts with which the e-business tester should be familiar. Beyond the most basic issues, there are a number of more advanced topics that the tester should have, at least, a passing familiarity with. In addition, you may need to understand many more technology issues specific to your system, although you probably don't have time to study them deeply. The concepts listed in Appendix A are a reasonable starting point for understanding the architecture of the Web; they are also the foundation for most of the Internet-based products now in use. For a basic introduction to these and many other Internet concepts, Preston Gralla's book, *How the Internet Works* [1], covers virtually all of the architectural aspects of the Internet.

Some of the test techniques presented in Part III require a programmer's level of knowledge as they are most appropriate for unit and integration testing. It is important that testers understand the technical issues enough to know where developer testing stops and system testing starts.

Testing Considerations

Here are some broad issues to consider when formulating an e-business test strategy. If testing is to keep pace with development, we need to squeeze the testing into the develop and release cycle.

Developer Testing

Kent Beck's book, *Extreme Programming Explained* [2], promotes a set of disciplines for developers that encourages them to do significantly more and better testing. Pair programming, continuous automated testing, and permanently maintained regression tests all combine to improve the development test process if (and this is a big if) the developers are prepared to work this way.

Consider asking the developers to use a variety of browsers (and versions) for their testing, rather than only using the company's chosen browser. This might help flush out compatibility issues across different browser types. You may be able to reduce or eliminate later configuration testing.

Consider Using Test Drivers

In terms of user interfaces, Web applications are often relatively simple compared with traditional client/server or mainframe-based systems. A common design goal with Web applications is to place as much functionality on servers as possible, rather than relying on code that executes on the client browser. Where the Web is being used as a front-end to existing legacy systems, the testing of the back-end systems is as complicated as ever. The user interface of Web applications is sometimes the very last thing to be developed, and the integration of automated tools with browser-based applications is not always perfect, so consider using test drivers to execute functional tests of server-based code.

Test drivers are (usually) small, simple programs that accept test data, construct the call to the server-based code, execute the test transactions, and store the results for later evaluation. Some drivers can be enhanced to perform simple comparisons with previously run benchmarks. Suppose you wanted to execute hundreds of tests of a particular screen-based transaction. You might prepare a manual (or automated) test script that used the browser user interface, but the browser acts only as a means of capturing data from a user and constructing an HTTP message to send to a Web server. If you were concerned about the functionality of the server-based code, you would only be interested in the server response to the HTTP message being sent. As an alternative to using the browser, you could build a driver that could construct the HTTP message reliably, send the message to your Web server, and accept the response. Such a driver would allow you to separate the tests of server-based functionality from four other test objectives:

1. Validating the HTML received from the server (which can be done using HTML validators);

2. Demonstrating that a browser displays the HTML correctly (which can only be done visually);

3. Demonstrating that the browser captures data through the user interface and constructs the HTTP message correctly (which can be done by transaction link testing and examining Web server logs);

4. Checking client-side code (e.g., JavaScript embedded in HTML pages).

The benefit of using a test driver is that the driver can execute hundreds of tests without incurring the delay and potential complexity of using the browser interface. In addition, cosmetic changes in the user interface do not affect the format or content of the HTTP messages, so driver-based tests are easier to maintain. There are proprietary tools that can help, but you should consider writing your own in as few as a hundred lines of Visual Basic, Perl, or C++ code. Usually, developers build test drivers for use in their unit testing, but these drivers can often be reused for system testing. Custom-built drivers might be viable where the testers have large numbers of tests to automate and either a capture-replay tool is not available or the user interface makes such tests difficult to implement or execute quickly.

The test strategy should indicate where and how test drivers might be used to automate server-based components. Further guidance on the use of drivers is given in Chapter 17.

Configurations

One of the challenges to e-business testers is configuration testing. The most common configuration problems and approaches to addressing them are well documented. Chapter 11 provides general guidance on configuration testing and [3, 4] provide further background. The point to consider regarding test strategy is scope. There are hundreds of variations in browser and OS technologies, as well as in their versions, so there are thousands of potential combinations in use. The number of configurations you can test is limited, so you should consider who your users are and what technologies they might be using. Further, prioritization of these combinations (most likely by their popularity) will help you to maximize the number of users covered and minimize the number of users who might be adversely affected by configuration issues.

What browsers and versions will your Web site support? Do you need to worry about no-frames browsers? Do you need to consider nongraphic browsers? These questions are important because they help you to determine the scale of regression testing across a range of browsers and versions. Even if you will support only IE and Netscape, which versions of these browsers should you test against?

You must propose a scope for the testing, estimate the potential cost, and review that data with the stakeholders, management, and technical experts in the project. This will help to force a decision as to what will actually be supported, which may be much less than previously envisaged by management. If you are going to test many of the browsers and versions, you will be committed to doing an awful lot of regression testing.

Consider and propose an alternative: that the developers work to the HTML standards supported by the chosen browsers. Tools can then be used to validate the HTML in your Web pages. The number of browser platforms available is steadily growing. In the future, it looks increasingly likely that standards-based development and automated HTML validation will be a more practical approach than expensive regression testing across a wide range of platforms. This topic considered in greater depth in Chapter 12.

Web Conventions and Accessibility

The World Wide Web Consortium (W3C) Web Accessibility Initiative (WAI), (http://www.w3c.org/WAI), explains how to make Web content accessible to people with disabilities. Accessibility guidelines are intended for Web page authors (as well as developers of authoring tools). Following the guidelines will, however, make Web content more accessible to all users, whatever user agent they are using. Accessibility guidelines cover all user agents from desktop browsers, voice browsers, mobile phones to automobile-based personal computers and the like, as well as the environmental constraints users might experience (e.g., noisy surroundings, under- or over-illuminated rooms, hands-free environments). The Web conventions that the guidelines promote will help people find information on the Web more quickly in addition to making Web sites more usable.

Although adherence to conventions is never mandatory, following Web conventions can make a big difference to your users. A Web site that behaves differently from 90% of other sites might look good superficially, but cause users so much hassle that they stop using it. For example, will your application support a user's turning off graphics? Dial-up users sometimes switch off graphics to speed things up. Will the site work if users reject cookies or the cookies time out prematurely? Must users always have the required plug-ins? As a tester, you need to establish what conventions will apply to you, so you can test against them and ignore other contraventions. The best thing about Web conventions is that they are widely documented and the browser defaults support them; therefore testing becomes straightforward.

The WAI guidelines paper [5] and the associated checklist [6] are ideal documents for testers to use as baselines. Any contravention can be reported as a bug to the developers. Either get your project to obey some or all conventions and use a baseline to test against, or eliminate Web conventions from consideration in your test plan (but be prepared for usability problems later).

From the point of view of test strategy, Web conventions are a set of requirements that can be tested against, and there are tools available to execute checks of site pages against these conventions. If system requirements reference these Web conventions, then the conventions are legitimate baselines for testing. Even if not referenced, most of the conventions can still provide a baseline to test against. Web guidelines are a good thing for users and testers alike, but they restrict the Web site developers somewhat because adherence to conventions might mean that the developers must write more code to make pages accessible.

The level of adherence to Web conventions should ideally be defined in the system requirements from the start. If Web conventions have not been defined as part of the system requirements, the developers may not respond well to bug reports relating to violations of Web conventions. You need to liaise with the users, developers, and project management to determine the degree of adherence that users require and that developers will aspire to before defining the scope of testing. Only then can you deem tests against Web conventions to be in scope.

Although some Web conventions relate to good usability design, others relate to the shortcomings of certain browsers (or previous versions of the mainstream browsers) and some browser configuration options available to users (e.g., turning off images or rejecting cookies).

Less well-covered in many test strategies is the area of user browser configuration. Will you test situations in which users turn off graphics to speed up access or reject cookies because of security concerns? These scenarios, athough they may seem irrelevant to developers and may be less common, are still possible, and they may adversely affect end users of your Web site. Other concerns relate to the plug-ins that users have installed. The need fora plug-in can be accommodated by most Web site implementations, and the user may download and install plug-in options on demand. Many users refuse to do this, however, partly because some downloads take a long time to perform and partly because many users are wary of unsolicitied requests to install software at all. Such scenarios may be covered in the risk analysis, but could also be considered as a standard set of scoping issues for all Web sites.

Using a Test Process Framework to Build Your Test Strategy

The test techniques described in Part III each aim to address one or more risks or failure modes. Given a risk analysis that generates a list of risks in scope, techniques are selected based on their matching these risks. Next, the test types are structured into a series of stages that address the risks most efficiently. The test process framework presented in Table 7.1 is intended to assist testers in constructing their own test process when they know the test types that will be used. The framework will help you to construct the detailed test stages from the test types.

Seven Categories of Tests

To address the risks of the e-business project, we have identified 24 distinct test types, each of which addresses a different risk area. The test types are grouped into seven main categories:

1. Static;
2. Web page integration;
3. Functional;

4. Service;

5. Usability;

6. Security;

7. Large-scale integration.

Table 7.1
Test Process Framework

Test Type	Test Priorities					Test Types Mapped to Test Stages						Tool Type[5]
	Smoke	Usability	Performance	Functionality	Static/Dynamic	Desktop Development	Infrastructure	System	Integration	Postdeployment Monitoring	
Static											
Content checking	Y[1]				S	A/M[2]					SC
HTML validation	Y				S	A[3]				A	HV
Browser syntax compatibility checking	Y				S	A					BC
Visual browser validation		Y			D	M[4]		M			
Web Page Integration											
Link checking	Y				D	A	A		A		LC
Object load and timing		Y	Y		D	A	A		A		LC
Transaction verification	Y				S	A/M		A/M			TE
Functional											
Browser page testing	Y				D	A/M					TE
Server-based component testing	Y				D			A/M			TD
Transaction link testing				Y	D			A/M	A		TE
Application system testing				Y	D			A/M			TE
Context testing		Y			D			A/M			TE
Localization		Y			D	A/M		A/M			TE
Configuration testing	Y				D	M		A/M	M		TE

Table 7.1 (continued)

Test Type	Test Priorities				Test Types Mapped to Test Stages						
	Smoke	Usability	Performance	Functionality	Static/Dynamic	Desktop Development	Infrastructure	System	Integration	Postdeployment Monitoring	Tool Type[5]
Service											
Performance and stress testing			Y		D		A	A		A	LP
Reliability/failover testing	Y				D	A	A	A	A		LP
Service management testing					D			M	M		TE/ TD/ SC
Usability											
Collaborative usability inspection	Y				S	M	M	M			
Usability testing				Y	D			M			
Web accessibility checking	Y				S	A		A		A	WA
Security											
Security assessment				Y	S			A/M	A/M	A/M	SS
Penetration testing				Y	D			A/M	A/M	A/M	SS
Large-Scale Integration											
Systems integration testing				Y	D			A/M	A/M		TE
Business integration testing	Y				D				A/M		TE

1. Y implies the test is economic in order to be considered part of the test priority.
2. The test can be done manually or using a tool.
3. The test can only be done using a tool.
4. The test can only be done manually.
5. See section below entitled "Tests Can Be Automated or Manual" for code definitions.

Essential Testing Priorities

An interesting aspect of the e-business project is its sometimes extreme pace. In mature companies trying to establish a Web presence, the existing IT department may be responsible for development and may follow its standard, staged development and test process. Some projects operate in Web time, however. If you are working in a start-up environment where speed to market is the first priority, you may have to squeeze testing into a few days or even a few hours. Release cycles may occur daily. How can the traditional test process be fitted into this kind of schedule?

Clearly, the tester must be prepared to adopt test practices that complement these two very different scenarios. Our proposal is that a range of test priorities be set in line with the project development process. Table 7.2 presents one way of looking at the four most important testable attributes of your Web site. These four levels of priority are introduced here to give you an impression of the stark choices that you may face in your projects.

In Table 7.1 the test types have been allocated to one of the four test priorities detailed in Table 7.2. Test types that fall into the smoke (testing)

Table 7.2
Essential Testing Priorities

Testing Priority	When to Use
Smoke	• Smoke testing measures whether the application can survive one user session without crashing.
	• If you are under severe time pressure (e.g., you have only hours to do the testing), smoke testing may have to suffice.
Usability	• If your site is hard to use, the user won't hesitate to leave your site before reaching the functionality.
	• Usability testing involves inspection, review, and heuristic evaluation.
Performance	• If your site is usable but slow, users may give up on the functionality and leave.
	• Performance tests measure the speed of the site; flush out weak points, and measure limits.
Functionality	• These tests are likely to be the hardest to implement and in scope after all the other tests have been included.
	• Functionality is obviously tested in all projects, but is often covered during development and user evaluation superficially.

column are typically automated and should entail the minimum number of tests to address the maximum number of risks in the shortest time. The tests that fall into the functionality (testing) column are typically the most expensive and time consuming to implement and execute. The purpose of the Essential Testing Priorities columns is to help you to select the test types to include in your test process. The essential testing priorities are an approximate way of prioritizing the tests based on the time and effort required to implement them.

Tests Types Can Be Static or Dynamic

Test types can be static or dynamic. For example, static tests are those relating to inspection, review, or automated static analysis of development deliverables. There are six static test types in the framework.

Stages of Testing

We have found that the test types do not always fit into the traditional unit, integration, system, and acceptance test stages. So, we provide a structure that has test stages that categorize the test types in a technical way:

- Desktop development testing (broadly, of software that executes under the control of the browser);
- Infrastructure testing (of what runs on the servers);
- System testing (of the complete system in isolation);
- Large-scale integration (with other systems and business processes);
- Postdeployment monitoring (of live sites, retaining automated tests and using external services).

Tests Can Be Automated or Manual

The A and M entries under the Test Types Mapped to Test Stages columns in Table 7.1 denote whether or not the test can be automated:

- *M:* The test can only be done manually.
- *A:* The test can only be done using a tool.
- *A/M:* The test can be done manually or using a tool.

In addition, there are eight common tool types that support the test types in the test process framework. These are described in much more detail in Chapters 9 through 15. The codes in the rightmost column of the test process framework shown in Table 7.1 refer to the following tool types:

- Spelling and grammar checkers (SC);
- HTML validators (HV);
- Web-accessibility checkers (WA);
- Browser compatibility checkers (BC);
- Link checkers (LC);
- Browser test execution tools (TE);
- Test drivers for server-based code (TD);
- Load and performance test tools (LP);
- Security scanning tools (SS).

Guidelines for Using the Test Process Framework (Table 7.1)

Not all test types are appropriate to or possible in all circumstances. We are not suggesting that you perform every test type in the framework, but that you gain a consensus view on the risks of most concern, match the resulting test objectives and test techniques to your development methodology, and use the framework to help construct your test process.

The sequence of tasks required to construct the test process is as follows:

1. Identify the risks of concern with the project stakeholders, management, users, and technologists, and prioritize those that must be addressed by the testing.

2. For each risk to be addressed, identify one or more test types that can help to address the risk. Be sure to document those risks that will not be addressed by the testing.

3. Using the text of the risk description, write up test objectives (e.g., to demonstrate that the Web application operates reliably in a range of configurations) to show how this risk will be addressed.

4. Assign the test type to a test stage and nominate the responsible party within the project.

5. Estimate the time required to plan and execute the test.

6. Review the scope of the testing (what is in scope and what is out of scope), test objectives, stage definitions, responsibilities, and estimates, and refine.

The framework is a guideline to be considered and adapted—tailor it to your environment.

Postdeployment Monitoring

Postdeployment monitoring is done after implementation in a production environment. The reason for including this in your test strategy is that production e-business sites can fail, but it may be that none of your prospective customers will tell you. They'll simply go elsewhere. Furthermore, degradation of site performance may not be noticeable day by day, but statistics derived by using a tool can provide early warning of performance problems while there is still time to recover the situation. You might consider revising existing automated tests to monitor the site yourself. Services aimed at monitoring your site remotely are available, so this is an alternative worth considering.

What can be monitored? In theory, any repeatable test could be executed in the live environment. Realistically, the following can be considered for postdeployment monitoring:

- Server and Web service availability;
- Web content availability;
- Static testing of Web pages (HTML validation, link checking, accessibility, download times);
- Performance (response times);
- Security (audits, scanning, and penetration testing);
- End-to-end functionality.

Chapter 16 describes postdeployment monitoring options in greater detail.

References

[1]   Gralla, P., *How the Internet Works*, Indianapolis, IN: QUE, 1999.

[2]   Beck, K., *Extreme Programming Explained*, Boston, MA: Addison-Wesley, 2000.

[3]   Nguyen, H. Q., *Testing Applications on the Web*, New York: John Wiley & Sons, 2001.

[4]   Splaine, S., and S. P. Jaskiel, *The Web Testing Handbook*, Orange Park, FL: STQE Publishing, 2001.

[5]   World Wide Web Consortium, "Web Content Accessibility Guidelines," http://www.w3.org/TR/WCAG10, 2002.

[6]   World Wide Web Consortium, "Checklist of Checkpoints for Web Content Accessibility Guidelines," http://www.w3.org/TR/WCAG10/full-checklist.html, 2002.

8

From Risk Analysis to a Test Process

The risk analysis and assessment that we covered in Part I of the book showed how to arrive at a scope for the testing to be done. The risks of most concern were assessed and a set of test objectives derived from those risks, leaving us then with a set of tasks that we may have assigned to one or another test stage in our overall test process. We might also have assigned responsibility for each task and developed a clear idea of how it would be achieved. In Part I, we assumed this to be a straightforward task. Although in the risk assessment workshop the manner in which a test process should be structured might seem clear, achieving what might be called an optimal test process is influenced by several factors. Some constraints make the test process less than optimal. In this section, we'll explore these constraints.

Many Focused Stages or Bigger, Broader Test Stages?

Should we split the test process into a long series of test stages with highly focused objectives? Although this might make the test planning and preparation most effective, there are management overheads associated with having many stages. Because the stages are sequential, a delay in the completion of one stage will have a domino effect on later stages. Each stage might each have its own rather inflexible exit criteria, and a stage cannot complete if the exit criteria are not met, can it? Where the stages are sequential, they might all lie along a critical path as well, so that where test stages are dependent on their predecessors, a delay in one stage delays the whole project. It becomes difficult to adhere to rigid test stage entry and exit criteria when tests are organized this way.

Multiple test stages occurring in sequence and performed by different teams often increase the need for test environments. Setting up test environments can be a time-consuming and expensive affair. Test environments are often owned by one development or test group, so late handover of environments and shared access to environments often cause a problem. Conflicts occur between groups who need to share test environments. In the ideal world, sequential test stages run by different groups are most efficient, but suffer from the problems above. What are the advantages and disadvantages of larger, more complex test stages?

Bundling several test activities into a single stage eliminates some problems, but causes others. One serious aspect is the fact that a larger, complex test stage might become unwieldy. Reporting and understanding progress within the complexities of such test stages become more difficult because progress through the stage may be held up by problems in any of the separate tests types that have been combined. Is it sensible to have a combined report of functional, usability, and security tests all in one stage? Managing and reporting the tests separately can overcome this problem. Difficulties arise, however, when some tests complete and others are held up because bugs are found. It may be that later test stages could proceed (e.g., performance tests), but these are held up because the current test stage as a whole is prevented from completing as one type of test (e.g., a browser compatibility test) is experiencing problems.

Suppose, for example, the current test stage comprises application-system and usability testing, and the next test stage comprises performance and security tests. It would be prudent to identify the dependencies between these test types across the test stage boundaries. It is possible that the tests in a subsequent stage could start before all of the test types in the previous stage are passed in their entirety. For example, performance testing might be dependent on the application-system testing, but not on usability tests.

We recommend that test types be grouped into test stages using the following broad criteria:

- Test types should be performed as early as practical [i.e., when the object under test is available (built)].

- Tests are performed by one group or are the responsibility of one manager.

- There are no conflicting test environment requirements.

- Test types should have no dependencies on test types in later stages. A test type may have a dependency on other test types in the same stage, but these interdependent tests must be run in the correct sequence.

These criteria may help you specify the test types for each test stage in your overall test process.

Know Your Users

Risk-based testing aims to provide information to the project stakeholders on which to base a decision about the system's acceptability. The risks to be addressed by testing will have been discussed at a high level during the risk analysis. Sometimes, the mode of failure that a risk relates to must be discussed in more detail before the approach to that risk can be formalized. Where user behavior or the client OS or browser technology being used has a bearing on the risk, it is most helpful to understand who the users will actually be. For example, such an understanding might help you predict the most likely causes of failures or the most likely impacts of such failures. With this knowledge, you may be able to focus or reduce the amount of testing effort required and squeeze the testing into the budget available to you.

There are several areas where this knowledge will be most helpful. The browsers and OSs used by your customers may be easy to determine if, for instance, you are selling to Microsoft software developers who are likely to be using the latest versions of IE and Windows. Are your customers likely to have all of the latest plug-ins? Technically advanced users are likely to have high-specification machines and the latest versions of browsers, plug-ins, and Java virtual machines. Users based in schools may have older, lower-specification machines and older versions of browsers and plug-ins (if they have them at all). How do you obtain the details of who your customers are and what technologies they use? There are several sources of such information:

- Analyze your current Web server logs. If you are implementing a new service on an existing Web site, it is likely that the profile of your new users will match that of your existing users. Web server logs provide a good indication of the technologies used by your visitors, including their client OSs and browser types and versions.

- Research the free information on the Web. There are several sites that provide free analyses of Web user and technological data. These are identified in Chapters 9 through 11.

- Survey your current or prospective users and analyze the results. You might conduct the survey yourself as a paper exercise, put a survey questionnaire on the Web site itself, or commission an external organization to conduct the survey.

- Use your existing Web site to gather information. It is possible, using JavaScript, for example, to gather information about the user's client machine and store it in a cookie or transmit it to your Web or database server. Although this is easy to do, your users may object. After all, a lot of the information you collect could be of as much interest to hackers. Provision of this data should be voluntary, of course, and your Web site should always ask permission to do this.

- Buy the information. There are many organizations offering up-to-date surveys and analyses of user expectations and behavior at a price.

- If you have an existing Web site with a registration facility, consider using the user-profile data to analyze your current users. Note that users tend to volunteer personal information if it is given only for the purpose of using your site and services and will be treated as confidential. Although most would not consider the use of these details in statistical analyses a breach of privacy, check that your privacy policy allows for this before you use personal data in this way.

User demographics have a bearing on the following risk areas:

- Configurations to be tested;

- Popularity and take up of plug-ins;

- User configurations (e.g., images turned off, cookie rejection, and attitudes about downloading software from the Web);

- User agents to be supported (PDAs, WebTV, WAP devices).

Part III will provide more detail about each test type affected.

Where Do Nonfunctional Tests Fit?

Traditionally, nonfunctional tests are performed after functional system testing is complete. That is, the system should be free of major bugs before any of the nonfunctional tests are performed. In the case of performance testing, it makes no sense to subject a system to hundreds of thousands of transactions if it is so bug-ridden that it fails at the first transaction. There are several exceptions to this rule of course.

First, usability assessment is possible before a system is complete. Usability assessments can take place as part of the requirements-gathering process, during system design (using prototypes), or later in the project when the complete system is available. The test strategy should make it clear that the objectives of these tests might include eliciting requirements or refining a system design, rather than demonstrating the usability of a complete system.

Second, performance testing of a complete technical architecture cannot be done before the entire system is available and relatively stable. It is possible, however, to perform (comparative) benchmarking exercises of hardware and large-scale performance tests of infrastructure without having the complete application in place. Further, it is possible to conduct informal tests of single components using test drivers to gain some insight into how they will perform in isolation and to flush out obvious problems in code.

Third, security assessments may be done on partial environments. For example, the networking infrastructure could be scanned and evaluated for vulnerabilities before the system that will use it is available. Source code can also be scanned for insecure coding practices before a complete integrated system is available.

Build-and-Integration Strategies—an Example

Most e-business systems are built from a number of components. Figure 8.1 shows a typical architecture of an e-commerce system; we will use it to illustrate some of the issues related to build-and-integration strategies affecting the test process. The main components are as follows:

- The Web server running ASP or CGI scripts;
- The application or object server, which might be running COM objects or Enterprise Java Bean (EJB) components;
- The database server, running the DBMS-SQL Server, Oracle, DB2, or MySQL, such as;

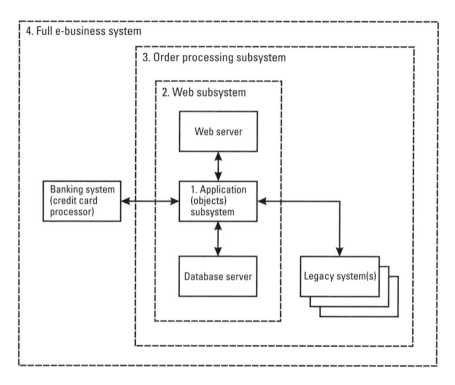

Figure 8.1 Typical e-commerce system.

- Legacy systems, maybe running on several other servers and perhaps holding customer databases, order processing, financial accounting, and customer relationship management (CRM) systems;

- External banking system that provides the credit checking, credit-card authorization, and processing facilities.

The developers might be split into four groups each working on a separate component because the skill sets for each component are quite different. For example:

- Group A builds Web server–based components.

- Group B builds application server objects.

- Group C builds the database and stored procedures.

- Group D builds interfaces to legacy systems and banking systems.

Let us assume the legacy systems do not need to change. The overall system architecture might require that all of the components be available to provide a useful service to customers. If so, system testing probably requires that all of the architectural components be available and integrated in a single test environment. When components are built and assembled in a test environment and "big bang" integration tested, integration bugs tend to make the tester's job much harder. Bugs tend to be deeply embedded in code and difficult to track down because the level of complexity has increased from single components to a huge system. Assuming that a system built this way will work the first time is as realistic as throwing twenty thousand automobile parts in the air and expecting an operational automobile to hit the ground. Most of the components will have to be built and tested in isolation before being integrated into the complete system. This usually requires building stubs and drivers. The build-and-integration sequence is primarily a technical decision, but it affects the test strategy significantly.

The test process that might result is summarized in Table 8.1. There are two integration test stages, but the processes of integration and integration testing occur at every test stage after the component test. The system test would include some integration testing of the Web subsystem, as well as most of the functional system testing of the application, with the legacy

Table 8.1
E-Commerce Test Stages

Test Stage	Technical Components to Be Tested	Notes
Component test	Individual components	All software components are built and unit-tested in isolation.
Integration test	Application (objects) subsystem	The application server objects are integrated and tested as a subsystem. Interfaces to all other components are stubbed out.
System test	Web subsystem	The Web server, application objects, and database server are integration tested.
Large-scale integration test	Order processing subsystem	The interfaces to legacy systems are activated and integration tested.
Bank integration test	Full e-commerce system	The interfaces to the banking systems are activated, and the complete end-to-end integration testing takes place.

systems and the banking system stubbed out. The large-scale integration test stage covers the integration of the legacy systems, and the bank integration test addresses the process of connecting to the bank's test environment. Other test types would be merged into one or another of the five test stages. Performance testing might take place as part of large-scale integration. The usability assessment might be done as part of the system test, and so on.

Taking integration as an incremental activity forces developers at least to build stubs and drivers to test components in isolation, then in subsystems. No developer likes to write code that is thrown away after use, which is exactly what might be done with the stubs and drivers when testing is completed. The developers may therefore argue that integration testing isn't required. They may ask, "Why not test all of the components together when they are all available?" Although this would simplify their job, it pushes the integration test activity backwards and effectively embeds it into the system test. Systems with integration bugs tend to be very fragile, and those bugs are often deeply embedded in the technical architecture. Consequently, these are often the most difficult bugs to track down, diagnose, and fix. When integration testing is not done, later system tests tend to be more traumatic, take longer to perform, and end up being more expensive. Unfortunately, many organizations treat integration testing as something that happens as if by magic in a system test, and they then wonder why system testing is so difficult.

The test strategy must reflect the fact that skipping integration testing is a false economy: the time saved by developers is lost when obscure integration bugs hold up the system testing for days, weeks, or even months. Where interfaces between components are poorly defined, the developers may argue that it isn't possible to define a precise build sequence as the design isn't finalized. The test strategist must press the designers to partition the architecture in as testable a way as possible so that the stages of integration can be identified. When this is done, some form of integration testing can take place at the end of each stage of integration.

Automated Regression Testing

One of the tenets of *Extreme Programming Explained* [1] is that component-level tests are run and rerun so often that automation of these tests is essential. This is an effective way of managing the stability of a product through continuous change where requirements are unstable. You might consider including this approach to automation in your test strategy. Designing tests to be automated from the start forces both developers and system testers to be disciplined in making their tests automatable and establishes a regime of continuous regression testing.

Many project plans put off the automation of regression tests until the end. We don't recommend this. Most projects are littered with good intentions that were never achieved. If a project slips, the pressure on testers will be to get the manual testing completed and the system delivered on time. Under these circumstances, there probably won't be enough time to build the automated tests before the project closes. Consequently, we recommend that automated scripts be built and maintained right from the start for regression purposes during subsystem- or system-test stages. There just won't be enough time to automate manual tests later. This approach should be stated explicitly in your plans. The problem with this approach, however, is that introduces a delay in turning around tests where, perhaps, the user interface is changing regularly (it will be difficult to maintain tests as fast as the user interface changes). The overhead of implementing automated tests in parallel with manual testing should also be identified in your plans.

One of the benefits of having developers build automated scripts is that a programming background is required to use most tools effectively. Developers can often build automated scripts faster than system testers (who might be less technically inclined). Developer-written automated test scripts can be reused for system testing. Data-driven scripts can be reused to execute the tests prepared by system testers; scripts can provide code that can be adapted or cannibalized for system test scripts.

It might help if system testers work with the developers to automate their tests. If both groups use the same test tool, the transition between development and system testing will be smoother. Developers can more easily reproduce the faults reported by later system testers because they are using the same test technology, methods, and approach.

Further Thoughts on Tools

There are many opportunities to use automation in the implementation of tests across almost all of the e-business test techniques. In Part III, we discuss the techniques and the tools that are available to support them. From the point of view of test strategy, however, it is worth considering some of the influences that tools have on the overall approach to testing.

Typically, the tools that execute functional tests require a significant amount of technical expertise to operate. Using a test execution tool, few, if any, tests can simply be captured, then replayed as regression tests by end users, for example. System test teams normally include a small number of test automation specialists who look after the automation within the team. The testers provide the tests for the automation specialists to implement using the tool.

The tools that detect static faults in HTML are very easy to use (so they can be used by nontechnical testers), but the information they generate is only of use to developers. Developers don't make as much use of static test tools as they perhaps should, even though static test tools are extremely easy to implement as compared with, say, test execution tools. We recommend that developers use the static analysis tools to provide evidence of successful HTML validation. Further, we suggest that this evidence be defined as a deliverable from the developers to accompany the (functionally tested) code that they write. System testers might use the same tools later to ensure that the HTML is compliant. It is in the developers' interest to adhere to Web conventions and HTML standards because finding and fixing bugs early is so much easier. If the system testers will be using these tools to find, say, HTML bugs, you had better agree on the rules of engagement with the development manager before documenting this in your test strategy.

One further complication is that many tools support more than one type of test. For example, some capture-replay tools support link checking; some tools support HTML validation, link checking, spell checking, and image optimization, all in one. The more sophisticated tools might, therefore, be used in more than one test stage. The number of licenses you have to buy might rise if different groups use different features of the same tool. It would be a far more serious situation were multiple tools with largely overlapping functionalities to be purchased for use by different groups. The waste of money incurred by having more tools than are required might be substantial, so do your tools research in conjunction with the developers, system testers, and any other potential tools users first to ensure the best combination of tools is procured.

Tools are discussed in more detail in Chapters 9 through 15 and 17.

Reference

[1]   Beck, K., *Extreme Programming Explained*, Boston, MA: Addison-Wesley, 2000.

Part III
E-Business Test Techniques and Tools

9

Static Testing

Overview

Static tests are those that do not involve executing software under test by inputting data and commands and comparing the software behavior with expected results. Static tests do involve inspections and reviews of project documentation, specifications, or code. Static analysis of code using automated tools also counts as a static test and is an effective way of detecting not only faults, but also poor programming practices. Table 9.1 lists the risks that static testing addresses.

Content Checking

The accuracy, completeness, consistency, correct spelling, and accessibility of Web page content might be deemed cosmetic but cosmetic no longer means unimportant, as perhaps it might in terms of internal IT systems. For example, if a testing services company misspelled the word "quality" as "kwality" on its home page it might not reflect well on the organization. Delivery of content might be the only purpose for many e-business sites. If content is the product for sale or if customers will use it to conduct their own business, faults might be regarded as serious threats to success. Web site content should be checked. Where a Web site contains downloadable documents,

Table 9.1
Risks Addressed by Static Testing

ID	Risk	Test Objective	Technique
C1	Spelling and other content-oriented mistakes on pages detract from the user's perceived quality of the product.	Ensure that all text in pages is spelled correctly.	Content checking
C2	Printouts of Web pages crop content are illegible, or poorly laid out.	Demonstrate that printed pages are complete, legible, and usable.	Content checking
C3	Web pages become distorted and illegible when viewed with varying window sizes, screen resolutions, or font sizes.	Demonstrate that Web pages are usable at varying window sizes, screen resolutions, and font sizes.	Content checking
C4	Incorrect or poorly written text on pages confuses or misleads users.	Verify that all text, messages, help screens, and information provided are accurate, concise, helpful, and understandable.	Content checking See also usability assessment (Chapter 14).
C5	Poorly designed or nonstandard HTML affects the layout or functionality of Web pages.	Verify that HTML on Web pages complies with the HTML standard.	HTML validation
C6	Poorly designed or nonstandard cascading style sheets (CSS) affect the appearance of Web pages.	Verify that CSS files comply with the CSS standard.	HTML validation
C7	Web page HTML is not supported by all browsers; layout and functionality work inconsistently across browsers.	Demonstrate that Web pages appear and behave consistently across the browsers in scope.	Browser syntax compatibility checking See also configuration testing (Chapter 11).
C8	The layout or general appearance of Web pages varies across different browser types.	Verify by inspection that the appearance of Web pages is consistent across browsers in scope.	Visual browser validation

such as white papers, catalogs, or brochures, these should undergo the usual checks and reviews. We are not concerned with those issues here. It is the Web pages themselves, downloaded from Web servers or generated by applications, that we are concerned with.

All of the popular Web page editors incorporate spell checkers to validate the text displayed in pages. Of course, we encourage the authors to use these to ensure correctness in the content. A problem with dynamic Web pages, however, is that the page content is generated from within some form of server-based code rather than static HTML files. In these cases, the pages must be first displayed in a browser and then checked.

Many of the tools that perform HTML validation also have built-in spell checkers. They have their own dictionaries (usually based on U.S. spellings), but are configurable. For example, the NetMechanic validation tool (http://www.netmechanic.com) allows you to store your own dictionary of terms in the home directory of your Web site, which will be used for checking. The Doctor HTML™ validator (http://www2.imagiware.com/RxHTML/) allows you to set up and maintain your own dictionary on the tool's Web site, which will be used for subsequent checking. One technique we have used is to take the displayed Web page in a browser window, copy it, and paste it into a word processor. You then spell check the text, and in the case of articles or longer documents, you can validate the text using a thesaurus or grammar checker and even generate readability scores.

Web users frequently encounter Web pages that appear differently when printed on a page. Any page on your Web site could be printed out. Most people prefer to print long pages and read them off-line as opposed to scrolling through them. It is irritating to see wide text forced off a printed page, making the document useless, and it is probably worse still to make users print pages with colorful backgrounds and unreadable text (using up all their printer toner in the process!) On an aesthetic note, Vincent Flanders and Michael Willis's book *Web Pages That Suck* [1] provides many examples of the pitfalls in page design, text layout, and content. Jakob Nielsen [2] recommends that any material intended to be printed have two formats: the on-screen format and a version intended for printing, in perhaps PDF or postscript format. Pages should be sized to fit on the most common paper sizes: U.S. letter format and European A4 format, namely. With 1-inch margins, the page size would be 6.25×9 inches (159×229 mm).

Just like any documentation, Web pages should be independently reviewed to ensure they are consistent, grammatically correct, and usable. This task might be included in a usability test.

HTML Validation

It is worth looking at the way that browsers support HTML in a little more detail. In principle, all browsers should support the HTML standard. The standard is defined by the World Wide Web Consortium (W3C) and is freely available from their Web site (http://www.w3c.org) [3]. In its early implementation, HTML was principally a markup language with a built-in mechanism, CGI, for invoking functionality that resided on Web servers. Later developments included the ability to incorporate functionality to run on browsers using embedded VBScript or JavaScript. Cascading style sheets (CSS) are separate files containing style information used with HTML pages. The CSS standard can also be found on the W3C Web site [4]. CSS allows the formatting controls to be separated from content by implementing reusable styles in Web pages. In parallel with these enhancements, Java applets could also be embedded in HTML and executed within browsers; fully functional applications have been implemented this way. Over time, the richness of layout features increased and dynamic HTML facilities dealing with events relating to page loading and closing, button clicks, and rollovers were added.

As this book goes to press, HTML version 4.01 is the current standard (version 5 is being developed). HTML has come a long way since it was first defined, and there is no doubt that it has some way to go before it stops evolving. As the HTML standard has evolved, so have browsers. To varying degrees, they adhere to the HTML standard. If we look closely at three of them, you will understand the nature of the problems that developers and users of Web sites face.

The two leading browsers, Netscape and Microsoft IE, are long established. For several years, at the height of the browser wars, competing browser vendors worked on the basis of "embracing and enhancing" the HTML standard. Their browsers broadly supported the standard, but offered extensions so that Web sites built to exploit these features would have a Best Viewed with Netscape or Best Viewed with Internet Explorer button to allow users to download the browser "that worked." If a browser didn't support some features, it would appear to end users to be inferior. Nowadays, it seems that the browsers are falling behind the standard, but Microsoft in particular continues to offer many formatting features and a broader range of events in its implementation that are beyond the standard specifications. The Opera browser probably offers the implementation that is closest to the standard, but Opera is still far less popular than Netscape and IE.

Browsers Can Interpret HTML Differently

Browsers download HTML pages from Web servers, interpret the HTML text, and render the page within the browser window. In most ways, this is a similar process to software interpretation. Unlike software interpreters, however, browsers are very forgiving of poor quality code. The good news (for users, at least) is that if a browser encounters a tag or attribute in the HTML that it does not recognize, the browser will ignore it. There are no unsightly and confusing syntax error messages displayed to users. In general, the browsers do their best with invalid HTML, but if the programmer has got the HTML wrong, the required layout effects or functionality may not work. Web page developers and testers may not see problems, but users may experience obscure difficulties later. Developers need to use tools and services that can validate HTML (and XML or WML) against rules defined in established and emerging standards before they deploy their Web pages.

Opera has gone some way to help Web developers identify bad code in the pages they are testing. It has a facility that will send any open Web page to the W3C HTML Validation Service (validator.w3.org) that then reports the errors found.

Browsers Treat HTML Faults Differently

There are further anomalies. IE is much more relaxed about poor HTML than Netscape. For example, leaving off a closing </TABLE> tag is a violation of the HTML rules. IE might forgive this error and display the table correctly; Netscape cannot recover from this error and doesn't display the table at all. Whether you are using validation tools or not, we recommend that your developers test their Web pages using a browser that is more sensitive to nonstandard HTML to increase the chances of detecting faults earlier.

Browsers Display HTML Differently

One example of where browsers differ involves an attribute of the <TABLE> tag. The BACKGROUND attribute is nonstandard. It can be used in an HTML table definition and has a defined value. The syntax is BACKGROUND = "url" where url indicates the address of an image to display as a background to the table cells. Netscape displays the image in each cell. IE displays the image as a background to the whole table. Clearly, the two browsers interpret this attribute differently. This feature should be avoided!

Tools that can inspect and validate HTML for syntax faults and compatibility with the various browsers are listed in Table 9.2 at the end of this chapter. Although tools can validate the underlying HTML, we recommend that you also perform a visual check to ensure differences between browsers do not cause problems for users.

Development Tools May Generate Poor HTML

Development tools usually have settings that restrict the generation of non-standard HTML. In most of these tools, it is possible to restrict the tool to generating code that is compatible with one of the following:

- IE only;
- Netscape only;
- Both IE and Netscape;
- WebTV.

Alternatively, a custom option allows the user to turn on or off specific code-generation features in the tool. The facilities can also be restricted to older browser versions. Although this should help to reduce the amount of problematic HTML code generated by the tool, it will not eliminate it. Developers may forget to turn these features on, but developers may not always use the graphical page editor in any case. Most of the time, the fine-tuning of Web pages is done by editing the HTML text directly.

Remote Validation or In-House Tools?

Some tools operate as portals that can be used to validate your Web pages remotely. You provide the URL for the page to be checked, and the portal performs the validation immediately or schedules its robot to visit your site and perform the test. When complete, the robot e-mails you a link to the results on a results server. This method requires that your site be hosted on the Web, which might not be convenient or even possible (for security reasons). Remote validation services tend to be free or inexpensive.

A better solution, perhaps, is to have a tool that you can operate internally within your development or test environment. These tools scan your pages and the results can be inspected without your having to expose your test site to the outside world. These tools are more likely to be proprietary, but still relatively inexpensive. One consideration worth noting is that some tool providers will make their source code available for you to implement (or even customize) on your own site. These tools are typically written as Perl scripts or C++ programs and are aimed at developers, of course.

We strongly suggest you discuss with your developers how they write their HTML and conduct their ad hoc testing, as well as what levels of validation are appropriate before selecting your particular validation method or tool.

Examples of HTML Validators

Figure 9.1 shows an example of how the free W3C Validation Service works. Like most of the remote validation services, you provide a URL (in this case the Evolutif home page) and select a document type. There are various reporting options that produce more or less detail in the report, and when you click the validate button (obscured), the page is checked immediately.

The results of the analysis are shown in Figure 9.2. You can see that the errors are listed in order by line number with a rather terse description of the problem. In this case, strict adherence to HTML 4.01 requires that all text formatting be done using CSS, rather than explicit FONT control. (We'll fix that problem shortly, I promise!) Validator isn't the most informative tool,

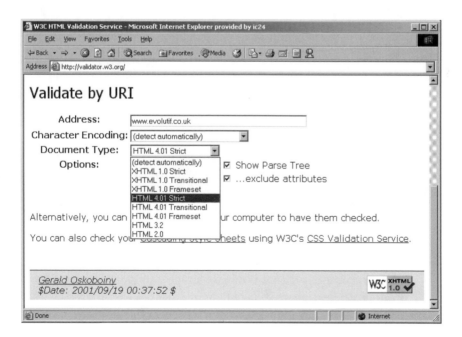

Figure 9.1 The W3C Validator.

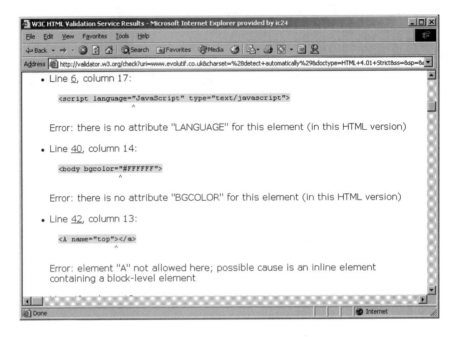

Figure 9.2 Typical validation results.

but it can be trusted to report the existence of faults. Other tools provide more explanation and some can generate corrected HTML where the tool can interpret and resolve the problem.

CSE's HTML Validator can be downloaded and run on your own PC. This tool retails for under $100 if you buy more than one copy. It can scan and validate single pages or whole directories of HTML files using its batch validation feature. The tool can be used to edit HTML files and save them back to the directory. Of more interest to testers, it incorporates a built-in browser based on IE. This neat feature means that you can navigate through a Web application, and for each new page displayed, validate the page on the fly. This eliminates the problem that most validation tools encounter in which pages generated by CGI or other server-based technologies (ASP, JSP) can only be reached by executing a coherent set of screen transactions. Most Web sites will not allow tools to do this.

Figure 9.3 shows a typical display. In the center pane, a Web page is displayed. The top pane displays the HTML source code for the page. Pressing the F6 key initiates validation, and the resulting error messages are summarized in the lower left pane. In the lower right pane, the highlighted error message is displayed in full.

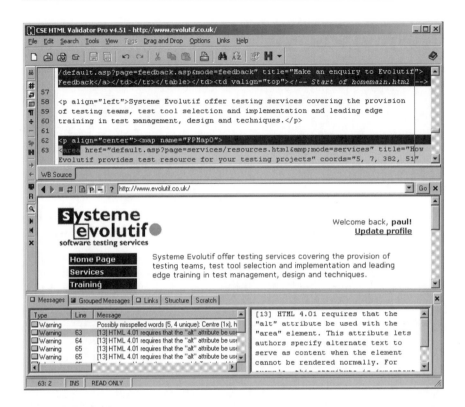

Figure 9.3 HTML Validator window. © 2002 AI Internet Solutions. Reproduced with permission.

Varying the Depth of Testing

Validation tools can be configured to compare HTML against stricter or more relaxed versions of the standard:

- The HTML 4.01 Strict Document Type Definition (DTD) includes all elements and attributes that have not been deprecated or do not appear in frameset documents.

- The HTML 4.01 Transitional DTD includes everything in the strict DTD, plus deprecated elements and attributes (most of which concern visual presentation).

- The HTML 4.01 Frameset DTD includes everything in the transitional DTD, plus frames as well. This includes the least strict version of the standard.

There are other ways of reducing the depth of testing:

- Advise developers to comply with specific conventions and fix only certain types of faults.
- Configure the validation tools to display all warnings or only the most serious warnings.

If you plan to support the two leading browsers, there are three possible approaches:

1. Adopt a reduced set of HTML elements within the HTML standard that is supported by both browsers and restricts developers to those.
2. Build parallel HTML implementations for each browser and determine which should be used at runtime (potentially complicated and more costly).
3. Adopt one browser as standard and ignore all others (viable only if you are building an intranet and have control over your users' technology platforms).

Once a strategy has been selected, you must agree with the developers whether (and how) they are adopting this strategy. You can then use the available tools in a consistent way to report faults.

Browser Syntax Compatibility Checking

Most of the tools that validate HTML against standards can also validate HTML against particular browsers. Figure 9.4 shows part of a typical report from the Doctor HTML tool from Imagiware. The figure shows that the HTML elements identified are compatible with IE 4 and up and match the standard requirements. The errors relate to elements not supported in IE 3 or Netscape and Opera. Obviously, meeting the requirements of the HTML standard does not guarantee that all of the browsers will interpret your HTML as intended.

You need to use a tool that covers as many of the target platforms you intend to support as possible. Given that these tests are automated, the choice you have is whether to report (and correct) the faults that make your HTML incompatible with your selected browsers. The decision to test more or less is really influenced by the scope of browsers to be supported.

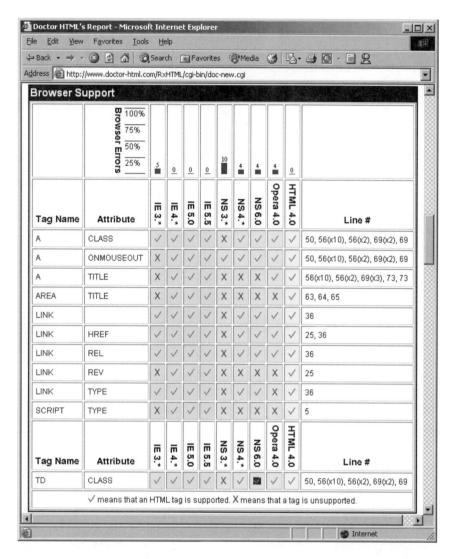

Figure 9.4 Sample browser compatibility report. © 2000, with permission of Imagiware, Inc.

Visual Browser Validation

It should be obvious from the previous discussion that there will be significant differences not only in the appearance of Web pages displayed by the different browsers, but also in their behavior. Take, for example, the screen dumps of a test version of the Evolutif Web site. Figure 9.5(a) shows the registration page in IE 6.0. Figure 9.5(b) shows the same page displayed using Netscape 4.51. The windows have been sized to display the same Web page area. The appearance of the same page in the two browsers varies dramatically. The differences here are cosmetic, rather than functional, but if your intention is to avoid the need to scroll pages in a set resolution setting, then the whole problem of pushing fields or buttons off the visible window arises. Although it is common practice, most users dislike having to scroll through forms to reach data entry fields and buttons.

Other, more serious problems have been reported, but are most commonly associated with differences in the following:

- The colors of standard objects (e.g., horizontal lines, borders);
- The centering and scaling of objects in windows;

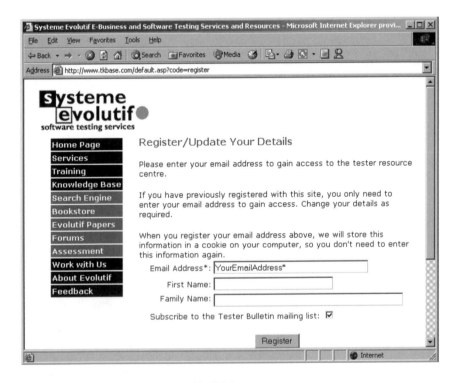

Figure 9.5(a) Sample page displayed in IE 6.0.

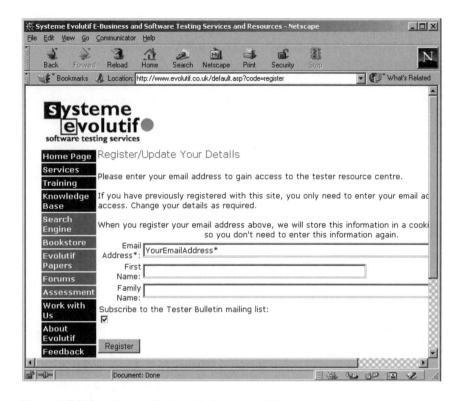

Figure 9.5(b) Sample page displayed in Netscape 4.51.

- Display of scrolling marquees;
- Table layouts (automatic sizing gives different results);
- Table background and border colors.

The webreview Web site (http://www.webreview.com) [5] summarizes common browser implementation issues and suggests safer approaches.

Consider testing on one platform and verifying visually that the appearance of pages on the other browsers is acceptable. We recommend, for example, that developers use the earliest (i.e., least capable) versions of the browsers to be supported, as well as the more common later versions. Multiple versions of IE cannot normally be installed on a single machine, so you may need to dual boot your test environment or have a spare machine to implement this. Netscape allows multiple versions to be installed as long as they are in different directories.

Recently, NetMechanic (http://www.netmechanic.com) [6] introduced a new feature on its site validation toolkit. The BrowserPhoto™ facility takes snapshots of your Web pages as viewed in a variety of browsers, versions, and screen resolutions. It is clear that this facility could reduce dramatically the number of configurations you need to have available in your test environment and could speed up the process of checking each one.

The depth of testing in this case has three dimensions:

1. How many configurations do you need to test? This decision is explored in more detail in the configuration testing discussion (frequently, visual browser validation is performed as part of configuration testing).

2. How many of your screens should be examined visually? You might consider only doing critical screens, those you believe are most sensitive to compatibility problems, or those that comprise the critical business functions.

3. Which problems should you focus on? You might focus only on particular types of problems, such as the layout of forms and the accessibility of all fields, buttons, and images. If a font is wrongly sized or if fields have moved across the screen, perhaps you needn't worry.

Tools for Static Testing

Tools that perform automated HTML validation and compatibility often perform other functions, such as link, spelling, and accessibility checks. These tools are now widely available; some are free, and others can be obtained at a small cost. Most of the HTML development tools have some form of built-in validation. Some tool vendors bundle validation functionality with their proprietary test tool suites. If you acquire tools that incorporate validation facilities, we recommend that you compare the validation results of these with one of the (free) independent validation services to ensure they report the same faults. It is common for validation code to be licensed for reuse in other services and products, so some of the tools listed in Table 9.2 share the same functionality.

Table 9.2
Browser and HTML Validation Tools

Tool Name	URL
A Real Validator	http://arealvalidator.com
Bobby	http://www.cast.org/bobby
CSE HTML Validator	http://www.htmlvalidator.com
Doctor HTML	http://www2.imagiware.com/RxHTML/
Dr. Watson	http://watson.addy.com
HTML Tidy	http://www.w3c.org/People/Raggett/tidy/
META Medic	http://northernwebs.com/set/setsimjr.html
Microsoft StyleT CSS Style Testing Tool	http://msdn.microsoft.com
Net Mechanic	http://www.netmechanic.com
W3C CSS Validation Service	http://jigsaw.w3.org/css-validator/validator-uri.html
W3C HTML Validation Service	http://validator.w3.org
WDG HTML Validator	http://www.htmlhelp.com/tools/validator/
Web Page Backward Compatibility Viewer	http://www.delorie.com/web/wpbcv.html
Web Page Purifier	http://www.delorie.com/web/purify.html
Web Site Garage	http://websitegarage.netscape.com

References

[1]   Flanders, V., and M. Willis, *Web Pages That Suck: Learn Good Design by Looking at Bad Design,* San Francisco, CA: Sybex, 1998.

[2]   Nielsen, J., *Designing Web Usability,* Indianapolis, IN: New Riders, 2000.

[3]   World Wide Web Consortium, "HTML 4.01 Specification," http://www.w3.org/TR/html4/, 2002.

[4]   World Wide Web Consortium, "Cascading Style Sheets, Level 2 CSS2 Specification," http://www.w3.org/TR/REC-CSS2/, 2002.

[5]   webreview.com, "Browser Guide," http://www.webreview.com/browsers/index.shtml, 2002.

[6]   NetMechanic.com, "BrowserPhoto™," http://www.netmechanic.com/browser-index.htm, 2002.

10

Web Page Integration Testing

Overview

The risks listed in Table 10.1 all relate to failures that would be noticeable as soon as a user first navigates to a page, clicks on a link or button to navigate to another page, or invokes a server-based component. These risks are grouped together because they relate to the integration of HTML pages to embedded objects, linked pages, or server-based functionality. Collecting these risks together means that the testing required to address them can be performed on a single Web page component when the linked objects are available. As each component is developed and combined with its linked components, the links to other pages and objects can be checked within a development environment. Essentially, this is an integration process, and the tests that accompany it are integration tests. One of the biggest benefits of these tests is that they can largely be automated.

When the complete system is assembled in a system test environment, many of these tests should become redundant. Link checking, in particular, can be a quick and easy way of determining whether all components of the system have been delivered and installed. A successful automated link check is a convenient test to set as an entry criterion for systems testing. If Web page integration tests are performed as part of developer testing, integration problems can be found early, instead of later when they would cause serious avoidable disruption to system testing.

Web page integration testing also aims to check that the correct objects are loaded quickly. We have seen Web pages reference perhaps 100 separate

Table 10.1
Risks Addressed by Web Page Integration Testing

ID	Risk	Test Objective	Technique
I1	Graphical or other objects do not load onto Web pages, marring the appearance or affecting the functionality.	Demonstrate that all objects (frame page HTML, images, sounds, applets) referenced by the pages are available and can load.	Link checking
I2	Links to other on-site objects do not work.	Verify that links to on-site objects load correctly when clicked.	Link checking
I3	Links to other off-site objects do not work.	Verify that links to off-site objects load correctly when clicked.	Link checking
I4	The HTML page or objects embedded in the page are so large that the page downloads too slowly.	Verify that objects are small enough to download within an acceptable time.	Object load and timing
I5	Links to server-based functionality do not work.	Verify the following: • Correct components are referenced; • Component exists and can be executed; • Data passed to the component is transferred correctly; • Results are returned and presented.	Transaction verification

objects that together need to be loaded and displayed. (This is an exceptionally large number of page elements and isn't recommended!) For any Web page to display, not only must each of its objects exist in the location referenced by the HTML of the page, the objects themselves should not be overly large, making the page unacceptably slow to load.

Transaction verification aims to ensure that the integration of Web pages with the server-based components that handle HTML forms is correct. The right component must be called with the correct parameters. The rules governing the validity of data transferred using parameters or shared between components and its usage should be consistent across interfacing components. There are very few useful references on integration testing, and none that help with the Web-specific issues detailed above. The principles of integration testing, however, are universal and are well covered in Beizer's and Hetzel's books [1, 2]. We recommend you consult both for the principles and details concerning how to construct integration test cases.

Web page integration testing is focused primarily on technical issues, and we recommend that developers conduct these tests as part of their unit and integration testing. System testers might perform only link checks using automated tools.

Link Checking

Missing Embedded Web Page Objects

We navigate to a new Web page by typing a URL into the address window of a browser, by clicking on a link in a displayed Web page, or by filling in Web page form fields and clicking on the submit button. When we take any of these actions, the browser sends an HTTP message to the Web server identified in the domain name of the link or form and requests that the page be returned or that a server-based component be invoked. Either way, the Web server responds by sending an HTTP message that contains the HTML for the new page (or executes a server-based component that generates the new HTML page as its output). The browser parses, interprets, and displays the page, depending on the content of the HTML.

An HTML Web page may reference other embedded objects such as the following:

- Other HTML pages to be displayed in frames;
- Images (in JPEG, TIFF or other formats);
- Videos (in AVI, MPEG format);
- Sounds (in SND, MP3 or other format);
- Java Applets.

The browser displays the page and its embedded objects just as the page designer intended, with images, videos, and sounds (providing the multimedia experience). All too often, Web sites that contain a large number of embedded objects fail because the Web server cannot return some objects for the browser to display or replay. When an embedded object cannot be retrieved from the Web server, the browser normally displays a simple icon denoting that an object is not available, and if the page author has been conscientious, it may show a message describing what should have been displayed. If a missing graphic was a button with text in the image describing its function, the Web page may be made unusable because the cue that informs the user what to do next may be missing. By the way, alternate text, defined in HTML and displayed by browsers when images are not loaded, is covered as an accessibility issue in Chapter 13.

Missing Linked Objects

Within the body of a Web page, there are usually linked objects that are only requested when the user clicks on a link or on the active buttons in an interactive form. In this case, the new page, document, downloadable file, or server-based component is requested from the Web server; if it is not returned, the browser usually displays the warning screen and the dreaded HTTP 404 message. Figures 10.1 and 10.2 show the IE and Netscape versions of this warning screen, respectively.

Why Do Objects Go Missing?

Link failures typically occur when new or changed pages are not checked or where linked objects are moved or renamed. These problems are symptoms of either a lack of control over Web site change and release processes or a lack of attention to unit and integration testing. Internal links are links to objects that reside on the same Web server as the pages containing them and are under your control, so problems are relatively easy to spot and correct. External links are not usually under your control. If you have links to the off-site pages of business partners, customers, or suppliers, or if you link to reference material on other sites, you must ensure that these links work because off-site pages (and the Web sites that host them) are regularly moved, renamed, or deleted. Their Web masters will not consult you when they do this. Link checking is a perpetual chore because over time your off-site links are bound to become out-dated as all sites change. Continuous link checking is an important aspect of postdeployment monitoring, covered in Chapter 16. Many of the link checking portals referenced at the end of this chapter offer continuous monitoring options.

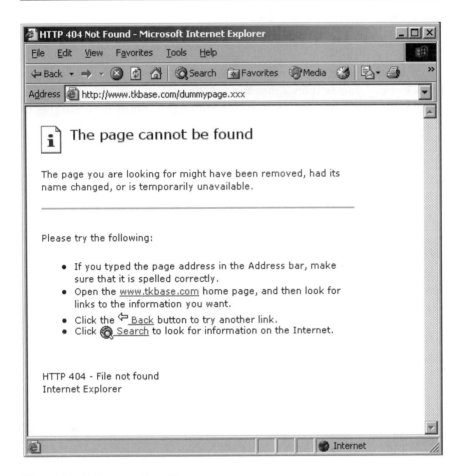

Figure 10.1 IE "page not found" warning screen.

Other Return Codes from Web Servers

When a Web server receives an HTTP request, the server sends a return code to the client browser. Return codes indicate the status of the request, and there are a large number of them. For example, a return code of 200 means the page or object was successfully downloaded, and 404 means the object was not found on the Web server. Rather than letting the user's browser display the 404 error page, it is preferable for the Web server to be configured so as to present users with a prepared error page that allows them to search the Web site for the page they want or to go elsewhere. Many sites set up special pages on the Web server to "soften" the erroneous response to users and offer

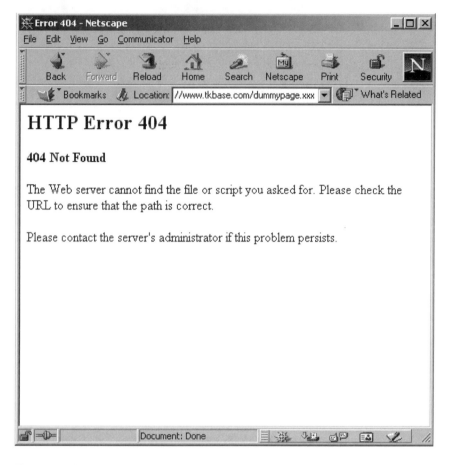

Figure 10.2 Netscape "page not found" warning screen.

help or advice on what to do next. The error codes are split into five bands or categories as displayed in Table 10.2.

Browsers are generally "silent" when they receive codes in the 100 to 399 range. Errors in the 400 to 599 code range, such as those listed in Table 10.3, are reported back to the user; they may also be handled by a dedicated page on the Web server.

If your Web server software has this facility and you decide to provide your own custom error pages, you should check that these have been properly configured. If you cannot easily simulate the error condition, you may have to verify the configuration by inspection of the Web server settings.

Table 10.2
Server-Response Code Ranges and Meanings

Code Range	Response Meaning
100–199	Informational
200–299	Client request successful
300–399	Client request redirected
400–499	Client request incomplete
500–599	Server errors

Table 10.3
Example Server-Response Error Codes and Meanings

Error Code	Response Meaning
400	Failed: bad request
401	Failed: unauthorized
402	Failed: payment required
403	Failed: forbidden
404	Failed: not found
500	Failed: internal error
501	Failed: not implemented
502	Failed: overloaded temporarily
503	Failed: gateway timeout

Automated Link Checkers

Link checkers scan the HTML of a starting page, then identify and check that all of the linked objects on the page exist and can be loaded. These linked objects can be any of the following:

- Linked pages (other pages to be navigated to by clicking on hyper-links);

- Frame pages (where a page is partitioned into frames and each frame has its own HTML page to create the image displayed in the browser window);

- Images used for graphical appearance or as navigation buttons (e.g., GIFs and JPEGs);

- Form handlers, where these are CGI scripts, ASP, and so forth;

- ActiveX, Java applets, and other objects that are downloaded and executed within the browser;

- Other content files, such as video (AVI, MPEG) and audio (WAV, AU, MIDI, MPEG) files;

- Other Internet protocols, such as e-mail, FTP, newsgroup links.

Typically, the tools that link check using robots perform two functions: They first identify all of the linked objects on a page, then attempt to download them. In doing so, the robots determine whether the object exists and can be loaded. Some tools report on the size and download time for the object. Typically, the reports produced list the objects linked, their validity, and their size. Some tools provide download times for each object based on selected network connection speeds. Nowadays, a 56K modem is the norm for dial-up users (although these normally connect at around 40 Kbps). This connection speed is reasonable for most business-to-consumer applications. For business-to-business applications, end users might be connected at much higher speeds using their corporate LAN. (Under these circumstances, object sizes and download speeds are of less concern.)

Some tools work as portal-based services, where you request a Web robot or agent to visit your site on the Web, traverse all of the links and objects, and then produce a report. Other tools can be installed to run on your intranet or test environment. Be aware that some site managers prefer not to be visited by remote agents and search engines and will configure their sites and firewalls accordingly. An article posted on the Global Positioning site, "Excluding Pages from Search Engines" [3], explains how this can be done for a Web server. Check that your Web server and network administrator have not imposed restrictions that stop remote link checking agents from working.

Web page authoring tools usually offer link-checking facilities. Because the download speed of an object over a fixed bandwidth is mainly determined by the object's size, most of these tools also report download speeds for your preferred bandwidth. Some of the link checking and authoring tools provide graphical output of the links for a site with the home page at the center of such graphics. These diagrams normally resemble a collection of connected spidery shapes. This is less useful for large sites (although the diagrams can be pretty!).

Figure 10.3 shows the starting window of the Xenu Link Sleuth tool. The user enters the URL of a page, and the tool then checks all the pages and objects linked to this starting point. By default, the tool will check all of the pages linked to linked pages, and the pages that link to them, and so on, until a whole site has been checked. The tool has the option to check off-site pages to make sure they are available, but the tool ventures no further into the Web after it has encountered an off-site link (for obvious reasons).

Figure 10.4 shows the results of the Xenu analysis. There are various reporting options, but you can see from the figure that there are several linked pages missing.

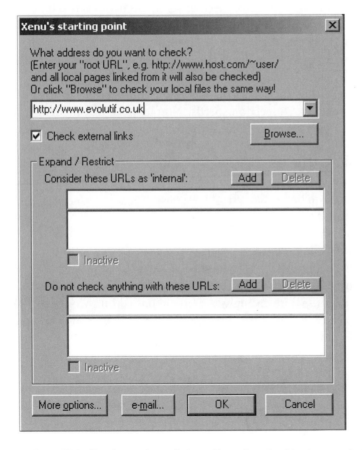

Figure 10.3 Xenu Link Sleuth starting window. Reproduced with the permission of Tilman Hausherr.

Figure 10.4 Xenu Link Sleuth results page. Reproduced with the permission of Tilman Hausherr.

One of the tools that performs static analysis of HTML code is HTML Validator™ [4]. This tool allows the user to navigate through the Web application using the built-in browser facility and scan the displayed HTML. It will also check links on the displayed page as you visit new screens, so it is useful for doing link checking on the fly.

Object Load and Timing

Jakob Nielsen's Web site, useit.com (http://www.useit.com), is an excellent reference for Web usability issues. He quotes the following response-time limit for the speed of a Web transaction, derived from his book *Usability Engineering*:

10 seconds is about the limit for keeping the user's attention focused on the dialogue. For longer delays, users will want to perform other tasks while waiting for the computer to finish, so they should be given feedback indicating when the computer expects to be done. Feedback during the delay is especially important if the response time is likely to be highly variable, since users will then not know what to expect [5].

If a Web page has to download in fewer than 10 seconds and a user has a 33K modem, then the size of the page and all of its embedded objects cannot exceed 330,000 bits, or 41.25 KB. If a user accesses the Web using a fast 10-Mbps connection, the page size can be as great as 1.25 MB and still download in 10 seconds. Clearly, before you get concerned about page size, you need to understand how your users are connecting to the Web.

Bear in mind that most home-based and small office–based users may be accessing the Web through 28K, 33K, or 56K modems. You remember accessing the Web using your 9,600-bps modem, don't you? In those days you probably turned graphics off entirely. Nowadays, the standard modem speed is around 33K. This is what you should use for assessing the speed of downloads. Until new broadband technologies are fully established, the size of pages will remain a big issue for consumer users. In a report entitled, "Hooked on Dial-up: Consumer ISP Trends and Market Share" [6], Cahners In-Stat Group forecasts that by 2005, dial-up will still remain the dominant form of Internet access. For the foreseeable future, the size of your Web pages must remain a concern, and you should test for this.

The main concern with speed of page loading is page design, not the speed of your infrastructure and the net itself (although these naturally affect download speed; we'll cover performance testing in Chapter 12). Normally, if page graphics are not the main content offered on a Web site, the images used to illustrate the site and provide graphical buttons for navigation and transactions are the main concern. Normal recommendations for good (and fast) page design are as follows:

- HTML IMG tags have WIDTH and HEIGHT attributes to define image size explicitly.

- The home page should be less than 30K in size total.

- All other pages should be less than 45K.

- Background and button or icon pictures should be less than 5K.

- If you must use an image for the page background, use the same image for all pages.

- Photos should be in JPEG format; computer generated images and schematics should be GIFs.

- All GIFs should be interlaced.

- Images should not be duplicated; use the same images repeatedly to avoid reloads.

- Limit table text size to 2K.

- Size tables explicitly rather than allowing browsers to format them automatically.

Vincent Flanders and Michael Willis provide comprehensive guidance for fixing a broad range of graphics problems in their book [7]. These include a range of tools for optimizing JPEG and GIF formatted images.

Figure 10.5 shows a typical report from the NetMechanic tool [8]. You can see that the checked page would load in 10.73 seconds using a 28.8K modem and in 6.44 seconds using a 56K modem. The sizes of all the embedded objects (usually images) are listed and the larger ones are highlighted in red. Many large images can be reduced in size by optimizing the image file. This is mostly achieved by reducing the number of colors in the image. NetMechanic has a neat facility called GifBot that can take the images on your Web site and show you examples of various optimization levels and their effect on the image quality. Typically, size savings of 50% are achievable without noticeable degradation of image quality. For large images, these savings can make or break the acceptability of a Web page.

Transaction Verification

The most common mechanism used to implement functionality on Web sites is CGI. When an HTML form is filled in and submitted using one of the form buttons, the form handler referenced by the form definition is invoked on the server. The browser sends the data captured on visible fields and the preset information defined on invisible fields as parameters to the server-based form handler.

Server-based forms handlers are CGI programs. On Linux/Unix systems these are most often Perl scripts or programs written in C++. In the Windows environment, these programs can be C++ programs, DLLs, ASPs, JSPs, PHPs, and other server-based HTML embedded-code interpreters that implement the CGI mechanism, so the same principles apply.

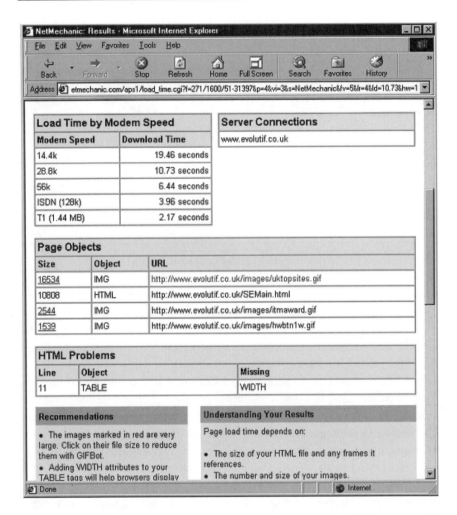

Figure 10.5 Sample NetMechanic results. © 2002, NetMechanic.com. Reproduced with permission.

Figure 10.6 shows a typical user dialog that invokes several transactions on different screens in order to buy a CD or book a flight, for example. From the first login page, the user enters a user id and password and clicks the login button. The resulting HTTP message to the Web server invokes a CGI script. This script validates the user id and password, generates the HTML for the options page, and sends it back to the user's browser, which then displays it. The options page has a forms handler script, which works in a similar way. In general, all Web applications are constructed from scripts that

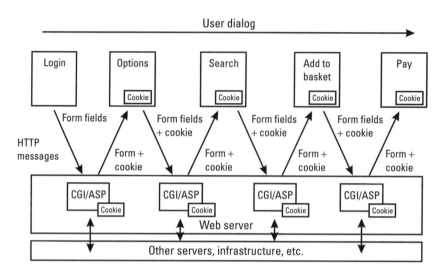

Figure 10.6 Typical user dialog showing Web pages and handlers.

generate HTML forms that are matched with a CGI handler script. Every form has a matching handler script.

On the server, the forms handler extracts the parameters supplied in the message sent by the browser and uses this data to perform the server-based transaction. Typically, forms handlers execute query or update transactions on databases, then generate a new page to be posted back to the client browser. Increasingly, handlers invoke other server-based components or objects that themselves access databases or networked legacy systems.

Transaction verification aims at ensuring that the correct forms handler is invoked and that the parameters passed to the forms handler are correct. Part of the forms definition is the method by which the HTTP message is sent to the server. HTTP has several methods, but the two we are concerned with are GET and POST, which cover almost all of the situations of interest to us here. For more detailed descriptions of CGI, GETs and POSTs, see [9, 10].

HTTP GET

When a CGI program is invoked by an HTTP GET message, the parameters are appended to the URL of the forms handler. For example, a form having two fields, reptype and sortorder, that generates a report might generate a URL (displayed in the address window of the browser) such as:

```
http://www.mysite.com/cgi-bin/doreport.pl?reptype=
ProdList&sortorder=ByPrice
```

The full URL above would invoke the program doreport.pl in directory cgi-bin on the Web server http://www.mysite.com and use two parameter values. In an HTTP GET, the parameters are appended to the program's URL in the text starting with the question mark character. The parameters are separated by an ampersand (&) character. Each parameter appears as a name-value pair. In this case, `reptype=ProdList` and `sortorder=By Price`.

To check whether the doreport.pl script has been invoked correctly with all of its parameters supplied, one can simply look at the URL that is generated and displayed in the browser address window. Sometimes the URL text for complex transactions is very long. In this case, you might copy the text string and paste it into a Notepad document. You could then print it out and inspect it carefully.

HTTP POST

When a CGI program is invoked by an HTTP POST message, the parameters are incorporated into the body of the HTTP message (not into the URL, as with GETs). The browser does not display the form parameters appended to the URL in the URL window. You cannot see the parameters from the address window. POSTs are used either because the programmer wants to hide sensitive information or the URL string would be too large for HTTP to handle. The forms handler obtains these values from the body of the HTTP message. You cannot see this HTTP message from within the browser, unfortunately. In this case, in order to verify that the parameters have been passed correctly, the programmer would need to incorporate a small amount of code to write out the parameters as received by the forms handler program. This code would be commented out when any anomalies were fixed and the code was working correctly, of course.

As an ASP example, the code below could be used to display all the parameters collected on an HTML form. The file is called handler.asp.

```
<H2>The ASP Request Object</H2>
<H3>Variables POSTed</H3>
<%
For Each objItem In Request.Form
   Response.Write objItem & " = " &
      Request.Form(objItem) & "<BR>"
Next
```

```
%>
<!--
<H3>Variables in the URL</H3>
<%
For Each objItem In Request.QueryString
   Response.Write objItem & " = " &
       Request.QueryString(objItem) & "<BR>"
Next
%>
<!--
...having printed out the parameters passed to this script (via
an HTTP GET or POST call) the remainder of the HTML and ASP
code appears here and operates on the parameters supplied...
-->
```

When this handler is called from a form in a Web page, it displays all of the
parameters collected off the form fields and also those embedded in the URL
referenced in the FORM HTML. The first HTML statement in the form
definition is displayed below:

```
<FORM ACTION="handler.asp?thisis=atest&sample=form"
      METHOD="POST">
  ...
  ...
```

The output from the handler is printed below:

```
The ASP Request Object
Variables POSTed
FirstName = Priscilla
Reading = on
LastName = Descartes
Swimming = on
Country = America
OtherHobby = Computers, Mountaineering,
Comments = Type your comments here...
SelectAge = 21-30
btnSubmit = Submit

Variables in the URL
sample = form
thisis = atest
```

Developers could test the forms in any Web page by using the test handler
code above and referencing that code in the development version of their
forms. Before writing the handler, they could unit test their forms' HTML

using the handler as a stub to display the data captured in the form. When the handler has been written and is ready to test, the form definition can reference the real handler. Of course, these techniques are really only appropriate for developers to use in their unit and integration tests.

Tools for Web Page Integration Testing

Tools that perform automated link checking often perform other functions, such as HTML validation, spelling, and accessibility checks. These tools are now widely available; some are free and others can be obtained at a small cost. Most of the HTML development tools also have some form of link-checking built-in. Table 10.4 presents a selection of tools available.

Table 10.4
Tools for Web Page Integration Testing

Tool Name	URL
Alért LinkRunner	http://www.alertbookmarks.com/lr/download.htm
Big Brother	http://pauillac.inria.fr/~fpottier/brother.html.en
Bobby	http://www.cast.org/bobby
CSE HTML Validator	http://www.htmlvalidator.com
CyberSpider Link Test	http://www.cyberspyder.com
Doctor HTML	http://www2.imagiware.com/RxHTML/
Dr. Watson	http://watson.addy.com
HTML Link Validator	http://lithops.mastak.com
InfoLink	http://www.biggbyte.com
Link Alarm	http://www.linkalarm.com
LinkBot	http://www.watchfire.com
LinkGuard	http://www.linkguard.com
Link Lint	http://www.linklint.org
LinkScan	http://www.elsop.com
NetMechanic	http://www.netmechanic.com
Xenu's Link Sleuth	http://home.snafu.de/tilman/xenulink.html
W3C Link Checker Service	http://validator.w3.org/checklink
WebART	http://www.oclc.org/webart
Web Site Garage	http://websitegarage.netscape.com

References

[1] Beizer, B., *Software System Testing and Quality Assurance*, New York: Van Nostrand Reinhold, 1984.

[2] Hetzel, W. C., *The Complete Guide to Software Testing*, Wellesley, MA: QED Information Sciences, 1988.

[3] Global Positioning, "Excluding Pages from Search Engines," http://www.global-positioning.com/robots_text_file/index.html, 2002.

[4] CSE HTML Validator™, "HTML and Link Validation Tool," http://www.html-validator.com, 2002.

[5] Nielsen J., *Usability Engineering*, San Francisco, CA: Morgan Kaufmann, 1994.

[6] Cahners In-Stat, "Hooked on Dial-up: Consumer ISP Trends and Market Share," http://www.instat.com/abstracts/ia/2001/is0102es_abs.htm, 2002.

[7] Flanders V., and M. Willis, *Web Pages That Suck: Learn Good Design by Looking at Bad Design*, San Francisco, CA: Sybex, 2001.

[8] NetMechanic, "NetMechanic Portal Service for Checking Links, HTML, GIF Images, etc.," http://www.netmechanic.com, 2002.

[9] Gralla, P., *How the Internet Works*, Indianapolis, IN: QUE, 1999.

[10] Spainhour, S., and V. Quercias, *Webmaster in a Nutshell*, Sebastopol, CA: O'Reilly, 1996.

11

Functional Testing

Overview

Table 11.1 lists the risks addressed by functional testing, though this chapter takes some liberty perhaps with the strict definition of that term. Strictly speaking, functional tests demonstrate that software meets its functional requirements, which describe what the system must do. Nonfunctional requirements, by and large, describe how the system must deliver its functionality. (Is it fast? Is it usable? Is it secure?) Performance, usability, and security testing are therefore nonfunctional test types. Configuration testing could also be regarded as a nonfunctional test, but for most practical purposes, configuration testing is dominated by functional regression tests using a variety of platforms and configurations. For this reason, configuration testing has been included in the functional testing chapter. Localization testing may also be regarded as a nonfunctional test, but again we have squeezed this test type into this chapter. We apologize to the purists.

The textbook strategy for staged testing is to conduct component-level tests first, then to link test the trusted components in testable combinations or subsystems. This is small-scale integration testing. Integration testing is incremental, usually builds up as the number of components assembled increases, and ends when a complete system is available. Then, system and acceptance teams finish the test cycle, using functional and business requirements as baselines.

This chapter is not intended to match the traditional test life cycle of component, link, and system test stages. Rather, it is intended to illustrate

Table 11.1
Risks Addressed by Functional Testing

ID	Risk	Test Objective	Technique
F1	Web page's embedded components fail to meet requirements.	Demonstrate that Web page user interface meets requirements.	Browser page testing
F2	Web pages with embedded scripts are unusable by users with script support turned off.	Demonstrate that pages provide warnings, alternative functionality, or both for users with script support disabled.	Browser page testing These checks might also be performed as part of HTML validation (Chapter 9), configuration testing (this chapter), or Web accessibility checking (Chapter 13).
F3	Web pages with embedded Java applets are unusable by users with applet support turned off.	Demonstrate that pages provide warnings, alternative functionality, or both for users with applet support disabled.	Browser page testing These checks might also be performed as part of HTML validation (Chapter 9), configuration testing (this chapter), or Web accessibility checking (Chapter 13).
F4	Web pages requiring plug-ins are unusable by users not having that plug-in or with plug-in support turned off. No alternative functionality is provided.	Demonstrate that pages provide warnings, alternative functionality, or both for users without plug-ins or with plug-in support disabled.	Browser page testing
F5	A server-based component fails to meet its functional requirements.	Demonstrate that the server-based component meets its functional requirements.	Server-based component testing
F6	A custom-built infrastructure component fails to meet its functional requirements.	Demonstrate that the infrastructure component meets its functional requirements.	Server-based component testing

Table 11.1 (continued)

ID	Risk	Test Objective	Technique
F7	Components are not integrated (data transfer).	Demonstrate that components are integrated and perform data transfer correctly.	Transaction link testing
F8	Components are not integrated (data reconciliation across interfaces).	Demonstrate that components are integrated [data transferred across the interface is consistently used (e.g., currency, language, metrics, timings, accuracy, tolerances)].	Transaction link testing
F9	Components are not integrated (transfer of control).	Demonstrate that components are integrated (transfer of control with required parameters is done correctly).	Transaction link testing
F10	Middleware, connectivity, or custom-built components fail or crash when used for an extended period.	Demonstrate that integrated components do not fail with repeated use or use over an extended period.	Transaction link testing
F11	System fails to meet functional requirements.	Demonstrate that the integrated system meets its functional requirements.	Application system testing
F12	System fails when connection or session is disrupted midtransaction.	Demonstrate that the system will operate with loss of context or fail gracefully.	Context testing
F13	Weird paths (connect, reconnect, disconnect) allow users to execute transactions out of normal sequence or context.	Demonstrate that the system will operate with loss of connection and reconnection without compromising the system or user.	Context testing
F14	Weird paths (back, forward, reload or refresh buttons) allow users to execute transactions out of normal sequence or context.	Demonstrate that the system will either prohibit such operations or not fail if they are performed.	Context testing

Table 11.1 (continued)

ID	Risk	Test Objective	Technique
F15	System is unusable or exhibits unacceptable behavior if cookies are disabled, expire, or are interfered with on the client machine.	Demonstrate that the system operates correctly (does not use cookies) or gives error message if sessions are interrupted or cookies are interfered with.	Context testing
F16	Cookies that are deleted or expire prematurely cause the Web service to fail.	Verify that where cookies are deleted, the Web site continues to provide service.	Context testing
F17	A multilingual system is not accurately translated (e.g., screens, reports, help screens, manuals).	Verify that all language-specific text has been translated across all components.	Localization
F18	Local address formats (zip code, postcode, department) are not handled correctly.	Verify that local address formats for the countries in scope can be accommodated.	Localization
F19	The system doesn't handle local variety in personal set-up and usage (e.g., bank account number, social security number).	Where local variations in data formats exist, demonstrate that these can be handled correctly.	Localization
F20	The system cannot accommodate local currencies, taxes, or other arrangements.	Demonstrate that the system can process local currencies for the countries in scope.	Localization
F21	The system does not work with nominated browsers and versions to be supported.	Demonstrate that the system operates correctly on all browser versions to be supported.	Configuration testing
F22	The system cannot be used on new platforms (e.g., Web TV, mobile phones, PDAs).	Demonstrate that the system can operate correctly on new platforms in scope.	Configuration testing
F23	Client configuration (e.g., screen resolution) makes the system unusable.	Demonstrate that the system can be operated at the minimum specified screen resolution.	Configuration testing

Table 11.1 (continued)

ID	Risk	Test Objective	Technique
F24	Web page appearance or behavior is adversely affected by user browser configuration options.	Demonstrate that the Web page functions correctly in the following situations, for instance: • User turns off graphics or sound; • User has a no-frames browser; • User has a text-only browser.	Configuration testing
F25	Connection through commercial services (e.g., AOL) fails.	Demonstrate that system can be used through commercial services and operate correctly.	Configuration testing
F26	Client configuration unusable; local character sets being rejected by software or database.	Demonstrate that the system can accept and process data from computers with a non-English set up.	Configuration testing or localization (this chapter)
F27	Minimum supported client platform cannot be supported.	Demonstrate that minimum specification configuration supports the system.	Configuration testing
F28	Browsers with different JavaScript support cause the embedded scripts to fail (or not run at all).	Demonstrate that browsers and versions in scope support the JavaScript features and operate correctly.	Configuration testing

the particular challenges appropriate to Web technology. The traditional view, however, that functional testing builds in stages from small- to large-scale activities is still appropriate.

Browser page testing relates to the functionality available within a Web page that does not exercise components on a Web server. Server-based component testing covers those components that exist on Web servers and are invoked by Web page transactions. We do not discuss (to any great degree) the testing of other components or objects based on Web, object, application, or database servers or, indeed, legacy systems. These are normally tested by traditional client/server techniques, and references to appropriate methods are provided. Transaction link testing describes the particular challenge of integrating the Web page, server-based components and back-end services. Application system testing represents the traditional approach to a system test that covers the functional requirements of a system as a whole.

Client/server-based systems are normally hosted on reliable networks and implement applications that constrain users to specific navigation paths. Web applications, however, often rely on users to manage their own network connections (e.g., dial-up), and browsers allow users to retrace their steps through Web pages and to repeat, break off, and restart business transactions at any point. This "freedom" greatly increases the number of possible paths through applications that require additional, possibly complex coding to ensure safe handling. Context testing (or perhaps better, loss of context testing) addresses the risks that users will follow weird paths through the application or experience irregular network connectivity. Localization testing covers the particular requirements relating to address formats, multicurrency and tax arrangements, and the translation of language-specific content into alternative languages in scope. Configuration tests of the (potentially numerous) hardware and software combinations to be supported minimize the risk of the system failing because users have obscure configurations.

If there is no time to do formal test planning, or if the test objectives and requirements provide insufficient detail to plan any testing anyway, exploratory testing, mentioned in Chapter 4, could prove to be a useful method for deciding what tests to do next.

Architecture and Components

Before we look at the test types themselves in more detail, it is worth spending a little time looking at how Web applications are normally built from components. Nguyen's book, *Testing Applications on the Web* [1], provides a good overview of the most common architectures in use and the components that can be combined to implement them. The problem with architectures and components is that there are an almost infinite number of combinations and permutations of these architectures, and the technical detail required to understand and test all such components would be overwhelming. In this chapter, we'll focus specifically on the common browser-based functionality and the components residing on Web servers that are the next layer in these architectures. For more detail on approaches to testing various types of components residing on servers, we strongly recommend Nguyen's book [1].

Test Types and the Objects Under Test

Figure 11.1 presents a schematic of a typical architecture for a Web system. As with many larger, more complex Web sites, its four-tiered architecture comprises the following:

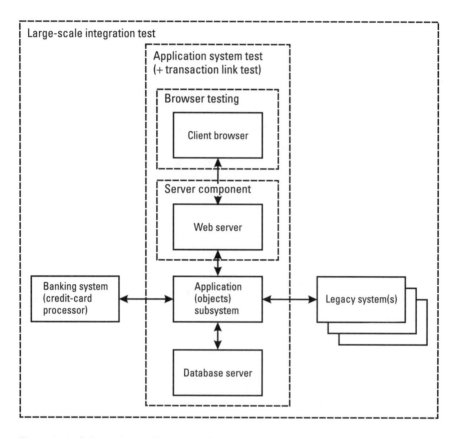

Figure 11.1 Schematic detailing scope of functional test types.

- *First tier:* client browser;
- *Second tier:* Web server(s) accessed through the Internet;
- *Third tier:* application or object server(s);
- *Fourth tier:*
  - Database server;
  - Other legacy systems;
  - External interfaces (e.g., banks).

The diagram sets out the boundaries for four test types, each of which indicates the system components that are within scope. In the real world, systems can be much larger and more complex, but they can also be smaller and simpler. Table 11.2 presents somewhat idealized descriptions of the test types

Table 11.2
Scope of Functional Test Types

Test Type	Scope
Browser testing	Covers the components executed under the control of the browser
Server component testing	Covers the components residing on the server and invoked by the browser components
Application system test	Covers the technical components specific to the application under test and excludes internal client legacy or external systems
Large-scale integration	Covers the entire technical architecture for the system being implemented

described here and their scopes in order to put them into context. You may find that the scope of your test stages and the test types they include are much less ordered and clear-cut.

Automated Test Execution

The test types described in this chapter dealing with functionality can all benefit from the use of automated test execution tools. In the server-based component testing section, we suggest that custom-built dummy HTML forms or test drivers can support this test activity, and these are described briefly. We will provide more detail in Chapter 17 on the range of tools available for e-business testing.

With regard to proprietary test-running tools that drive the user interface via a browser, it is clear that some of the tests that involve the user interface could be automated. We suggest that any repeatable test can be scripted in a proprietary tool for repeated automated execution. There are many texts that describe the selection and implementation of automated test-running tools, and we will not attempt to repeat that guidance here, except to say that the path to automation is littered will failure. It remains a sad fact that most test-running tools end up on the shelf. The promise of test automation is very high, but the achievement of this promise can be quite a challenge. At this point, we will say that test automation should be considered as early as test planning is undertaken. We will look briefly at the possibilities of automation and the challenges of selection and implementation further in Chapter 17. For the remainder of this chapter, you should note that automated tools could support all of the dynamic tests, in principle. You should look closely at the opportunities in your own project to implement automated tools that add value to your endeavors.

Browser Page Testing

Browser page tests cover the objects that execute within the browser, but do not exercise the server-based components. These components typically include the following:

- JavaScript (or VBScript) code embedded within an HTML page that implements special effects, or field validation;
- Java applets that implement screen functionality or graphical output;
- ActiveX components that execute within the context of a Web page;
- Plug-ins, such as QuickTime or RealPlayer.

These features of the Web pages should be tested in place using the browser. They are most easily tested against checklists of conventional requirements or the specific requirements for particular pages. Some systems implement a large amount of functionality in Java applets; some entire applications are implemented in applets. In these cases, test them like any other graphical user interface (GUI) application.

JavaScript is used for several purposes to enhance the behavior of the (normally) static Web page. It not only gives programmers more control over browser windows, but also allows them to delegate some functionality to the client machine to reduce the load on servers. As usual, however, the browsers (and even different versions of the browsers) implement JavaScript slightly differently, and this is a consideration. Programmers should reduce their dependency on the latest features of JavaScript, or there may be problems with earlier browsers.

Typically JavaScript is used to provide the following:

- *Web page enhancements:* Examples include scrolling messages in the browser status bar, providing dates and times to Web pages in the user's local time zone, rollover buttons and images that change appearance as the mouse pointer moves over them, and hierarchical menus that provide shortcuts to large numbers of pages on the Web site.

- *Window manipulation:* The JavaScript object model gives programmers a rich set of features that control window location, size, and attributes (e.g., existence of menus, buttons, resizability).

- *HTML form object manipulation:* JavaScript can access the properties of individual form fields. For example, if a user changes the value of a check box, the available options in a pull-down list can change to be consistent with the check-box option.

- *HTML form validation:* Data validation rules can be applied within the browser, rather than letting the Web server perform this function. Validation can take place at the field level, where the browser can report invalid data as it is entered, or when the user clicks a button to submit the form to the server.

- *Access to cookies:* JavaScript can read and write cookies.

If you are a developer, these JavaScript features should be tested as part of the component-level tests of new Web pages. It is common for JavaScript to be placed in include files so these routines can be written once and used many times. You should make sure that the common code you acquire by using these include files does not disturb the required behavior of your browser windows.

Only three browsers interpret JavaScript correctly: Netscape, IE, and Opera. As with the Java Virtual Machine, JavaScript implementation support varies across browsers. Netscape invented JavaScript, but Microsoft did not want to license this capability from Netscape, so they reverse engineered the JavaScript functionality into their browser and called it JScript. Although there were some inconsistencies across these implementations, a standard called ECMAScript (based on Netscape's JavaScript) was established in 1997. Netscape, IE, and Opera all support the ECMAScript standard. There are some discrepancies between the implementations of JavaScript, but these are mainly problems with early browser versions. The book *Pure JavaScript* by Wyke, Gilliam, and Ting [2] provides a comprehensive reference manual to the language and an overview of features that are affected.

What about VBScript? VBScript is a fully functional scripting language that provides pretty much the same functionality as JavaScript, but only Microsoft IE supports it. Consequently, it is not normally used on public Web sites, because it excludes Netscape and other browser users; however, it can be very useful on private Intranets, where all users have IE. It is not discussed further here.

Java Applets, ActiveX components, and plug-ins can, in some ways, be treated as miniapplications that execute within the context of the browser. Because these components are standalone applications or exist to support specific pages, the functionality in these components can be tested as part of a unit test of the Web pages. As such, they are prone to the usual methods for GUI testing. See [1] for an overview of these component types and guidance for testing them using checklists. Other sources of guidance on testing GUI applications can be found in [3–6].

One further consideration is that the browsers that support scripting languages have facilities to turn off support. In HTML, the <NOSCRIPT> tag can be used to deal with this situation. If a page with script code in it is opened by a browser with no support for the scripting language or with support turned off, the browser will execute the HTML code within the <NOSCRIPT>...</NOSCRIPT> tags instead. Typically, such code would say "JavaScript must be turned on to use this site," but it may invoke an alternative method of achieving the same functionality as the scripting code. If deemed significant, Web pages that contain script code should be checked against browsers that have scripting support disabled. Note that some HTML validators (e.g., Bobby [7]) can scan for these tags and highlight scripts where the NOSCRIPT tag is missing. Users normally turn off scripting as a security precaution. These checks are probably easiest to implement as either functional tests or as part of automated HTML validation or accessibility (see Chapter 13).

Users may also turn off or reject Java applets. The same considerations above apply to this situation. You should check that your Web pages provide either warnings that the site will not work or alternative functionality.

Server-Based Component Testing

Server-based component testing covers the objects that execute on the server, but are initiated by Java applets, ActiveX components, or HTML forms-based user interactions on the browser. These components typically perform standard processes, such as the following:

- Security checking and validation;
- Business logic to perform database enquiries or updates;
- Product catalog searches;

- Order processing;

- Credit checking and payment processing.

The components that handle the calls from HTML forms may be stand-alone components and perform all the required activities to deliver the required functionality to the end user. It is common, however, particularly in larger or more complex environments, for the Web server–based component to call upon other components, objects, or services resident on database, application, object, or other types of servers. The test methods described in this section relate only to the Web server–based components. Component-level tests of back-end objects or services normally require the building of special drivers and stubs, and practical approaches tend to be technology-specific. Testing objects is beyond the scope of this book, but [8, 9] provide comprehensive advice on testing object-based systems.

Usually, the server-based forms handlers are written at the same time as the forms that invoke them; however, we have found two problems with testing server-based code using the user interface:

1. In some projects, the user interface may actually be the last thing written, so server-based components cannot be tested completely until very late in the project.

2. It is common for server-based components to be programmed to deal with a very broad range of input parameters, invoking complex transactions that interface with legacy systems. Large numbers of tests may be difficult to implement manually, so an automated alternative can be more effective and economic.

We strongly recommend that you consider using dummy HTML pages or home-brew test drivers to test your server-based components. If the user interface is not yet available or stable, it might be easier to implement tests of Web server–based components using dummy Web pages. Although they are most appropriate for developers performing unit testing, there are advantages to later testers' adopting such methods to speed up their system or acceptance testing. Dummy forms and test drivers are discussed further in Appendix B.

For Java developers, there are tools that support the unit testing of Java applications. Several of these are listed at the end of the chapter with their vendors' Web addresses.

Transaction Link Testing

Transaction link testing (link testing) aims to address the problem of integrating the complete end-to-end functionality to ensure that the entire transaction is processed correctly from the user action on the browser interface to the back-end systems. Link testing focuses very much on selected test cases that exercise particular interfaces between components in the technical architecture to ensure that mismatches between components are minimized. Done well, it detects faults in the integration of components that cause system testers serious difficulties later. Link testing therefore incorporates the same technical components as application system testing (see Figure 11.1). In most development environments, link testing either is not done at all or receives only cursory attention. System testers are all too familiar with the delays that poorly integrated systems cause them early on in their own system test stage.

Typical link tests use selected transactions that invoke several components and interfaces that must collaborate to deliver a piece of functionality. Transaction link testing maps on a smaller scale to traditional integration testing in which a member of the programming team conducts tests to ensure the products of more than one programmer integrate before submitting integrated components for system test.

A transaction that processes the on-line payment for a book might involve the following:

- A button click on the user interface prompting validation of the fields on the screen (embedded JavaScript);
- Dispatch of an HTTP POST message to the Web server, with visible and hidden fields on the user screen being transmitted within the message body;
- Invocation of a Web server–based component that sends requests to various objects, such as the following:
  - Credit-checking object;
  - Order-posting object;
  - Database-update object;
  - Special offers and order confirmation e-mail generator object;
  - Thank you Web page generator object.
- The server component response would be a confirmation page with options to place more orders or log off.

The objects called by the server-based component should have been tested in isolation beforehand. They may have been tested as they were coded with stubbed-out interfaces and simple driver programs or dummy Web pages to exercise them in artificial circumstances. Link tests are designed to force the software to invoke the various components as a complete set and to investigate whether the direct and indirect interfaces work correctly. These test cases cover the following main concerns:

- Transfer of control between components;
- Transfer of data between components (in both directions);
- Consistency of use of data across components.

Typical test cases involve the following:

- Sequences of multiple browser page transactions to ensure that the handover of control from server component to browser page back to server component works correctly;
- Single shot transactions that query, add, update, or delete zero, one, several, or a large number of records;
- Reconciliation of pretest database content, data entered through screens, system outputs, and posttest database content.

Overall, link tests aim to cover the complete end-to-end functionality within a system, including the browser Web pages, Web server–based objects, other server-based objects, and back-end databases. It might only be possible, however, to perform this testing with the legacy system and other customer system interfaces stubbed out. This is often the case when a system supplier does not have access to its customer's legacy systems or other external interfaces. Large-scale integration testing (Chapter 15) would aim to verify that the complete technical architecture integrates by testing the complete system and its interfaces.

The interactions between components can be complex; there might be a significant amount of custom-built code in the server-based objects, or there could be custom-built middleware involved. In these circumstances, it is prudent to automate some of these transactions to ensure that such interfaces and custom code can support repeated use for an extended period. In our experience, custom code embedded deep in the technical architecture is prone to failure under stress or long-term use. Repeated transactions driven by a test execution tool (or possible reuse of the drivers mentioned earlier) can expose obscure memory leaks or synchronization problems that often dog custom-written components.

Application System Testing

Application system testing aims to cover functional testing of the application as a whole. Where a supplier providing the system is unable to build a complete test environment that includes, for example, the client's legacy systems and interfaces to banks or other partners, system testing would take place in an environment with client-supplied interfaces stubbed out (see Figure 11.1). Testing of the complete technical architecture is covered later in large-scale integration testing and is likely to be a key part of acceptance testing. Application system testing in the form described here is most likely to be performed by the suppliers of the system itself in an environment that allows the system to be tested in isolation from its external interfaces.

Because we have isolated the functional testing of a system, a traditional approach to this testing is appropriate. There are many standard texts that describe methods for functional system testing, including our own Evolutif system test methodology, SysTeMet [10]. Building a system test plan from good requirements is fairly straightforward, but we also discuss briefly some alternative methods for use when requirements are sketchy.

Testing When Requirements Are of High Quality

Where requirements are accurate, complete, and testable, the textbook black-box test-design techniques can help you systematically cover the documented features thoroughly. There are many such techniques, most of which are based on some form of model. Simple techniques, such as equivalence partitioning and boundary values, generate test cases that are extremely effective and thorough, and at the same time very easy for inexperienced testers to understand. Other techniques include state transition testing and logic-based testing, among others, and are appropriate in different situations where perhaps the requirements may be modeled in different ways. For example, a lot of object-oriented software can be modeled as state machines. State diagrams provide an easy-to-use model for testers to build comprehensive test plans. There are many textbooks that explain the use of these techniques, but we would recommend the following texts in particular:

- Boris Beizer's *Black-Box Testing* [11] covers the key black-box techniques comprehensively. For those requiring detail on their theoretical basis and other practical implementation issues, his *Software Test Techniques* [12] is worth reading (this book also covers white-box test techniques).

- Kaner, Falk, and Nguyen's *Testing Computer Software* [13] provides a more accessible introduction to basic techniques.

- BS 7925-2 [14] is a standard for software component testing. It provides a generic test process for component-level testing, but includes very precise definitions of the most useful and popular black- and white-box techniques. The standard also provides thorough guidelines for each of the techniques with examples. A prepublication version is freely downloadable from the British Computer Society Specialist Interest Group in Software Testing (BCS SIGIST) Working Party Web site (http://www.testingstandards.co.uk).

Testing When Requirements Are Poor

Test design techniques are fine, but black-box test-design techniques rely on good requirements. Many testers work in environments where requirements may be grossly inadequate for formal test design. Transaction flow testing, best described in [12], is based on the notion of modeling the behavior of a system and its users with a flow graph (or flowchart). Processes in the flow graph may be performed by the system under test, the user, or some other agent outside the system. Figure 11.2 shows a typical transaction flow graph that includes both automated and manual processes and decisions.

Typically, paths through the flow graph are traced to cover processes, links, and decision outcomes to give some confidence that the users, the system under test, and other processes can collaborate to meet business requirements. Where detailed system requirements are lacking, the way that a user operates the system and the assumed high-level behavior may be well understood, but not documented. Transaction flow graphs can usually be prepared quite quickly by working closely with users or designers and are both a valuable aid in refining the requirements and the design of a system and a valuable model to base tests on later. Using transaction flow graphs to plan tests without having requirements isn't strictly the correct implementation of this method, but in our experience they can jump-start the test planning

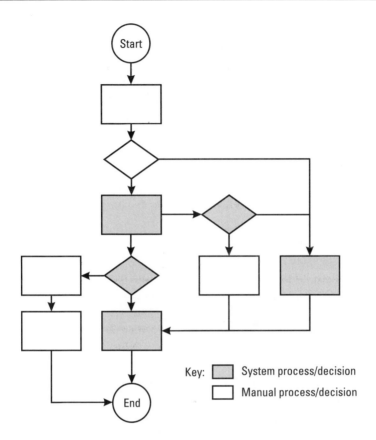

Figure 11.2 Sample transaction flow graph.

process when working with users who understand the way the system is to be used.

One final method worth mentioning is business simulation. One could say that this method is also based on transaction flows, but it relies on the testers (or users) of the system acting exactly like real users in their own working environment. When applied to intranets, one might set up a complete working office environment for users to conduct their business, supported by the system to do specific (not necessarily scripted) tasks. In the case of a publicly available Web site, the testers simply have to behave like end users. The Evolutif paper "Business Simulation Testing" [15] provides some background to the technique. Business simulation is discussed further in Chapter 15.

Context Testing

There are several risks relating to the context (or, perhaps more correctly, the loss of context) of Web transactions. One of the differences between client/server and Web applications is that for home-based users, the network connection is under the user's control. Dial-up connections are usually temporary and are generally less reliable than the permanent high-speed LAN connections most office-based workers use. Connection, disconnection, and reconnection anomalies cause serious disruption to most users when they access the Web. The behavior of Web sites under these scenarios varies widely across Web sites, and in many cases, poor design causes Web site owners and their users dismay.

Unlike with client/server applications, the user accesses a Web application through a browser. The browser itself has buttons and controls that allow the user to interfere with the normal operation of the Web site in the following ways:

- The back button allows the user to go back to a previously displayed Web page cached in the browser's memory. If that page is used to execute a purchase with a one-time discount, the transaction could be re-executed many times with the discount applied. To avoid this, the developer can make these pages expire immediately so that the browser cannot just restore them from its cache.

- Refresh (IE) and reload (Netscape) buttons allow users to re-execute transactions that produce the current Web page. Again, this could allow users to repeat a system transaction without having to repeat previous pages.

- The history facilities in browsers bookmark previously visited pages and navigate directly back to them, which re-executes the transaction that loaded the page. The application Web pages could therefore, in principle, be re-executed in any order the user wished, which could wreak havoc with the application.

Surely, users would not do this, you may think. Of course, they would. One obvious reason might be that they would prefer not to re-enter lots of personal data to place an order. By backtracking and changing selected form fields, they believe that they can submit a second order without having to re-enter the rest of the required data. When users get disconnected from a site, they might believe that by reconnecting and jumping straight to the page they were working on when the connection was lost, they can avoid the tedium of logging back in and re-entering the preparatory data for their purchase transaction. It is inevitable that users will inadvertently abuse your site in this way (and fraudulent attackers are bound to try it deliberately), so you really ought to test for it.

The Web is stateless, meaning that each HTTP message received by a Web server is processed by the server and then forgotten. Web servers do not store any details of the HTTP messages they service except a record of it written into the server log. The Web server cannot link a transaction that adds products to a shopping cart to a later transaction that pays for the goods unless one of several mechanisms is used. Given that it is easy to break the continuity of a series of Web transactions, you should discuss with your developers how they can achieve and maintain continuity in business transactions. With this knowledge, you can then attempt to subvert these mechanisms to demonstrate their resilience.

Cookies

Cookies are one way of maintaining the context of Web transactions. They are small amounts of data that can be stored on the user's hard drive by the browser at the request of the Web site being accessed. When the user clicks a button and sends a new HTTP request to the Web server to process a transaction, the cookie data is embedded into the HTTP message, and the server can extract this cookie data for its own purposes. When the server responds, the HTTP message sent back contains the (potentially changed) cookie data; the browser receives the cookie and stores it in memory or on the client machine's hard drive.

Typically, cookies contain such personal data as users' names, the date of their last visit, and so on. If you are using ASP, cookies contain a unique reference to identify a logged-in user session. All transactions posted to the Web server during the session are labeled with this session identifier in the cookie, so the server-based code can remember with whom it is dealing. Used sensibly, cookies are harmless enough; however, the programmer has total control over cookies and could put more sensitive data, such as passwords, credit-card numbers, and other more personal information into them. For this reason, browsers offer options that warn users that cookies are being sent and that reject them. If a user rejects a cookie, will your application still work, or will the transactions fall apart because there is no way to string them together?

There are also some limitations on the use of cookies, and these are prime candidates for test cases. Cookies have an expiration date. That is, the programmer sets a date on which the cookie will automatically be deleted from disk by the browser. If the expiration date is not set or is set in the past, the cookie will only last for the duration of the user session. Ask the developers how they are using cookies and how they set expiration dates. If the developers set cookies to expire, say, one year in the future, what happens to the application if the user comes back 366 days later?

Cookies have maximum size of 4K each, and there are conventional limits of 300 cookies on a client and 20 cookies for a single domain—are your developers exceeding these limits?

Hidden Fields

The most common alternative to using cookies to maintain the context of transactions is to use hidden HTML form fields. When a user completes an HTML form displayed on a Web page, the content of visible fields that the user has entered are appended to the HTTP message sent to the Web server. There is a facility in HTML, however, to include hidden fields with preset values within the form. These values are sent to the server at the same time in the same message. Programmers use this facility to include context information, such as a transaction identifier, in the forms that are returned to the browser. Because the hidden fields are invisible, the user never notices that data items like these accompany the data that they are entering. It is a simple mechanism, but very effective. There is, of course, a security hole here—you can view the HTML source code in the browser, change it to suit your purposes, and potentially affect the behavior of the system under test. Problems with hidden fields are well documented and are less common than they used to be.

It is essential that you discuss with your developers the mechanisms they use to get around the stateless nature of the Web and how they might be subverted. This will enable you to develop a set of tests that could expose faults in the design of the application.

Loss of Connection

The context of user transactions can be lost through other means. The first, most obvious one is a loss of connection between the client machine and the Web. Users with dial-up modems are used to connections timing out or failing. How does your application cope with this? When you lose the connection or close your browser completely, cookies with no expiration date will be lost. Can, or should, users retrace their steps in the application using the history facility in the browser?

Other Situations to Consider

What happens if a new user of the same client PC uses your application on the same Web site? Will the new user pick up the cookies of the previous user? Will the new user's cookies overwrite the previous user's cookies? Is this a problem? Ask your developers if (and how) they can accommodate the above scenarios. If they have a means of recovery or avoidance of problems, you should test it. If not, you may have exposed a problem in their design. See [1] and [16] for more detailed coverage of issues relating to cookies and testing for anomalies.

Localization Testing

Is your site intended to be used by, say, English-speaking users only? If not, what steps are being taken to make your site multilingual? If your site is to be accessible to people using more than one language, all material on your Web site, including screen-based text, error messages, help, reports, and electronically mailed output needs to be available in the language of choice. Multilingual sites are often built with all language-specific material codified into a database. Where a user requests a particular language, the site extracts the relevant language-specific elements from the database. In this case, localization testing is all about verifying that all user messages, prompts, and output are translated correctly and that the functionality delivered to the end user is identical. Checking translations isn't quite as simple as comparing text translation with a foreign dictionary. Have you ever seen the names of dishes on a foreign restaurant's menu translated literally? The people checking translations should speak the target language as their mother tongue so you can be sure that the translations are accurate, not just literal.

In effect, a regression test is required that verifies that the altered output has been correctly translated. Although the functionality may not be affected, it is common for the text of translated words to take up more space—a particular problem with small navigation buttons which include text with an image. Developers should make allowance for the growth in size of text.

One attractive possibility would be to automate a set of regression tests of the functionality and to parameterize the scripts with alternate translations of system input and output. If, however, the application has been developed to reuse tables of alternative messages, then it might be easier simply to inspect these language-specific text tables than to regression test functionality that does not change across languages.

In our experience, many sites adopt the rather cumbersome technique of hosting multiple copies of translated HTML pages on the same server, allowing the user to choose a language-specific Web site. These need more testing, and configuration management is a bigger headache for developers and testers.

Functional differences between localized Web sites should consider at least the following:

- *Local variations in taxing and other financial arrangements:* In the United States, different states have different tax arrangements; in Europe, the Value-Added Tax applies, but at different rates in each country. Different countries' banking systems have differently formatted bank account numbers and bank codes.

- *Address formats:* In the United States, there are zip codes; in the United Kingdom, there are postcodes; in France, there are departments, and so forth. Each country has a different format and validation process for its postal codes.

- *Foreign character sets:* In foreign countries, users may select a different character set than that used for English (British or U.S.). Russian, Greek, and Japanese character sets are dramatically different, aren't they? Will your validation or database settings allow for this?

There are many potential pitfalls in designing international Web sites. Resolving many of the issues requires extensive local knowledge. Given that few Web site developers are able to perform translations themselves, the translation work is often outsourced to other firms, which then verify that the translation is correct.

For an overview of localization testing, see [13], which introduces many other aspects of the localization problem, including issues relating to character sets, keyboards, character collation sequences, printers, and foreign date, time, and currency formats, among others.

Configuration Testing

Configuration testing aims to demonstrate that your Web application will operate correctly on your nominated range of client hardware, OS, and browser combinations. On the Internet, you have no control over the end users' platform, so to avoid problems later, it is best to test a range of configurations to ensure that you can support at least the most common combinations. The problem, of course, is that there is a virtually unlimited number of possible combinations. Table 11.3 provides some indication of the possibilities that face the tester.

Most of the component types listed in Table 11.3 have multiple versions. The number of combinations and permutations are in the hundreds, or even thousands. The essential difficulty of configuration testing is therefore deciding on the scope of the testing. The big questions include the following:

- What do your users actually use?
- Which configurations should you support? (Not all will be worth considering).
- Which can you test economically?
- Which can you test automatically?

If you intend to perform configuration testing on more than a handful of platforms, the first task is to analyze your market. What kind of hardware and software are your users most likely to have? One might reasonably expect your analysis to result in a small subset of what is available. For example, IE and Netscape used on Windows 98, NT4, and 2000 might cover the majority of business-to-business clients; but what about Unix and Macintosh users? Should you exclude these unknown, but potentially large, user communities?

If you are to look seriously at configuration testing, then you must also look at component commonality. Is there any reason to doubt that one browser version will work differently on two OS versions? If there is, what is the potential impact? Are you using any OS-specific features?

Table 11.3
Common Configuration Options

OS platforms	DOS, Windows 3.1, 95, 98, NT 3.51, NT 4, 2000, XP, Macintosh, Linux, Unix
Network connections	Dial-up modems, direct Internet lines, cable modems, ADSL, wireless
Commercial services	MSN, AOL, and others
Browsers	IE, Netscape, Opera, and many others—too many to mention.
Browser versions	All browsers have several versions perhaps with country-specific localizations.

There are two discussions to have:

1. *With the marketers:* What platform combinations are most likely?
2. *With the developers:* Are any platform-specific features being used that make configuration testing essential?

In our experience, only the largest, most mission critical projects or those that need to accommodate absolutely the maximum number of client platforms take configuration testing so seriously that they test large numbers of configurations. Although it might be practical to build your own test lab with a limited number of configurations, we find that it is at least as common to outsource the configuration testing. It is likely that only specialized companies have the resources to build such environments with dozens of distinct test platforms and relatively cheap resources to perform the (rather boring) testing itself.

Kaner, Faulk, and Nguyen's *Testing Computer Software* [13] sets out the broad issues in configuration testing and offers a seven-step guide to the process. Nguyen's *Testing Applications on the Web* [1] restates these guidelines in the context of Web systems and offers guidance in setting up and running configuration tests. The discussion of risk is also expanded to account for server-based components that might also be configuration tested. Dustin, Rashka, and McDiarmid's *Quality Web Systems* [17] discusses a very broad range of compatibility and configuration issues with examples of how programmers can accommodate multiple (usually two) browser types.

We Haven't the Time—Is There an Alternative?

If you are pressed for time and concerned with only the two leading browsers, IE and Netscape, then you might consider the following simple approach:

- Identify browser compatibility problems using the static-analysis tools that are now widely available. To the degree that they identify HTML features that are nonstandard and not compatible with one or more browser versions, they will detect most major issues more quickly than manual regression testing.
- Encourage your developers and testers to use a variety of browsers and versions. In this way, one would expect that in the day-to-day operation of the Web application, compatibility problems would be detected during development and unit testing.

If you are only concerned with the two leading browsers, anything that gets over these two hurdles is likely to be quite obscure. It will likely affect few users, and there's no guarantee that you would have found the problem anyway. Your organization might be prepared to take that risk and opt to display a "best viewed by brower *X* version *Y*" message on its home page, rather than pay for expensive configuration testing.

Tools for Functional Testing

There are now many tools that can help with automated test execution. These tools drive the application using the user interface, and in the main are quite expensive. The listing in Table 11.4 is quite comprehensive, but you should not rely on it to be completely up-to-date. Chapter 17 presents tool directory listings that are maintained.

Table 11.4
Tools for Functional Testing

Proprietary Tools	URL
Atesto FunctionChecker	http://www.atesto.com
ETester, Bean-Test (EJB testing)	http://www.empirix.com
eValid	http://www.soft.com
Astra QuickTest	http://www.mercuryinteractive.com
WebART	http://www.oclc.org/webart/
JavaPlayback (capture/replay for Java GUI)	http://www.softwareautomation.com
Jtest (Java unit testing)	http://www.parasoft.com
QARun, TestPartner	http://www.compuware.com
SilkTest, SilkTest International (localization testing), SilkPilot (EJB testing)	http://www.segue.com
TeamTest	http://www.rational.com
WebKing (development, testing, and Web management)	http://www.parasoft.com
WebFT	http://www.radview.com
Free Tools	**URL**
BigBen Tools	http://www.okchicken.com/~timm/bigben/
Common Software Test Tools	http://commontest.sourceforge.net
Doit	http://doit.sourceforge.net
Junit (Java component testing tool)	http://swww.junit.org

References

[1] Nguyen H. Q., *Testing Applications on the Web*, New York: John Wiley & Sons, 2001.

[2] Wyke, R. A., J. D. Gilliam, and C. Ting, *Pure JavaScript*, Indianapolis, IN: SAMS, 1999.

[3] Dustin E., J. Rashka, and J. Paul, *Automated Software Testing*, Boston, MA: Addison-Wesley, 1999.

[4] Gerrard P., "Testing GUI Applications," *EuroSTAR '97 Conf.*, Edinburgh, Scotland, November 1997 (also at http://www.evolutif.co.uk).

[5] Pettichord, B., "Success with Test Automation," http://www.io.com/~wazmo/, 2002.

[6] Bazman's Testing Pages, "GUI Testing Checklist," http://members.tripod.com/~bazman/, 2002.

[7] CAST, "Bobby HTML Accessibility Checking Tool," http://www.cast.org/bobby/, 2002.

[8] Marick, B., *The Craft of Software Testing*, Englewood Cliffs, NJ: Prentice Hall, 1995.

[9] Binder, R., *Testing Object-Oriented Systems: Models, Patterns, and Tools*, Boston, MA: Addison-Wesley, 1999.

[10] Systeme Evolutif Limited, *SysTeMet™ System Test Methodology*, Systeme Evolutif internal methodology, 1994.

[11] Beizer, B., *Black-Box Testing*, New York: John Wiley & Sons, 1995.

[12] Beizer, B., *Software Test Techniques*, 2nd ed., New York: Van Nostrand Reinhold, 1990.

[13] Kaner, C, J. Faulk, and H. Q. Nguyen, *Testing Computer Software*, New York: John Wiley & Sons, 1993.

[14] British Standards Institution, *BS-7925-2:1998 Software Testing—Software Component Testing*, London, BSI, United Kingdom, 1998, (a prepublication version of the standard is available at http://www.testingstandards.co.uk).

[15] Gerrard, P., "Business Simulation Testing," http://www.evolutif.co.uk, 2002.

[16] Splaine, S., and S. P. Jaskiel, *The Web Testing Handbook*, Orange Park, FL: STQE Publishing, 2001.

[17] Dustin, E., J. Rashka, and D. McDiarmid, *Quality Web Systems*, Boston, MA: Addison-Wesley, 2001.

12

Service Testing

Overview

Companies build e-business Web sites to provide a service to customers. In many cases, these sites also have to make money. If a Web site provides poor service, customers will stop using it and find an alternative. Quality of service as provided by a Web site could be defined to include such attributes as functionality, performance, reliability, usability, security, and so on. For our purposes, however, we are separating out three particular Web service objectives that come under the scrutiny of what we will call "Service Testing":

1. *Performance:* The Web site must be responsive to users while supporting the loads imposed upon it.
2. *Reliability:* The Web site must be reliable or continue to provide a service even when a failure occurs if it is designed to be resilient to failure.
3. *Manageability:* The Web site must be capable of being managed, configured, and changed without a degradation of service noticeable to end users.

We have grouped these three sets of service objectives together because there is a common thread to the testing we do to identify shortcomings. In all three cases, we need a simulation of user load to conduct the tests effectively. Performance, reliability, and manageability objectives exist in the context of live

customers using the site to do business. Table 12.1 lists the risks addressed by
service testing.

The responsiveness of a site is directly related to the resources available
within the technical architecture. As more customers use the Web site, fewer
technical resources are available to service each user's requests, and response
times degrade. Although it is possible to model performance of complex
environments, it normally falls to performance testers to simulate the projected loads on a comparable technical environment to establish confidence
in the performance of a new Web service. Formal performance modeling to
predict system behavior is beyond the scope of this book. See [1, 2] for a
thorough treatment of this subject.

Table 12.1
Risks Addressed by Service Testing

ID	Risk	Test Objective	Technique
S1	The technical infrastructure cannot support the design load and meet response time requirements.	Demonstrate that infrastructure components meet load and response time requirements.	Performance and stress testing
S2	The system cannot meet response time requirements while processing the design loads.	Demonstrate that the entire technical architecture meets load and response time requirements.	Performance and stress testing
S3	The system fails when subjected to extreme loads.	Demonstrate that system regulates and load balances incoming messages or at least fails gracefully as designed.	Performance and stress testing
S4	The system's capacity cannot be increased in line with anticipated growth in load (scalability).	Demonstrate scalability of key components that could cause bottlenecks.	Performance and stress testing
S5	The system cannot accommodate anticipated numbers of concurrent users.	Demonstrate that the system can accommodate through load balancing and regulation the anticipated numbers of concurrent users.	Performance and stress testing

Table 12.1 (continued)

ID	Risk	Test Objective	Technique
S6	Partial system failure causes the entire system to fail or become unavailable.	Simulate specified failure scenarios and demonstrate that failover capabilities operate correctly.	Reliability/failover testing
S7	The system cannot be relied upon to be available for extended periods.	Demonstrate that throughput and response-time requirements are met without degradation over an extended period.	Reliability/failover testing
S8	System management procedures (start-up, shutdown, installation, upgrade, configuration, security, backup, and restoration) fail.	Demonstrate that system management procedures (start-up, shutdown, installation, upgrade, configuration, security, backup, and restoration) work correctly.	Service management testing
S9	Backup and recovery in case of minor failure are not in place or fail.	Demonstrate that service can be recovered from selected modes of failure.	Service management testing
S10	Disaster recovery plans are not in place or fail.	Demonstrate that contingency planning measures restore service in the case of catastrophic failure.	Service management testing

Obviously, a Web site that is lightly loaded is less likely to fail. Much of the complexity of software and hardware exists to accommodate the demands for resources within the technical architecture when a site is heavily loaded. When a site is loaded (or overloaded), the conflicting requests for resources must be managed by various infrastructure components, such as server and network OSs, database management systems, Web server products, object request brokers, middleware, and so on. These infrastructure components are usually more reliable than the custom-built application code that demands the resource, but failures can occur in two ways:

1. Infrastructure components fail because application code (through poor design or implementation) imposes excessive demands on resources.

2. Application components fail because the resources they require may not always be available (in time).

By simulating typical and unusual production loads over an extended period, testers can expose flaws in the design or implementation of the system. When these flaws are resolved, the same tests will demonstrate the system to be resilient.

Service management procedures are often the last (and possibly) the least tested aspects of a Web service. When the service is up and running, there are usually a large number of critical management processes to be performed to keep the service running smoothly. On a lightly used Web site or an intranet where users access the service during normal working hours, it might be possible to shut down a service to do routine maintenance, like making backups or performing upgrades, for example. A retail-banking site, however, could be used at any time of the day or night. Who can say when users will access their bank accounts? For international sites, the work day of the Web site never ends. At any moment, there are active users. The global availability of the Web means that many Web sites never sleep. Inevitably, management procedures must be performed while the site is live and users are on the system. It's a bit like performing open-heart surgery on an athlete running a marathon. Management procedures need to be tested while there is a load on the system to ensure they do not adversely impact the live service.

Performance and associated issues, such as resilience and reliability, dominate many people's thinking when it comes to nonfunctional testing. Certainly, everyone has used Web sites that were slow to respond, and there have been many reports of sites that failed because large numbers of people visited them simultaneously. In such cases, failures occur because applications are undersized, poorly designed, untuned, and inadequately tested. We have split our discussion of performance testing into five sections:

1. What Is Performance Testing?

2. Prerequisites for Performance Testing

3. Performance Requirements

4. The Performance Test Process

5. Performance Testing Practicalities

These five sections provide a broad overview of the full range of performance test activities. The three remaining sections in the chapter discuss other aspects of service testing.

What Is Performance Testing?

In some respects, performance testing is easy. You need to simulate a number of users doing typical transactions. Simultaneously, some test transactions are executed and response times are measured as a user would experience them. Of course, we could use real people to simulate users in production, and on more than one occasion, we have been involved in tests like that; however, manual performance testing is labor intensive, difficult to automate, unreliable (in terms of measurement), and boring for those involved. In this chapter, we are only concerned with tests performed using automated tools.

The principles of performance testing are well-documented. Our paper "Client/Server Performance Testing" [3] provides an overview of the principles and methods used to simulate loads, measure response times, and manage the process of performance testing, analysis, and tuning. In this chapter, we won't provide a detailed description of how performance tests are planned, constructed, executed, and analyzed. See [4–7] for excellent technical advice, tips and techniques for performance testing, and advice on the selection of tools and methods for Web site tuning and optimization. In many ways, the technical issues involved in conducting performance testing are the easiest to deal with. (We are not saying that solving performance problems is easy; that is a topic for another book.) Here, we will focus particularly on the challenges of performance testing from a nontechnical point of view and on some specific difficulties of Web performance testing. In our experience, once the tools have been selected, organizational, logistical, and sometimes political issues pose the greatest problems.

An Analogy

Figure 12.1 shows an athlete on a treadmill being monitored by a technician. The system under test is the athlete. The source of load is the treadmill. The technician monitors vital signs, such as pulse rate, breathing rate, and volumes of oxygen inhaled and carbon dioxide exhaled, as the athlete performs the test. Other probes might measure blood pressure, lactic-acid level, perspiration, and even brain-wave activity. The test starts with the athlete at rest and quiescent measurements are taken. The treadmill is started. The athlete walks slowly, and measurements are taken again. The speed is increased to 4 mph. The athlete copes easily with the brisk walk and measurements are taken. The speed is increased to 6 mph, 8 mph, and 10 mph. The athlete is running steadily, breathing hard, but well in control. The speed is increased to 12 mph, 14 mph, and 16 mph. The athlete is panting hard now, showing

Figure 12.1 Performance testing an athlete.

signs of stress, but coping. The speed is increased to 17 mph, 18 mph, and 20 mph. The athlete is sprinting hard now, gasping for air, barely in control, but managing the pace. The speed is increased to 21 mph, 22 mph, and 23 mph. The athlete staggers, falls, collapses, and rolls off the end of the treadmill. And dies! Well, maybe not.

This sounds brutal doesn't it? Of course, we would never perform this kind of test with a real person (at least not to the degree that they die). This is, however, exactly the approach we adopt when performance testing computer systems. Performance testing consists of a range of tests at varying loads where the system reaches a steady state (loads and response times reach constant levels). We measure load and response times for each load simulated for a 15 to 30 minute period to get a statistically significant number of measurements. We also monitor and record the vital signs for each load simulated. These are the various resources in our system (e.g., CPU and memory usage, network bandwidth, and input-output rates, and so on).

We then plot a graph of these varying loads against the response times experienced by our virtual users. When plotted, our graph looks something like Figure 12.2. At zero-load, where there is only a single user on the system, that user has the entire resource to him- or herself, and response times are fast. As we increase the load and measure response times, they get

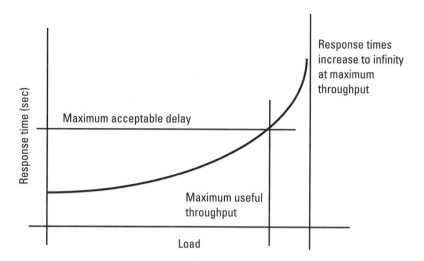

Figure 12.2 Load-response time graph.

progressively slower until we reach a point where the system is running at maximum capacity. It cannot process any more transactions beyond this maximum level. At this point, the response time for our test transactions is theoretically infinite because one of the key resources of the system is completely used up and no more transactions can be processed.

As we increase the loads from zero to the maximum, we also monitor the usage of various resource types. These resources include, for example, server processor usage, memory usage, network bandwidth, database locks, and so on. At the maximum load, one of these resources is 100% used up. This resource is the limiting resource, because it runs out first. Of course, at this point response times have degraded to the point that they are probably much slower than would be acceptable. Figure 12.3 shows a typical resource-usage load graph. To increase the throughput capacity or reduce response times for a system, we must do one of the following:

- Reduce the demand for the resource, typically by making the software that uses the resource more efficient (usually a development responsibility);

- Optimize the use of the hardware resource within the technical architecture, for example, by configuring the database to cache more data in memory or by prioritizing some processes above others on the application server;

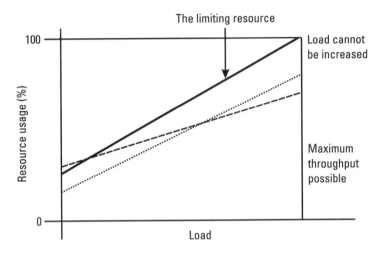

Figure 12.3 Resource usage-load graph.

- Make more of the resource available, normally by adding processors, memory, or network bandwidth, and so on.

Performance testing normally requires a team of people to help the testers. These are the technical architects, server administrators, network administrators, developers, and database designers and administrators. These technical experts are qualified to analyze the statistics generated by the resource monitoring tools and judge how best to adjust the application or to tune or upgrade the system. If you are the tester, unless you are a particular expert in these fields yourself, don't be tempted to pretend that you can interpret these statistics and make tuning and optimization decisions. It is essential to involve these experts early in the project to get their advice and commitment and, later, during testing, to ensure that bottlenecks are identified and resolved.

Performance Testing Objectives

The objective of a performance test is to demonstrate that the system meets requirements for transaction throughput and response times simultaneously. More formally, we can define the primary objective as follows:

> To demonstrate that the system functions to specification with acceptable response times while processing the required transaction volumes on a production sized database [3].

The main deliverables from such a test, prior to execution, are automated test scripts and an infrastructure to be used to execute automated tests for extended periods. This infrastructure is an asset and an expensive one too, so it pays to make as much use of this infrastructure as possible. Fortunately, the test infrastructure is a test bed that can be used for other tests with the following broader objectives:

- *Assessment of the system's capacity for growth:* The load and response data gained from the tests can be used to validate the capacity planning model and assist decision making.

- *Identification of weak points in the architecture:* The controlled load can be increased to extreme levels to stress the architecture and break it; bottlenecks and weak components can be fixed or replaced.

- *Tuning of the system:* Repeat runs of tests can be performed to verify that tuning activities are having the desired effect of improving performance.

- *Detection of obscure bugs in software:* Tests executed for extended periods can cause memory leaks, which lead to failures and reveal obscure contention problems or conflicts. (See the section on reliability/failover testing in this chapter.)

- *Verification of resilience and reliability:* Executing tests at production loads for extended periods is the only way to assess the system's resilience and reliability to ensure required service levels are likely to be met. (See the section on reliability/failover testing.)

Your test strategy should define the requirements for a test infrastructure to enable all these objectives to be met.

Prerequisites for Performance Testing

We can identify five prerequisites for a performance test. Not all of these need be in place prior to planning or preparing the test (although this might be helpful). Rather, the list below defines what is required before a test can be executed. If any of these prerequisites are missing, be very careful before you proceed to execute tests and publish results. The tests might be difficult or impossible to perform, or the credibility of any results that you publish may be seriously flawed and easy to undermine.

Quantitative, Relevant, Measurable, Realistic, and Achievable Requirements

As a foundation for all tests, performance requirements (objectives) should be agreed on beforehand so that a determination of whether the system meets those requirements can be made. Requirements for system throughput or response times, in order to be useful as a baseline for comparing performance results, must be:

- Quantifiable;
- Relevant to the task a user wants to perform;
- Measurable using a tool (or stopwatch);
- Realistic when compared with the duration of the user task;
- Economic.

These attributes are described in more detail in [3]. Often, performance requirements are vague or nonexistent. Seek out any documented requirements if you can, and if there are gaps, you may have to document them retrospectively. Performance requirements are discussed in more detail in the next section.

A Stable System

A test team attempting to construct a performance test of a system with poor-quality software is unlikely to be successful. If the software crashes regularly, it will probably not withstand the relatively minor stress of repeated use. Testers will not be able to record scripts in the first instance, or may not be able to execute a test for a reasonable length of time before the application, middleware, or operating system crashes. Performance tests stress all architectural components to some degree, but for performance testing to produce useful results, the system and the technical infrastructure have to be reasonably reliable and resilient to start with.

A Realistic Test Environment

The test environment should ideally be identical to the production environment, or at least a close simulation, dedicated to the performance test team for the duration of the test. Often this is not possible. For the results of the test to be meaningful, however, the test environment should be comparable to the final production environment. A test environment that bears no similarity to the final environment might be useful for finding obscure faults in the code, but it is useless for a performance analysis.

A simple example where a compromise might be acceptable would be where only one Web server is available for testing, but where the final architecture will balance the load between two identical servers. Reducing the load imposed to half during the test might provide a good test from the point of view of the Web server, but might understate the load on the network. In all cases, the compromise environment to be used should be discussed with the technical architect, who may be able to provide the required interpretations.

The performance test will be built to provide loads that simulate defined load profiles and scalable to impose higher loads. You would normally overload your system to some degree to see how much load it can support while still providing acceptable response times. You could interpret the system's ability to support a load 20% above your design load in two ways:

1. You have room for 20% growth beyond your design load.
2. There is a 20% margin of error for your projected load.

Either way, if your system supports a greater load, you will have somewhat more confidence in its capacity to support your business.

A Controlled Test Environment

Performance testers not only require stability in the hardware and software in terms of its reliability and resilience, but also need changes in the environment or software under test to be minimized. Automated scripts are extremely sensitive to changes in the behavior of the software under test. Test scripts designed to drive Web browsers are likely to fail immediately if the interface is changed even slightly. Changes in the operating system environment or database are equally likely to disrupt test preparation, as well as execution, and should be strictly controlled. The test team should ideally have the ability to refuse and postpone upgrades to any component of the architecture until they are ready to incorporate changes to their tests. Changes intended to improve the performance or reliability of the environment would normally be accepted as they become available.

The Performance Testing Toolkit

The five main tool requirements for our performance testing toolkit are summarized as follows:

- *Test database creation and maintenance:* It is necessary to create large volumes of data in the test database. We'd expect this to be a SQL-based utility or perhaps a PC-based product like Microsoft Access™ connected to your test database.

- *Load generation:* The common tools use test drivers that simulate virtual clients by sending HTTP messages to Web servers.

- *Application running tool:* This tool drives one or more instances of the application using the browser interface and records response time measurements. (This is usually the same tool used for load generation, but doesn't have to be.)

- *Resource monitoring:* This includes utilities that monitor and log client and server system resources, network traffic, database activity, and so forth.

- *Results analysis and reporting:* Test running and resource monitoring tools generate large volumes of results data. Although many such tools offer facilities for analysis, it is useful to combine results from these various sources and produce combined summary test reports. This can usually be achieved using PC spreadsheet, database, and word-processing tools.

Guidance on the selection and implementation of test tools can be found in [3–7]. A listing of commercially available and freeware performance test tools is presented at the end of this chapter.

Performance Requirements

Before a performance test can be specified and designed, requirements need to be agreed on for the following:

- Transaction response times;
- Load profiles (the number of users and transaction volumes to be simulated);
- Database volumes (the number of records in database tables expected in production).

It is common for performance requirements to be defined in vague terms. On more than one project, we have (as testers) had to prepare a statement of requirements upon which to base performance tests. Often, these requirements are based on forecasted business volumes that are sometimes unrealistic. Part of the tester's job may be to get business users to think about performance requirements realistically.

Response Time Requirements

When asked to specify performance requirements, users normally focus attention on response times and often wish to define requirements in terms of generic response times. A single response time requirement for all transactions might be simple to define from the user's point of view, but is unreasonable. Some functions are critical and require short response times; others are less critical and response-time requirements can be less stringent.

The following are some guidelines for defining response-time requirements:

- For an accurate representation of the performance experienced by a live user, response times should be defined as the period between a user's requesting the system to do something (e.g., clicking on a button) to the system's returning control to the user.

- Requirements can vary in criticality according to the different business scenarios envisaged. Subsecond response times are not always appropriate!

- Generic requirements are described as catch-all thresholds. Examples of generic requirements are times to load a page, navigate between pages, and so forth.

- Specific requirements define the requirements for identified system transactions. Examples might include the time to log in, search for a book by title, and so forth.

- Requirements are usually specified in terms of acceptable maximum, average, and 95th-percentile times.

The test team should set out to measure response times for all specific requirements and a selection of transactions that provide two or three examples of generic requirements.

Jakob Nielsen, in his book *Designing Web Usability* [8] and on his Web site, useit.com (http://www.useit.com), promotes a very simple three-tiered scheme based on work done by Robert B. Miller in 1968. After many years, these limits remain universally appropriate:

- One tenth of a second is the limit for having the user feel the system is reacting instantaneously.

- One second is the limit to allow the user's flow of thought to be uninterrupted.

- Ten seconds is about the limit for keeping the user's attention. Some might say this limit is 8, or even fewer, seconds.

It's up to you to decide whether to use these limits as the basis for your response-time requirements or to formulate your own, unique requirements in discussion with business users. Some sample response-time requirements and a discussion of them are provided in [3].

Load Profiles

The second component of performance requirements is a schedule of load profiles. A load profile is a definition of the level of system loading expected to occur during a specific business scenario. There are three types of scenarios to be simulated:

1. *Uncertain loads:* The mix of users and their activities is fixed, but the number of users and the size of load vary in each test. These tests reflect our expected or normal usage of the site, but the scale of the load is uncertain.

2. *Peak or unusual situations:* These include specific scenarios that relate, for example, to the response to a successful marketing campaign or special offer or to an event (which may be outside your control) that changes users' behavior.

3. *Extreme loads:* Although we might reasonably expect this never to occur, stress tests aim to break the architecture to identify weak points that can be repaired, tuned, or upgraded. In this way we can improve the resilience of the system.

We normally run a mix of tests, starting with a range of normal loads, followed by specific unusual-load scenarios, and finally stress tests to harden the architecture.

Requirements Realism

We probably know the load limits of an internal intranet. Intranets normally have a finite (and known) user base, so it should be possible to predict a workload to simulate. With Internets, however, there is no reasonable limit to how many users could browse and load your Web site. The calculations are primarily based on the success of marketing campaigns, word-of-mouth recommendations, and, in many cases, luck rather than judgment.

Where it is impossible to predict actual loads, it is perhaps better to think of performance testing less as a test with a defined target load, but as a measurement exercise to see how far the system can be loaded before selected response times become unacceptable. When management sees the capability of its technical infrastructure, it may realize how the technology constrains its ambitions; however, management might also decide to roll the new service out in a limited way to limit the risk of performance failures.

In our experience of dealing with both established firms and start-up companies, the predicted growth of business processed on their Web sites can be grossly overestimated. To acquire budget or venture capital and attention in the market, money is invested based on high expectations. High ambition has a part to play in the game of getting backing. Being overly ambitious, however, dramatically increases the cost of the infrastructure required and of performance testing. Ambitious targets for on-line business volumes require expensive test software licenses, more test hardware, more network infrastructure, and more time to plan, prepare, and execute.

On one occasion, a prospective client asked us to prepare a proposal to conduct a 2,000 concurrent-user performance test of their Web-based product. Without going into detail, their product was a highly specialized search engine that could be plugged into other vendor's Web sites. At our first meeting, we walked through some of the metrics they were using. They predicted the following:

- 100,000 users would register to use their search engine.
- 50,000 registered users would be active and would access the site once a week.
- Each user would connect to their service for an average of 10 minutes.
- Most users would access their system between 8 A.M. and 12 P.M.

We sketched out a quick calculation that surprised the management around the table:

- In an average week, if all active users connect for 10 minutes, the service would need to support 500,000 session minutes.
- If users connect between the hours of 8 A.M. to 12 P.M., these sessions are served in a live period of seven 16-hour days (equal to 126 hours or 7,560 minutes).
- The average number of concurrent sessions must therefore be 500,000 session minutes spread over 7,650 minutes of uptime.
- On average, the service needs to support 66.1 concurrent-user sessions.

The management team around the table was surprised to hear that their estimates of concurrent users might be far too high. Of course, this was an estimate of the average number of sessions. There must be peak levels of use at specific times of the day. Perhaps there are, but no one around the table could think of anything that would cause the user load to increase by a factor of 30! Be sure to qualify any requests to conduct huge tests by doing some simple calculations—just as a sanity check.

Database Volumes

Data volumes relate to the numbers of rows that should be present in the database tables after a specified period of live running. The database is a critical component, and we need to create a realistic volume of data to simulate the system in real use. Typically, we might use data volumes estimated to exist after one year's use of the system. Greater volumes might be used in some circumstances, depending on the application.

The Performance Test Process

There are four main activities in performance testing. An additional stage, tuning, accompanies the tester's activities and is normally performed by the technical experts. Tuning can be compared with the bug-fixing activity that usually accompanies functional test activities. Tuning may involve changes to the architectural infrastructure, but doesn't usually affect the functionality of the system under test. A schematic of the test process is presented in Figure 12.4. The five stages in the process are outlined in Table 12.2.

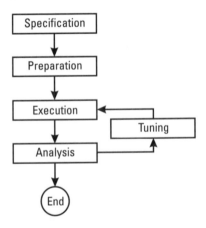

Figure 12.4 Performance test process.

Table 12.2
Performance Test Process Outline

Specification	• Documentation of the following performance requirements:
	   • Database volumes;
	   • Load profiles;
	   • Response time requirements.
	• Preparation of a schedule of load profile tests to be performed;
	• Inventory of system transactions comprising the loads to be tested;
	• Inventory of system transactions to be executed and response times measured;
	• Description of analyses and reports to be produced.

Preparation	• Preparation of a test database with appropriate data volumes; • Scripting of system transactions to comprise the load; • Scripting of system transactions whose response is to be measured (possibly the same as the load transactions); • Development of workload definitions (i.e., the implementations of load profiles); • Preparation of test data to parameterize automated scripts.
Execution	• Execution of interim tests; • Execution of performance tests; • Repeat test runs, as required.
Analysis	• Collection and archiving of test results; • Preparation of tabular and graphical analyses; • Preparation of reports, including interpretation and recommendations.
Tuning	• Performance improvements to application software, middleware, and database organization; • Changes to server system parameters; • Upgrades to client or server hardware, network capacity, or routing.

Incremental Test Development

Performance test development is usually performed incrementally in four stages:

1. Each test script is prepared and tested in isolation to debug it.

2. Scripts are integrated into the development version of the workload, and the workload is executed to test that the new script is compatible.

3. As the workload grows, the developing test framework is continually refined, debugged, and made more reliable. Experience and familiarity with the tools also grow.

4. When the last script is integrated into the workload, the test is executed as a dry run to ensure it is completely repeatable, reliable, and ready for the formal tests.

Interim tests can provide useful results. Runs of the partial workload and test transactions may expose performance problems. These can be reported and acted upon within the development groups or by network, system, or database administrators. Tests of low volume loads can also provide an early indication of network traffic and potential bottlenecks when the test is scaled up. Poor response times can be caused by poor application design and can be investigated and cleared up by the developers earlier. Inefficient SQL can also be identified and optimized. Repeatable test scripts can be run for extended periods as soak tests (see later). Such tests can reveal errors, such as memory leaks, which would not normally be found during functional tests.

Test Execution

The execution of formal performance tests requires some stage management or coordination. As the time approaches to run the test, team members who will execute the test need to liaise with those who will monitor the test. The test monitoring team members are often working in different locations and need to be kept very well informed if the test is to run smoothly and all results are to be captured correctly. They need to be aware of the time window in which the test will be run and when they should start and stop their monitoring tools. They also need to be aware of how much time they have to archive their data, preprocess it, and make it available to the person who will analyze the data fully and produce the required reports.

Beyond the coordination of the various team members, performance test execution tends to follow a standard routine:

1. Preparation of database (restored from backup, if required);

2. Preparation of test environment as required and verification of its state;

3. Start of monitoring processes (network, clients and servers, and database);

4. Start of load simulation and observation of system monitor(s);

5. If a separate tool is used, when the load is stable, start of the application test running tool and response time measurement;

6. Close supervision for the duration of the test;

7. Termination of the test when the test period ends, if the test-running tools do not stop automatically;

8. Stopping of monitoring tools and saving of results;

9. Archiving of all captured results and assurance that all results data is backed up securely;

10. Production of interim reports; conference with other team members concerning any anomalies;

11. Preparation of analyses and reports.

When a test run is complete, it is common for some tuning activity to be performed. If a test is a repeat test, it is essential that any changes in environment are recorded, so that any differences in system behavior, and hence performance results, can be matched with the changes in configuration. As a rule, it is wise to change only one thing at a time so that when differences in behavior are detected, they can be traced back to the changes made.

Results Analysis and Reporting

The application test running tool will capture a series of response times for each transaction executed. The most typical report for a test run will summarize these measurements and report the following for each measurement taken:

- Count of measurements;
- Minimum response time;
- Maximum response time;
- Mean response time;
- 95th-percentile response time.

The 95th percentile, it should be noted, is the time within which 95% of the measurements occur. Other percentiles are sometimes used, but this depends on the format of the response time requirements. The required response times are usually presented in the same report for comparison.

The other main requirement that must be verified by the test is system throughput. The load generation tool should record the count of each transaction type for the period of the test. Dividing these counts by the duration of the test gives the transaction rate or throughput actually achieved. These rates should match the load profile, but might not if the system responds slowly. If the transaction load rate depends on delays between transactions, a slow response will increase the delay between transactions and slow the rate. The throughput will also be lower than planned if the system cannot support the transaction load.

It is common to execute a series of test runs at varying loads. Using the results of a series of tests, a graph of response times for a transaction plotted against the load applied can be prepared. Such graphs provide an indication of the rate of degradation in performance as load is increased and the maximum throughput that can be achieved while providing acceptable response times.

Resource monitoring tools usually have statistical or graphical reporting facilities that plot resource usage over time. Enhanced reports of resource usage versus load applied are very useful and can assist in the identification of bottlenecks in a system's architecture.

Performance Testing Practicalities

Nowadays, there is a choice of approach to performance testing. There are many companies offering to do your performance testing for you, and performance testing portals that offer remote testing opportunities are emerging in importance. In planning, preparing, and executing performance tests, there are several aspects of the task that cause difficulties. The problems encountered most often relate to the software and environment. The predominant issue that concerns the performance tester is stability. Unfortunately, performance testers are often required to work with software that is imperfect or unfinished. These issues are discussed in the following sections.

Which Performance Test Architecture?

There are four options for conducting performance testing. All require automated test tools, of course. To implement a realistic performance test, you need the following:

- Load generation tool;
- Load generation tool host machine(s);
- High-capacity network connection for remote users;

- Test environment with fully configured system, production data volumes, and a security infrastructure implemented with production-scale Internet connection.

The cost and complexity of acquiring and maintaining the test tool licenses, skills, hardware, and software environments can be extremely high. For some years, the tool vendors and specialist testing companies have provided on-site consultants to perform the work in your environment. Other services are emerging that make it easy to hire resources or test facilities. There are four basic choices as to how you implement performance tests:

1. Doing it yourself;
2. Outsourcing (bring external resources into your environment);
3. Remote testing (use external resources and their remote testing facility);
4. Performance test portals (build your own tests on a remote testing facility).

Some of the advantages and disadvantages of each are summarized in Table 12.3.

Table 12.3
Four Methods for Performance Testing

Doing It Yourself	Outsourcing	Remote Testing	Performance Test Portals
Test tool license			
You acquire the licenses for performance test tools.	You acquire the licenses for performance test tools.	Included in the price.	You rent a timeslot on a portal service.
Test tool host			
You provide.	You provide.	Included in the price.	Included in the price.
Internet connections			
You organize.	You organize.	Use of the service provider's is included. You liaise with your own ISP.	Use of the service provider's is included. You liaise with your own ISP.

Table 12.3 (continued)

Doing It Yourself	Outsourcing	Remote Testing	Performance Test Portals
Simplicity			
Complicated—you do everything.	You manage the consultants. You build the tool environment.	Simplest—the service provider does it all.	A simple infrastructure and tools solution, but you are responsible for building and running the test.
Cost			
Resources are cheaper, but tools, licenses, and hosts are expensive. You still need to buy training and skills.	Probably most expensive: you buy everything and hire external resources.	Lower tool and infrastructure costs, but expensive services. May be cheaper as a package.	Low tool and infrastructure costs—your resources are cheaper.
Pros and cons			
You acquire expensive tools that may rarely be used in the future.	Most expensive of all potentially.	Potentially cheaper—if you would have hired consultants anyway.	Lowest tool and infrastructure costs, but you still need to buy and acquire skills.
You need to organize, through perhaps two ISPs, large network connections (not an issue for intranets).	You need to organize, through perhaps two ISPs, large network connections (not an issue for intranets).	Simpler—you need one arrangement with your own ISP only.	Simplest infrastructure solution—but you must manage and perform the tests.
You are in control.	You are in control at a high level.	You can specify the tests; the service provider builds and executes them. You manage the supplier.	You are in control.
Complicated—you do everything.	Less complicated—the outsourcer manages the consultants.	Simplest solution—the service provider does it all.	Simpler technically—but you must build and execute the tests.
You can test as many times as you like.	You can test as many times as you like.	Pricing per test makes repeat tests expensive.	Price per test depends on the deal. You may get "all you can test" for a fixed period.

Compressed Timescales

One serious challenge with e-business performance testing is the time allowed to plan, prepare, execute, and analyze performance tests. We normally budget 6 to 8 weeks to prepare a test on a medium-to-high complexity environment. How long a period exists between system testing's elimination of all but the trivial faults and delivery into production? Not as long as you might need. There may be simplifying factors that make testing Web applications easier, however:

- Web applications are relatively simple from the point of view of thin clients sending messages to servers. The scripts required to simulate user activity can be very simple so reasonably realistic tests can be constructed quickly.

- Because the HTTP calls to server-based objects and Web pages are simple, they are much less affected by functional changes that correct faults during development and system testing. Consequently, work on the creation of performance test scripts can often be started before the full application is available.

- Tests using drivers (and not using the browsers user interface) may be adequate to make the test simpler.

Normally, we subject the system under test to load using drivers that simulate real users by sending messages across the network to the Web servers, just like normal clients would. In the Internet environment, the time taken by a browser to render a Web page and present it to an end user may be short compared with the time taken for a system to receive the HTTP message, perform a transaction, and dispatch a response to a client machine. It may be a reasonable compromise to ignore the time taken by browsers to render and display Web pages and just use the response times measured by the performance test drivers to reflect what a user would experience.

Scripting performance test tool drivers is comparatively simple. Scripting GUI-oriented transactions to drive the browser interface can be much more complicated. If you do decide to ignore the time taken by browsers themselves, be sure to discuss this with your users, technical architect(s), and developers to ensure they understand the compromise being made. If they deem this approach unacceptable, advise them of the delay that additional GUI scripting might introduce into the project.

Software Quality

In many projects, the time allowed for functional and nonfunctional testing (including performance testing) is squeezed. Too little time is allocated overall, and development slippages reduce the time available for system testing. Under any circumstance, the time allowed for testing is reduced, and the quality of the software is poorer than required.

When the test team receives the software to test and attempts to record test scripts, the scripts themselves will probably not stretch the application in terms of its functionality. The paths taken through the application will be designed to execute specific transactions successfully. As a test script is recorded, made repeatable, and then run repeatedly, bugs that were not caught during functional testing may begin to emerge.

One typical problem found during this period is that repeated runs of specific scripts may gradually absorb more and more client resources, leading to a failure when a resource, usually memory, runs out. Program crashes often occur when repeated use of specific features within the application causes counters or internal array bounds to be exceeded. Sometimes these problems can be bypassed by using different paths through the software, but more often, these scripts have to be postponed until these faults can be fixed.

Dedicated Environment

During test preparation, testers will be recording, editing, and replaying automated test scripts. These activities should not disturb or be disturbed by the activities of other users on a shared system. When a single test script is integrated into the complete workload and the full load simulation is run, however, other users of the system will probably be very badly affected by the sudden application of such a large load on the system.

If at all possible, the test team should have access to a dedicated environment for test development. It need hardly be stated that when the actual tests are run, there should be no other activity on the test environment. Testing on a dedicated environment is sensible if the target production infrastructure is dedicated to the system under test. However, most systems are implemented on shared infrastructure. You should discuss with your technical architect(s) what the implication of this is for your testing.

Other Potential Problems

Underestimation of the effort required to prepare and conduct a performance can lead to problems. Performance testing a large Web application is a complex activity that usually has to be completed in a very limited timescale. Few project managers have direct experience of the tasks involved in pre- paring and executing such tests. As a result, they usually underestimate the length of time it takes to build the infrastructure required to conduct the test. If this is the case, tests are unlikely to be ready to execute in the time available.

Overambition, at least early in the project, is common. Project managers often assume that databases have to be populated with perfect data, that every transaction must be incorporated into the load, and every response time measured. Usually, the Pareto rule applies: 80% of the database volume will be taken up by 20% of the system tables; 80% of the system load will be generated by 20% of the system transactions; only 20% of system transactions need to be measured and so on. When you discuss the number of transactions to simulate and the tables to populate, you should discuss the practicalities of implementing a perfect simulation with business users, designers, and developers. Because you are always constrained by time, you need to agree on the design of the test that is achievable in time, but still meaningful.

The skills required to execute automated tests using proprietary tools are not always easy to find, but as with most software development and testing activities, there are principles that, if adhered to, should allow competent functional testers to build a performance test. It is common for managers or testers with no test automation experience to assume that the test process consists of two stages: test scripting and test running. As should be clear by now, the process is more complicated and, actually, is more like a small software development project in its own right. On top of this, the testers may have to build or customize the tools they use.

When software developers who have designed, coded, and functionally tested an application are asked to build an automated test suite for a performance test, their main difficulty is their lack of testing experience. Experienced testers who have no experience of the system under test, however, usually need a period to gain familiarity with the system to be tested. Allowance for this should be made in the early stages of test development; testers will have to grapple with the vagaries of the system under test before they can start to record scripts.

Building a performance test database may involve generating thousands or millions of database rows in selected tables. There are two risks involved in this activity. The first is that in creating the invented data in the database tables, the referential integrity of the database is not maintained. The second risk is that your data may not obey business rules, such as the reconciliation of financial data between fields in different tables. In both cases, the load simulation may be perfect, but the application may not be able to handle such data inconsistencies and fail. In these circumstances, test scripts developed on a small coherent database might no longer work on a prepared, production-size database. Clearly, it is important that the person preparing the test database understand the database design and the operation of the application.

This problem can of course be helped if the database itself has the referential constraints implemented and will reject invalid data (often, these facilities are not used because they impose a significant performance overhead). When using procedural SQL to create database rows, the usual technique is to replicate existing database rows with a new unique primary key. Where primary keys are created from combined foreign keys, you must generate new primary keys by combining the primary keys from the referenced tables.

Presenting Results to Customers and Suppliers

On a previous project, we were hired as consultants to specify and supervise performance testing to be done by a third party. The performance testing took place towards the end of the project and was going badly (the measured response times were totally unacceptable). Our role was to advise both client and supplier and to witness and review the testing. Biweekly checkpoint meetings were held in two stages. In the first stage, the customer and their consultants discussed the progress. We reported to the project board the interim test results and our interpretation of them. Then, the suppliers were invited to join in for the second half of the meeting. The test results were presented and discussed, and quite a lot of pressure was applied on the supplier to emphasize the importance of the current shortcomings.

The point to be made here is this: It is very common to have the customer, the supplier, and the testers discussing performance issues late in the project. The situation is usually grim. The testers present the results, and the suppliers defend themselves. Typically, they suggest the tests are flawed: The load requirements are excessive. The numbers of concurrent users, the transaction rates, and the database volumes are all too high. The testers aren't simulating the users correctly. Real users would never do that. This isn't a good simulation. And so on.

The suppliers may try to undermine the testers' work. As a tester, you need to be very careful and certain of your results. You need to understand the results data and be confident that your tests are sound. You must test your tests and make sure the experts (and not you) perform analyses of the resource monitoring statistics because it's likely that you will come under attack. Suppliers aren't above suggesting the testers are incompetent. Remember, successful performance tests are usually a major hurdle for the suppliers, and a lot of money may depend on the successful outcome of the performance testing. You have been warned.

Reliability/Failover Testing

Assuring the continuous availability of a Web service may be a key objective of your project. Reliability testing helps to flush out obscure faults that cause unexpected failures so they can be fixed. Failover testing helps to ensure that the measures designed for anticipated failures actually work.

Failover Testing

Where sites are required to be resilient, reliable, or both, they tend to be designed with reliable systems components with built-in redundancy and failover features that come into play when failures occur. These features may include diverse network routing, multiple servers configured as clusters, middleware, and distributed object technology that handles load balancing and rerouting of traffic in failure scenarios. The features that provide diversity and redundancy are also often the mechanisms used to allow the performance of backups, software and hardware upgrades, and other maintenance activities (see the section on service management testing).

These configuration options are often trusted to work adequately, and it is only when disaster strikes that their behavior is seen for the first time. Failover testing aims to explore the behavior of the system under selected failure scenarios before deployment and normally involves the following:

- Identification of the components that could fail and cause a loss of service (looking at failures from the inside out);

- Identification of the hazards that could cause a failure and loss of service (looking at threats from the outside in);

- Analysis of the failure modes or scenarios that could occur where you need confidence that the recovery measures will work;

- An automated test that can be used to load the system and explore its behavior over an extended period and monitor its behavior under failure conditions.

Mostly used in higher integrity environments, a technique called fault tree analysis (FTA) can help to understand the dependencies of a service on its underlying components. FTA and fault tree diagrams are a logical representation of a system or service and the ways in which it can fail. Figure 12.5 shows the relationship between basic component failure events, intermediate subsystem failure events, and the topmost service failure event. Of course, it might be possible to identify more than three levels of failure event. Further, events relationships can be more complicated. For example, if a server component fails, we might lose a Web server. If our service depends on a single Web server we might lose the entire service. If, however, we have two Web servers and facilities to balance loads across them, we might still be able to provide a service, albeit at a reduced level. We would lose the service altogether only if both servers failed simultaneously.

FTA documents the Boolean relationships between lower-level failure events to those above them. A complete fault tree documents the permutations of failures that can occur, but still allows a service to be provided. Figure 12.6 shows an example where the loss of any low-level component causes one of the Web servers to fail (an OR relationship). Both Web servers must fail to cause loss of the entire service (an AND relationship). This is only a superficial description of the technique. Nancy Leveson's book *Safeware* [9] provides a more extensive description.

FTA is most helpful for the technical architect designing the mechanisms for coping with failures. Fault tree diagrams are sometimes complicated with many Boolean symbols representing the dependencies of services on their subsystems and the dependencies of subsystems on their

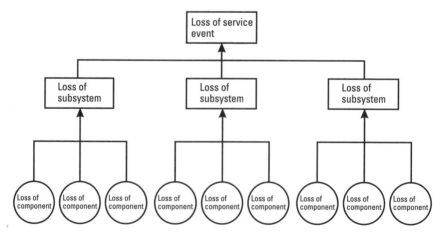

Figure 12.5 Failure event hierarchy.

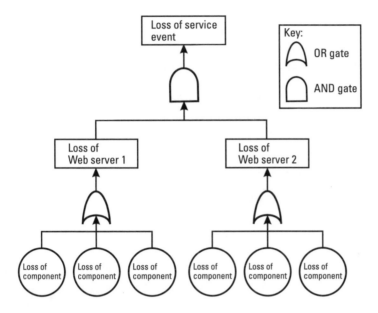

Figure 12.6 Example fault tree for a Web service.

components. These diagrams are used to identify the unusual, but possible, combinations of component failures that the system must withstand. For the tester, fault trees provide a simple model from which failover test scenarios can be derived. Typically, the tester would wish to identify all the modes of failure that the system is meant to be able to withstand and still provide a service. From these, the most likely scenarios would be subjected to testing.

Whether you use a sophisticated technique like FTA, or you are able to identify the main modes of failure easily just by discussing these with the technical experts, testing follows a straightforward approach. With an automated test running, early tests focus on individual component failures (e.g., you off-line a disk, power-down a server, break a network connection). Later tests simulate more complex (and presumably, less likely) multiple failure scenarios (e.g., simultaneous loss of a Web server and a network segment).

These tests need to be run with an automated load running to explore the system's behavior in production situations and to gain confidence in the designed-in recovery measures. In particular, you want to know the following:

- How does the architecture behave in failure situations?
- Do load-balancing facilities work correctly?

- Do failover capabilities absorb the load when a component fails?
- Does automatic recovery operate?
- Do restarted systems catch up?

Ultimately, the tests focus on determining whether the service to end users is maintained and whether the users actually notice the failure occurring.

Reliability (or Soak) Testing

Whereas failover testing addresses concern about the system's ability to withstand failures of one kind or another, reliability testing aims to address the concern over a failure occurring in the first place. Most hardware components are reliable to the degree that their mean time between failures may be measured in years. Proprietary software products may also have relatively high reliability (under normal working environments). The greatest reliability concerns typically revolve around the custom-built and bleeding-edge proprietary software that has not undergone extensive testing or use for long periods in a range of operating conditions.

Reliability tests require the use (or reuse) of automated tests in two ways to simulate the following:

1. Extreme loads on specific components or resources in the technical architecture;
2. Extended periods of normal (or extreme) loads on the complete system.

When focusing on specific components, we are looking to stress the component by subjecting it to an unreasonably large number of requests to perform its designed function. For example, if a single (nonredundant) object or application server is critical to the success of our system, we might stress test this server in isolation by subjecting it to a large number of concurrent requests to create new objects, process specific transactions, and then delete those same objects. Being critical, this server might be sized to handle several times the transaction load that the Web servers might encounter. We can't stress test this server in the context of the entire system (a stress test at the required volumes would always cause the Web servers to fail first, perhaps). By testing it in isolation, however, we gain confidence that it can support loads greater than other components whose reliability we already trust. Another example might be multiple application servers that service the requests from several Web servers. We might configure the Web servers to direct their traffic to a single application server to increase the load several times. This might be a more realistic scenario compared with a test of the application server in isolation; however, this test sounds very similar to the situation where the application servers fail, but the last one running supports the entire service. The similarity with failover testing is clear.

Soak tests subject a system to a load over an extended period of perhaps 24 or 48 hours or longer to find (what are usually) obscure problems. Early performance tests normally flush out obvious faults that cause a system to be unreliable, but these tests are left running for less than 1 hour. Obscure faults usually require testing over longer periods. The automated test does not necessarily have to be ramped up to extreme loads; stress testing covers that. We are particularly interested, however, in the system's ability to withstand continuous running of a wide variety of test transactions to find any obscure memory leaks, locking, or race conditions. As for performance testing, monitoring the resources used by the system helps to identify problems that might take a long time to cause an actual failure. Typically, the symptoms we are looking for are increases in the amount of resources being used over time. The allocation of memory to systems without return is a called a *memory leak*. Other system resources, such as locks, sockets, objects, and so on may also be subject to leakage over time. When leaks occur, a clear warning sign is that response times get progressively worse over the duration of the test. The system might not actually fail, but given enough testing time to show these trends, the symptom can be detected.

Service Management Testing

When the Web site is deployed in production, it has to be managed. Keeping a site up and running requires that it be monitored, upgraded, backed up, and fixed quickly when things go wrong. Postdeployment monitoring is covered in Chapter 16. The procedures that Web site managers use to perform upgrades, backups, releases, and restorations from failures are critical to providing a reliable service, so they need testing, particularly if the site will undergo rapid change after deployment.

The management procedures fall into five broad categories:

1. System shutdown and start-up procedures;
2. Server, network, and software infrastructure and application code installation and upgrades;

3. Server, network, and software infrastructure configuration and security changes;

4. Normal system backups;

5. System restoration (from various modes of failure) procedures.

The first four procedures are the routine, day-to-day procedures. The last one, system restoration, is less common and is very much the exception, as they deal with failures in the technical environment where more or less infrastructure may be out of service. The tests of the routine procedures will follow a similar pattern to failover testing in that the procedures are tested while the system is subjected to a simulated load. The particular problems to be addressed are as follows:

- Procedures fail to achieve the desired effect (e.g., an installation fails to implement a new version of a product, or a backup does not capture a restorable snapshot of the contents of a database).

- Procedures are unworkable or unusable (i.e., the procedures themselves cannot be performed easily by system management or operations staff. One example would be where a system upgrade must be performed on all servers in a cluster for the cluster to operate. This would require all machines to be off-lined, upgraded, and restarted at the same time).

- Procedures disrupt the live service (e.g., a backup requires a database to operate in read-only mode for the duration of the procedure, and this would make the live service unusable).

The tests should be run in as realistic a way as possible. System management staff must perform the procedures in exactly the same way as they would in production and not rely on familiar shortcuts or the fact that they do not have real users on the service. Typically, there are no test scripts used here, but a schedule of tasks to be followed identifies the system management procedures to be performed in a defined order. The impact on the virtual users should be monitored: response times or functional differences need to be noted and explained. Further, the overall performance of the systems involved should be monitored and any degradation in performance or significant changes in resource usage noted and justified.

Tools for Service Testing

As Table 12.4 shows, a large number of tools is available for performance testing. Most of the proprietary tools run on the Windows platform and a smaller number run under Unix. The proprietary tools all have GUI front-ends and sophisticated analysis and graphing capabilities. They tend to be easier to use.

Table 12.4
Tools for Service Testing

Proprietary Tools	URL
Astra LoadTest	http://www-svca.mercuryinteractive.com
Atesto Internet Loadmodeller	http://www.atesto.com
CapCal	http://www.capcal.com
e-Load, Bean-Test	http://www.empirix.com
eValid	http://www.soft.com
forecastweb	http://www.facilita.co.uk
OpenSTA	http://www.opensta.org
Portent	http://www.loadtesting.com
PureLoad	http://www.pureload.com
QAload, EcoTOOLS, File-AID/CS	http://www.compuware.com
silkperformer	http://www.segue.com
SiteLoad	http://www.rational.com
SiteTools Loader, SiteTools Monitor	http://www.softlight.com
Test Perspective	http://www.keynote.com
Web Performance Trainer	http://www.webperformanceinc.com
Web Server Stress Tool	http://www.paessler.com/tools/
WebART	http://www.oclc.org/webart
WebAvalanche, WebReflector	http://www.cawnetworks.com
WebLOAD	http://www.radview.com
Web Polygraph	http://www.web-polygraph.org
WebSizr	http://www.technovations.com
WebSpray	http://www.redhillnetworks.com

Table 12.4 (continued)

Free Tools	URL
ApacheBench	http://www.cpan.org/modules/by-module/HTTPD/
Deluge	http://deluge.sourceforge.net
DieselTest	http://sourceforge.net/projects/dieseltest/
Hammerhead 2	http://hammerhead.sourceforge.net
http_load	http://www.acme.com/software/http_load/
InetMonitor	http://www.microsoft.com/siteserver/site/DeployAdmin/InetMonitor.htm
Load	http://www.pushtotest.com
OpenLoad	http://openload.sourceforge.net
Siege	http://www.joedog.org
SSL Stress Tool	http://sslclient.sourceforge.net
Torture	http://stein.cshl.org/~lstein/torture/
Velometer	http://www.velometer.com
Wcat	http://www.microsoft.com/downloads/
Web Application Stress Tool	http://webtool.rte.microsoft.com
WTest	http://members.attcanada.ca/~bibhasb/

Of the free tools, the majority run under Unix and many are written in Perl. They have fewer features, they produce fewer, less comprehensive reports, and their scripting languages tend to be unsophisticated. They are less flexible than the proprietary tools and many have a command-line interface. They tend to lack many of the features of proprietary tools. They are less well documented and some assume users have a technical or programming background. They are free, however, and in most cases, you get the source code to play with too. If you need to enhance or customize the tools in some way, you can.

Being short of money is one reason for choosing a free tool. Even if you have a budget to spend, however, you still might consider using one of the free tools, at least temporarily. The principles of performance testing apply to all tools, so you might consider using a free tool to gain some experience, then make a better-informed decision to buy a commercially available tool when you know what you are doing.

References

[1]   Smith, C. U., *Performance Engineering of Software Systems*, Boston, MA: Addison-Wesley, 1990.

[2]   Menascé, D. A., and V. A. F. Almeida, *Scaling for E-Business*, Upper Saddle River, NJ: Prentice Hall, 2000.

[3]   Gerrard, P., "Client/Server Performance Testing," http://www.evolutif.co.uk, 2002.

[4]   Dustin, E., J. Rashka, and D. McDiarmid, *Quality Web Systems*, Boston, MA: Addison-Wesley, 2001.

[5]   Nguyen, H. Q., *Testing Applications on the Web*, New York: John Wiley & Sons, 2001.

[6]   Splaine, S., and S. P. Jaskiel, *The Web Testing Handbook*, Orange Park, FL: STQE Publishing, 2001.

[7]   Kolish, T., and T. Doyle, *Gain E-Confidence*, Lexington, MA: Segue Software, 1999.

[8]   Nielsen, J., *Designing Web Usability*, Indianapolis, IN: New Riders, 2000.

[9]   Leveson, N. G., *Safeware*, Reading, MA: Addison-Wesley, 1995.

13

Usability Assessment

Overview

We have all experienced difficulty using everyday things. Video recorders, mobile phones, and microwave ovens are technological miracles, when you think about it, but they aim to help us perform relatively simple tasks. So, why aren't they easier to use? Door handles, can openers, pushchairs, and food packaging may seem relatively basic in terms of their technology, but these mundane products confuse, perplex, and frustrate us when they appear impossible to use. Donald Norman's book, *The Design of Everyday Things* [1], provides many examples of usability failures and explains the challenges of and possible routes towards user-centered design.

Since the first computers were built, much of the mystique surrounding the software systems that run on them stems from the fact that software is rarely intuitive. Many people work for companies that have implemented difficult-to-use applications. Anyone observing the people at supermarket checkouts, hotel reception desks, or the next desk at his or her own office will have seen and heard frustration expressed at the system being used. If a company implements an unusable system, its employees will probably get on with their jobs, but they are likely to be less efficient and comfortable than should be the case. But these are captive users. Put an unusable site onto the Web, and your users will not stick around very long. Your users have the freedom to abandon your site and visit your competitors'. It may have been possible to implement difficult-to-use systems in the past, but it is no longer.

One of the key selling points for Web sites is their ease of use, and Table 13.1 presents the risks addressed by usability assessment.

A *usability fault* is a potential problem in the appearance or organization of a system that makes it less easy for users to use. Operationally, a

Table 13.1
Risks Addressed by Usability Assessment

ID	Risk	Test Objective	Technique
U1	Use of bleeding-edge technologies is excessive or inappropriate.	Verify that sophisticated plug-ins, page objects, or design techniques are not used where they add no value or where simpler methods would work just as well.	Collaborative usability inspection
U2	Site privacy statement is missing or inaccurate.	Verify that privacy guidelines are observed and that an accurate privacy statement exists on the site.	Collaborative usability inspection
U3	Screen appearance is adversely affected by changes to resolution and window resizing.	Verify that Web pages are readable on monochrome devices, low-resolution monitors, and in small windows.	Collaborative usability inspection
U4	Site uses frames in an inappropriate way.	Verify that frames are not used (if proscribed by requirements) or that frames do not adversely affect usability.	Collaborative usability inspection
U5	Text layout and formatting problems make the page unpleasant, confusing, or too long.	Verify that text layout is logical, consistent, and understandable, not fragmented or compiled into overly large pages.	Collaborative usability inspection
U6	Graphics problems make the page unpleasant, confusing, clichéd, or pretentious.	Verify that graphics are relevant, sympathetic to the appearance of the site, correctly sized, appropriate to anticipated users, and in keeping with the purpose of the site.	Collaborative usability inspection
U7	On-line user documentation and help is of poor quality.	Verify that on-line documentation is accurate, relevant, concise, and useful.	Collaborative usability inspection
U8	Users find the system time-consuming, error-prone, and inconsistent.	Demonstrate that selected tasks can be performed efficiently, accurately, and reliably.	Collaborative usability inspection

Table 13.1 (continued)

ID	Risk	Test Objective	Technique
U9	Site navigation is difficult to understand, illogical, or disorganized and obstructs the user.	Demonstrate that the navigation through pages is intuitive, consistent, and makes the user feel in control.	Usability test
U10	Site lacks a personalization facility (or the facility does not work).	Demonstrate that users may personalize the site to work in their preferred manner without being intrusive and without capturing personal data unnecessarily.	Usability test
U11	Site or pages are not accessible to people with disabilities.	Verify that accessibility conventions are adhered to.	Web accessibility checking
U12	Incorrect or poorly written text on pages confuses or misleads users.	Verify that all text, messages, and help screens, as well as the information provided, are accurate, concise, helpful, and understandable.	Previously covered by content checking (Chapter 9)
U13	The HTML page or objects embedded in the page are so large that the page is too slow to download.	Verify that objects are small enough to download within an acceptable time.	Previously covered by object load and timing (Chapter 10)
U14	The system cannot meet response time requirements while processing the design loads.	Demonstrate that the entire technical architecture meets load and response-time requirements.	Previously covered by performance and stress testing (Chapter 12)

usability fault is any clear or evident violation of an established usability principle or guideline; or it is any aspect of a system that is likely to lead to confusion, error, delay, or failure to complete some task on the part of the user. Usability faults have two dimensions:

1. The location and identity of a fault;
2. The problem and rationale for identifying it.

Applying the user-interface design principles set forth in Constantine and Lockwood's book, *Software for Use* [2], some examples of Web usability faults are summarized in Table 13.2.

Usability and usability assessment have never been as important as they are now. Typical Web site users have low boredom, frustration, inconvenience, and insecurity thresholds. Home-based users may never have been trained in the use of a computer, let alone browsers and your Web applications. Regardless of the user's level of sophistication, if your Web application doesn't allow enquiries to be made and orders to be placed easily, quickly, and reliably, the site will fail. If the user cannot easily understand from your Web site how to proceed, the user will leave your site and go elsewhere.

The first two methods of usability assessment discussed here, collaborative usability inspection and usability testing, are derived from the work of Larry Constantine and Lucy Lockwood in their book *Software for Use* [2]. We are grateful to the authors and publishers, Addison-Wesley, for allowing us to adapt their material for this chapter. For a more thorough discussion of the method and related references, you should refer to this work. Their Web site at http://www.foruse.com has numerous other resources on usability.

In his presentation to the User Interface '99 Conference [3], Larry Constantine identifies six methods for improving Web usability categorized as either expensive in the long term or most effective (Table 13.3).

Of the three methods deemed most effective, usability inspections stand out as the easiest and cheapest to implement, and early inspection is more efficient that later testing. This is consistent with all studies of inspection versus dynamic testing methods. Usability testing has its place, and we promote that as a method for addressing the specific areas of usefulness, ease of navigation, and personalization. Usage-centered design is, of course, an

Table 13.2
Some Examples of Usability Faults and Their Classifications

Location: Identity	Rationale: Problem
Personalization page: there is no cancel button	Tolerance principle: forced selection if dialogue opened mistakenly
Corporate home page: navigation links are unclear	Simplicity principle: user has to click on links to see where they lead
All pages: the hundreds of links on home page appear on all pages; required button is not easily found.	Visibility principle: the continue button is hidden among hundreds of other links

Table 13.3
Comparison of Methods for Improving Web Usability

Method	Expensive in the Long Term	Most Effective
Rapid iterative refinement: build something, try it, build it again	Yes	
Style guides: standard style and good guidelines		
Usability testing: actual trials, real users, no demos	Yes	Yes
Usability design metrics: hard numbers from designs and sketches		
Usability inspections: taking an informed, critical look		Yes
Usage-centered design: building in usability from the start		Yes

Source: [3]. Reproduced with permission.

approach to the overall design, implementation, and assessment of user interfaces, and its principles should be promoted in all development projects. It is not specifically a test activity.

Web accessibility checking, if done manually, might be deemed to be part of usability inspection as it could be performed at the same time as other checking. Accessibility guidelines, however, have been prepared, and it is now possible to perform the checking of a Web page against these guidelines using automated tools. Because it can be automated, Web accessibility testing has been described as a distinct test type in this chapter.

Other Methods

Beta testing is a commonly used method for gaining feedback from interested potential customers or friendly existing customers. Although it appears to be an inexpensive technique for the system supplier to employ, the feedback obtained is highly colored by the fact that usually only a self-selecting minority of beta testers respond. Even if all your beta testers give feedback, you have no control over their personal agendas or preferences. It is common for beta testers to blame product usability problems on themselves and figure out alternative ways of doing things. Usability problems may never come to light if this happens. Beta testing has the benefit of being cheap, but it can also be ineffective or misleading.

There are a number of other recognized techniques for usability assessment. Cognitive walkthroughs [4] are a detailed review of a sequence of steps that an interface requires a user to perform in order to accomplish some task. The reviewers check each step for potential usability problems. Usually, the main focus of the cognitive walkthrough is limited to understanding how easy a system is to learn. Questionnaire-based methods, such as SUMI [5] and WAMMI [6], collect subjective evaluation data and analyze it to product statistical scores on key attributes of the system under evaluation.

Collaborative Usability Inspection

Collaborative usability inspection is a systematic examination of a finished product, design, or prototype from the point of view of its usability by intended end users. The process is a team effort that includes developers, end users, application or domain experts, and usability specialists working in collaboration. A major benefit of the method is its own usability: It is easy to learn. Experienced inspection teams have been known to detect 100 usability faults per hour. The collaborative nature of these inspections means that users and developers understand the relationship between user interactions and design constraints and decisions. These inspections can be performed at any stage of development from the assessment of prototypes to the finished Web site, but, of course, the cost of fault correction increases the later the inspections take place. Collaborative usability inspection draws from other inspection techniques, most notably heuristic evaluation, a technique devised by Jakob Nielsen and succinctly described on his Web site at http:// www.useit.com [7]. This same Web site also has a wealth of Web-related usability articles, papers, and guidance.

Heuristics on Which to Base Inspections

Inspections are guided by a set of rules or heuristics for good user-interface design. These are used as a framework for identifying and categorizing usability faults. Constantine and Lockwood [2] propose a set of five usability rules and six generic user interface design principles reproduced in Tables 13.4 and 13.5.

Nielsen promotes a (popular) set of 10 Web design heuristics [8] summarized in Table 13.6. His book, *Designing Web Usability* [9], is packed with usability design guidelines from which you can extract your own preferred rules if you care to.

Table 13.4
Five Usability Rules

Rule	Description
Access	The system should be usable, without help or instruction, by a user who has knowledge and experience in the application domain, but no prior experience with the system.
Efficacy	The system should not interfere with or impede efficient use by a skilled user who has substantial experience with the system.
Progression	The system should facilitate continuous advancement in knowledge, skill, and facility and accommodate progressive change in usage as the user gains experience with the system.
Support	The system should support the real work that users are trying to accomplish by making it easier, simpler, faster, or more fun or by making new things possible.
Context	The system should be suited to the real conditions and actual environment of the operational context within which it will be deployed and used.

Source: [2]. Reproduced with permission.

Table 13.5
Six Usability Design Principles

Principle	Description
Structure	Organize the user interface purposefully in meaningful and useful ways based on clear, consistent models that are apparent and recognizable to users, putting related things together and separating unrelated things, differentiating dissimilar things, and making similar things resemble one another.
Simplicity	Make simple, common tasks simple to do, communicating clearly and simply in the user's own language and providing good shortcuts that are meaningfully related to longer procedures.
Visibility	Keep all needed options and materials for a given task visible without distracting the user with extraneous or redundant information.
Feedback	Keep users informed of actions or interpretations, changes of state or conditions, and errors or exceptions that are relevant and of interest to the user through clear, concise, and unambiguous language familiar to users.
Tolerance	Be flexible and tolerant, reducing the cost of mistakes and misuse by allowing undoing and redoing, while also preventing errors wherever possible by tolerating varied inputs and sequences and by interpreting all reasonable actions reasonably.
Reuse	Reuse internal and external components and behaviors, maintaining consistency with purpose rather than merely arbitrary consistency, thus reducing the need for users to rethink and remember.

Source: [2]. Reproduced with permission.

Table 13.6
Usability Heuristics

1.	Visibility of system status
2.	Match between system and the real world
3.	User control and freedom
4.	Consistency and standards
5.	Error prevention
6.	Recognition rather than recall
7.	Flexibility and efficiency of use
8.	Aesthetic and minimalist design
9.	Help for users to recognize, diagnose, and recover from errors
10.	Help and documentation

After: [8].

Other rules can be used, and several collections of checklists are available. See [10–12] for substantial checklists of usability design issues that could be employed, but probably need to be summarized to be useful as inspection rules. One of the benefits of using heuristics is that the rules can be distributed between the inspection participants to spread the workload a little—it is difficult for anyone to keep an eye on 10 heuristics at once.

Vincent Flanders and Michael Willis's book, *Web Pages That Suck* [13], takes a different approach to learning good design—studying bad design. Their book is a good source of practical recommendations that could also be used as a checklist.

Approach

Inspection is a pure fault-finding activity and its objectives are to detect usability faults and user-interface inconsistencies. The inspection team should adopt the tester mentality and act like impatient, intolerant, and difficult users. Inspection is intensive work and requires the team to be focused, persistent, and nitpicking. Somewhat like proofreading a book, the inspection demands that both the superficial appearance and underlying structure of the system be examined. Having users on the team makes it easier for the team to become more user-focused.

Because the developers are involved in the inspection it can be a little uncomfortable for them to see their work pulled to pieces by others. The traditional view of testing applies: Finding faults is good. Faults found can be fixed and the system improved. Celebrating faults and mocking the developers are not helpful. Faults should be discussed in technical terms with a view to getting the developers to accept them and understand their impact so they can formulate a better design. Where the system exhibits highly usable or well-designed features, these should be noted to ensure the developers do not change them when the faults are corrected.

When faults are reported, the developers should not dispute the faults, criticize the users, or get defensive, which might suppress the team's willingness to report faults. When a reviewer gets stuck, the developers should not suggest alternative methods of completing the desired task. This would hide the fact that the reviewers are lacking some information, and that is a fault. It is not helpful to discuss or argue the pros and cons of a particular fault: The team should focus on finding and logging faults as quickly as possible. Some faults may eventually be deemed so trivial that they are not fixed, but this decision to act and change the system is made by the stakeholders.

Inspection Roles

The members of the inspection team fulfill distinct roles. Teams can be as small as 3 or 4 people or as large as 20, but 6 to 12 is the optimum range of team size. The common roles allocated to inspection team members are summarized in Table 13.7.

Preparation for the Inspection

The lead reviewer briefs the other reviewers and organizes the room, equipment, servers, network for the inspection. This might include obtaining large monitors or projection screens so all reviewers can see the system in use and compiling paper copies of all Web pages under test or having a printer nearby to capture hardcopy versions of problem pages. The reviewers should not prepare before the inspection meeting so they can approach the inspection with a fresh outlook. With the help of the users and developers, the lead reviewer should assemble a collection of scenarios or test cases (see an example below) to be exercised in the inspection. It is important to set aside enough time to conduct the inspections, but it is also important not to let them drag on for too long. Systems that cannot be inspected in less than 3 or 4 hours need to be inspected over multiple sessions, each lasting a half day or less. The inspection will be performed in two phases.

Table 13.7
Usability Inspection Roles

Role	Description
Lead reviewer	Convenes and leads the inspection. Manages the team; ensures the process is followed; keeps the team focused. Contributes to the inspection, but does not dominate.
Inspection recorder	Maintains the records of faults found and their classification. Assesses and records the severity of the faults. Lead reviewer or continuity reviewer may fulfill this role in small teams.
Continuity reviewer	Optional role. Focuses on gaps in continuity or inconsistencies. In some projects, this role may be delegated to the entire team. In other projects, a separate continuity inspection may be justified.
Developers	Act as dedicated reviewers. Forbidden to argue, challenge, defend, design, or promise anything to other reviewers. The lead reviewer enforces this discipline.
Users and domain experts	Genuine end users to act as reviewers. If not users, then involve domain experts who are asked to think and act like users. User-reported problems should be taken most seriously, and users should be encouraged to raise as many faults as possible.
Usability specialists	Act as consultants to facilitate and explore the faults raised by the reviewers. Do not act as arbiters of fault severity.

Interactive Inspection Phase

In the first phase of inspection, the system is used to perform selected tasks. These tasks are defined prior to the meeting, but not scripted like a test script. Rather, they define a series of scenarios, such as the following:

> Register as a new user. Search for a book entitled *Web Page Testing* and buy it online using your credit card (number 9999 9999 9999 9999). Read the confirmation e-mail sent by the Web site and, using the e-mail instructions, obtain the status of your order.

Larry Constantine recommends, "The Lead Reviewer or someone else should drive the system in response to user statements about what they would do next. This is also the only practical way to deal with multiple users who have divergent approaches ... you should recommend against having more than two users in an inspection—too chaotic" (personal communication).

Comments from users or any of the other reviewers should be noted if a fault is detected. All of the reviewers should be looking for problems. The lead reviewer should prompt the team to note any observations in the following instances:

- When a new page appears (and note any immediately observable problems);
- At the end of each step or stage in the scenario;
- At the end of the scenario to summarize the views of the team.

Of course, the reviewers may make observations at any time. The lead reviewer facilitates the generation of comments and controls the flow of the inspection to allow the recorder to keep up with the logging. Observations on usable and effective features are also logged to ensure the developers do not change things that work well.

Static Inspection Phase

In the second phase, the inspection team visits as many of the pages in as many contexts as possible and examines each page in finer detail. It is probably impossible to visit all pages via the various navigation paths through the system, so the lead reviewer needs to manage the scope of this activity to ensure as many pages are inspected as possible in the time available. At this point, the reviewers should examine the details of all images and other embedded objects, the graphical detail on the page, form fields, buttons, drop-down lists, radio buttons, and check boxes to make sure there is no conflict with the usability rules.

Follow-Up

At the end of the inspection, the inspection team should review the fault list that has been logged by the inspection recorder. The faults should be evaluated by the inspection team and project manager (for a small project) or may be submitted to a project acceptance team on larger projects. The decision to be made is, does this fault make the system unacceptable?

The cost of correction (and the impact of change) is an important consideration and where the potential impact is less severe, these faults might not be fixed at all. This is ultimately a decision for the stakeholders—some faults may be deemed less severe and deferred to later releases. Faults need to be allocated a severity in line with their impact in production, then corrected by the developers.

Other Inspections

Two variations exist on the standard inspection method. Consistency inspections are required where there are particular concerns over the consistency of various pages that users access in their interactions and also within the content of individual pages. Selected groups of features are inspected for their consistency, and typical groupings you might use could include the following:

- Menu bars and buttons;
- Dialog boxes;
- Data fields and text labels;
- Error messages.

The important issue with consistency inspections is to be able to compare the contents of each group. Pinning hardcopy screenshots of Web pages or dialog boxes to the wall and looking at them is the simplest method. The inspection is focused on inconsistencies, not other usability issues, because broadening the scope makes these inspections less efficient.

Usability Testing

Usability testing aims to detect usability faults in a system by using the system to perform selected tasks. There are two broad ways of performing usability testing: in a usability laboratory or in the field. We will only consider field usability testing here. For a broader description of both methods, see [2].

Usability testing of a finished system is effective for finding certain faults, but is no substitute for good usability design. Experience shows that usability tests uncover fewer faults than inspections, but the faults that are found are often more subtle or unusual in nature, and they can be more serious. Usability testing requires that a working system be available, so these tests tend to be possible only late in the project. If there isn't time to fix these faults, they may be left in the released product. Overall, usability tests are most effective when used to investigate specific areas of an application or to explore particular issues.

Testing in the Field

Testing in the field requires that the system be used in the workplace. Users are invited to use the system to do real work; they may be asked to perform selected tasks and, perhaps, to repeat those tasks (with variations) many times. At its most formal, field testing simulates testing in a laboratory with video and sound equipment, mixers, and monitors being used by the trained observers. At its least formal, the observer watches the user operate the system and takes notes. It is possible to ask the users to keep their own notes for later analysis, but this distracts the user from the task and may influence the results of the test. The benefit of field use is the greater realism and possibly the comfort factor for the users: They are at their normal place of work. Where users are acting like home-based personal users, you could let them work at home, but to observe them at home might be regarded as too intrusive. An alternative would be to get volunteer users to come to your site and to put them in as comfortable and relaxed an environment as possible to conduct the test. However formally the test is arranged, observers should take care not to influence or disturb the user testers. The way in which instructions are given or the body language displayed by observers during the test itself may have a detrimental effect.

Test Process

Usability tests in the field are usually organized, observed, and analyzed by the usability testers. The volunteer users (or subjects) perform the tests—they are asked to perform selected tasks using the system under test. The system under test need not necessarily be a finished product, but it must incorporate all the features required to perform the specified tasks. It could be an alpha or beta version, but should be stable enough not to crash during these tests.

A key discipline of such tests is that the testers should observe the tests, but not interact with the subjects in a way that unduly influences their behavior. In particular, the testers should not comment on the users actions, answer questions, or suggest alternative ways of completing the task. To guarantee this objectivity, the testers might set up a camcorder to record the subjects' activities and display the live pictures in another room. The testers can take notes based on the actions they witness and study the recordings for later analysis.

User-subjects can be encouraged to talk out loud while performing the tests. In this way, the thoughts that go through each user's mind are captured live, as the action happens. This provides a more complete reflection of the user's experience and thought processes while using the system under test. It is easy to imagine what is happening in the following scenerio:

> I've added the printer cable to my shopping basket, but the system tells me to register as a user before I proceed to the checkout. Register user...nope, can't find that button. Ahhh, perhaps the New Customers link is the one to try. Yes it is. Why didn't they say that before?

This narrative makes it obvious what the user is having difficulty with. If the user didn't record these comments, the few seconds lost finding the right command might never have registered as a problem in his or her mind. Even if the user had recorded the fact that he or she had difficulty, it might not occur to the developers reading the test log what the problem was. The developers would see what they wanted to see, of course, because they designed and built the screens in the first place. This approach is not infallible, however, because the subjects, knowing they are being recorded, may self-censor their comments or become self-conscious. They might suppress certain comments because they don't want to look slow or incompetent or to be seen as unsystematic or lacking in confidence. Some people might simply find it difficult to work on the system and comment on their own actions at the same time. The users may need some coaching and encouragement to speak their minds.

An alternative approach that has some merit is testing done in pairs. This requires one person to use the keyboard and mouse with another talking through the task and reading the documentation. Both users observe the system's behavior and comment on or discuss what they see on screen. Although this might be a more natural way to operate the system and comfortable way to extract comments, it does of course require two people rather than one, so the pace of testing might be reduced as a consequence.

One final alternative is to record the expressions of users while they perform the tasks. Although a user might not say anything, a perplexed expression might indicate that something is wrong. When the subject sees the replay of their face, they can usually recall what gave them difficulty. Arranging a mirror attached to the PC monitor could bring the users expression onto the same field of view as the screen, so the two can be seen and filmed together. Otherwise, a second video recorder would be required. The user would not be asked to provide a running commentary, so this usage would be closer to normal usage. After the session is over, the testers use the facial expressions as a trigger for questions like, You looked confused. What was going through your mind just then?

After the test, the users should be debriefed. This is mainly to obtain their impressions of the system, feedback on what worked well and not so well, and suggestions for improvement. When taken in the round, these observations may reveal trends that greatly assist with the diagnosis of problems and possible solutions.

Among other things, Web usability testing aims to expose difficulties that a user experiences when engaged in the following activities:

- Performing particular business transactions using the Web site (e.g., searching for and buying a book, locating and reserving a flight to an unusual destination);

- Navigating a Web site (probably to find information or access a particular resource);

- Personalizing a site to achieve the faster, more efficient browsing experience the personalization is meant to deliver.

Test cases or scenarios should be selected to cover any particular tasks of concern.

Web Accessibility Checking

It is possible to conduct manual inspections of a system to detect departures from user-interface standards or accessibility guidelines. In the context of the Web, accessibility refers to the ease with which anyone can make use of the Web, regardless of his or her technology, location, or disability. The most important accessibility guidelines for Web-based systems are defined as part of the Web Accessibility Initiative (WAI), whose stated mission is "… to lead the Web to its full potential including promoting a high degree of usability for people with disabilities." Their most important guidelines are the "Web Content Accessibility Guidelines" [14]. This document defines a comprehensive collection of guidelines to make your Web pages more accessible to users with disabilities, although the vast majority of guidelines would make a site more accessible (or usable) to all users. Consequently, these guidelines provide a ready-made checklist of points to inspect Web pages against. Guidance for evaluating Web sites for accessibility can be found in [15], which includes a step-by-step process for accessibility evaluation. A major benefit of these guidelines is that they can be used as objective requirements. Failure to adhere to these guidelines can be raised as incidents.

There are several assistive technologies now available to help users with disabilities use the Web. These include the following:

- Text-to-speech (TTS) browsers that use synthesized speech to read text on Web sites to a user;

- Text-only browsers that render Web sites in a text-only format;

- Voice-enabled browsers that navigate Web sites using speech commands;

- Specialized keyboards and mice;

- Voice-recognition software;

- Refreshable braille devices that transfer text onto a special device;

- Screen magnification or enhancement software.

Standard HTML has features that specifically support the use of these technologies and, as a consequence, feature strongly in the accessibility guidelines. One simple example is that images must have some associated or alternate text, should the user turn them off or be blind. This alternate text is used by voice-enabled browsers to provide the user with an audible narrative describing what is visible on the Web page.

These accessibility recommendations will become increasingly important as it is likely that some or all may become mandatory in some applications. Section 508 [16] is a U.S. federal mandate requiring that information technology be made accessible to people with disabilities. In 1998, the Workforce Investment Act established Section 508 as an amendment to the Rehabilitation Act of 1973. It requires that electronic and information technology developed, procured, maintained, or used by the federal government be accessible to people with disabilities.

Much of Section 508 compliance concerns making Web sites, intranets, and Web-enabled applications more accessible. This affects government agencies as well as private-sector institutions. Government agencies must make their Web sites and intranets accessible according to the standards and can only create or purchase Web-enabled applications that are compliant with 508 standards. The law impacts corporations doing business with the government because those corporations need to make their Web-enabled applications and any Web sites built for government clients accessible as well.

Fortunately, these guidelines can be verified using automated tools. The best known of these is produced by the CAST organization and is called

Bobby [17]. Bobby verifies Web pages against the WAI recommendations and reports anomalies. It can be used on-line or downloaded for use on your intranet. Automated verification of accessibility is possible to do at any point where a Web page is available to test, so it is probably a job that the developers perform.

Tools for Assessing Web Page Accessibility

Evaluating the usability of the human/computer interface is somewhat subjective, and the areas where tools can replace manual or visual assessment are limited. One particular area where tools do offer some support is in verifying accessibility. Because the majority of accessibility guidelines set out by the WAI can be related directly to the Web page's HTML, it is possible for automated tools to scan HTML and compare it with the accessibility rules. There are also some specific issues, such as color blindness, that can also be checked. Table 13.8 lists some of the proprietary and free tools that are available on the Web. For a more comprehensive listing, visit the W3C Web site at http://www.w3c.org.

Table 13.8
Tools for Usability Assessment

Proprietary Tools	URL
AccVerify	http://www.hisoftware.com/access/
InSight	http://www.ssbtechnologies.com
Colorfield Insight	http://www.colorfield.com
A User Friendliness Checklist	http://www.pantos.org/atw/35317.html
Lift	http://www.usablenet.com
Web Metrics Testbed	http://www.nist.gov/webmet
Vischeck	http://www.vischeck.com
Free Tools	**URL**
Tool to verify page on varying screen sizes	http://www.anybrowser.com
Bobby	http://www.cast.org/bobby/
WebSat, WebCat tools	http://www.nist.gov/webmet

References

[1]   Norman, D. A., *The Design of Everyday Things*, New York: Doubleday, 1988.

[2]   Constantine, L. L., and L. A. D. Lockwood, *Software for Use*, Boston, MA: Addison-Wesley, 1999.

[3]   Constantine, L., "Web Usability Inspections," *Proc. User Interface '99 Conf.*, San Francisco, California, March 1999 (also available at http://www.foruse.com/).

[4]   Wharton, C., et al., "The Cognitive Walkthrough Method: A Practitioner's Guide." In *Usability Inspection Methods*, pp.105–141, J. Nielsen and R. L. Mack (Eds.), New York: John Wiley & Sons, 1994.

[5]   Human Factors Research Group, "Software Usability Measurement Inventory (SUMI)," University College Cork, Ireland, http://www.ucc.ie/hfrg/questionnaires/sumi/index.html, 2002.

[6]   HFRG Ireland and Nomos Management AB Sweden, "WAMMI Web Usability Questionnaire," http://www.nomos.se/wammi/, 2002.

[7]   Neilsen J., "How to Conduct an Heuristic Evaluation," http://www.useit.com, 2002.

[8]   Neilsen, J., "Ten Usability Heuristics," http://www.useit.com/papers/heuristic/heuristic_list.html, 2002.

[9]   Nielsen, J., *Designing Web Usability*, Indianapolis, IN: New Riders, 2000.

[10] Dustin, E., J. Rashka, and D. McDiarmid, *Quality Web Systems*, Boston, MA: Addison-Wesley, 2001.

[11] Nguyen, H. Q., *Testing Applications on the Web*, New York: John Wiley & Sons, 2001.

[12] Abeleto, Ltd., "Objective Evaluation of Likely Usability Hazards—Preliminaries for User Testing," http://www.abeleto.com, 2002.

[13] Flanders V., and M. Willis, *Web Pages That Suck*, San Francisco, CA: Sybex, 1998.

[14] World Wide Web Consortium (W3C), "Web Accessibility Initiative, Web Content Accessibility Guidelines 1.0," http://www.w3.org/TR/WCAG10/, 2002.

[15] World Wide Web Consortium (W3C), "Evaluating Web Sites for Accessibility," http://www.w3.org/WAI/eval/, 2002.

[16] Architectural and Transportation Barriers Compliance Board, "Electronic and Information Technology Accessibility Standards," http://www.access-board.gov/sec508/508standards.htm, 2002.

[17] CAST, "Bobby Web Page Accessibility Checker," http://www.cast.org/bobby/, 2002.

14

Security Testing

Overview

Table 14.1 presents risks addressed by security testing and associated test objectives. These have been derived from [1, 2]. When most people think of security (and the challenge that hackers present to it), they have a vision of longhaired college dropouts working into the wee hours at a furious pace, trying to crack a remote system. By guessing passwords and through perseverance, luck, and ingenuity, they break into the bank, government department, or evil mastermind's mainframe system. Although this image works well for the movies, it isn't helpful to our understanding of the security threats that face e-business systems. Determined attackers often work in teams, they work almost entirely with automated tools, and they may wait patiently for months before attacking perhaps hundreds of sites in a single day. Many of them adopt a scattergun approach to acquiring targets, but they really are more sophisticated than the movies usually represent them.

Although outsiders are a serious threat, it should be borne in mind that insiders perform many break-ins. Whatever their motives (frustration, anger, or a grudge against an employer), insiders are particularly dangerous. If they are still employed, not only do they have access to your systems, they probably also know your network topology and the servers that host critical services and are trusted within your organization—what they don't know, they can find out easily. Even if they have left your company, their knowledge gives them a head start in their intrusion efforts. Either way, your internal security policies should be regularly reviewed and thoroughly implemented.

Table 14.1

Risks Addressed by Security Testing

ID	Risk	Test Objective	Technique
X1	Inadequately configured border firewalls may allow intruders to connect using vulnerable services or ports.	Verify that requests to ports and services that are not required are filtered out.	Security assessment
X2	Unsecured and unmonitored remote-access points make your network vulnerable to attack.	Verify that remote access password policy or smart cards are properly implemented.	Security assessment
X3	Excessive trusts between machines allow hackers to gain unauthorized access.	Verify that only essential trust relationships between machines are implemented.	Security assessment
X4	Unnecessary user or test accounts are available for hackers to exploit.	Verify that accounts have minimum required privileges and that all unnecessary accounts are removed.	Security assessment
X5	Operating-system or service-related software vulnerabilities exist and are available for attackers to exploit.	Verify that known vulnerabilities in the operating system and service products have countermeasures implemented.	Security assessment
X6	Security policies and procedures are poor or are not fully implemented.	Verify that security policies are stringent, in line with best practices, and properly implemented.	Security assessment
X7	Excessive shares and weak directory access controls allow attackers to gain access to data and operating-system features.	Verify that minimum resource access and shares are set up to provide the Web service.	Security assessment
X8	Services, such as X-Windows, that are not required for the Web service itself, are available for hackers to exploit.	Verify that all operating-system and Web server features that are not needed to provide the service are removed from servers.	Security assessment
X9	Attackers can easily guess weak passwords on workstations, allowing them to gain access to vulnerable systems.	Verify that user-password policies are strict and fully implemented.	Security assessment

Table 14.1 (continued)

ID	Risk	Test Objective	Technique
X10	Internet-service products (e.g., Web, CGI, FTP) are poorly configured, allowing attackers to gain access.	Verify that services are configured securely and that all unnecessary features and CGI scripts are removed, in line with manufacturer's recommendations.	Security assessment
X11	Servers run Internet services with unnecessary vulnerabilities.	Verify that all unnecessary services are removed from servers.	Security assessment
X12	Servers running unnecessary or poorly configured services leak information to attackers, making it easier for them to compromise your systems.	Verify that services such as SMTP, SNMP, Telnet, and NetBIOS are turned off or configured securely.	Security assessment
X13	Service is vulnerable to denial of service (DoS) attack.	Verify that DoS countermeasures are in place and operate correctly.	Security assessment
X14	Vulnerabilities in CGI-script processing allow server-side directives to be used.	Verify that the Web server has the latest patches implemented and insecure facilities are removed or disabled.	Security assessment
X15	Inadequate monitoring, detection, and logging facilities on servers allow attacker activities to go undetected.	Verify that monitoring, detection, and logging services are securely configured.	Penetration testing
X16	Hidden fields on Web pages contain sensitive material and can be changed by attackers.	Verify that hidden fields on pages do not contain sensitive data and cannot be changed by attackers.	Penetration testing
X17	System transactions that pass sensitive data between Web servers and clients are not encrypted.	Verify that all sensitive system transactions are encrypted.	Penetration testing
X18	Hidden fields on HTML forms contain sensitive data and can be manipulated.	Verify that hidden fields do not contain data that can be changed to corrupt system transactions.	Penetration testing
X19	Cookies contain sensitive data, such as passwords or credit-card numbers that can be manipulated to impersonate users or defraud you.	Verify that cookies do not contain sensitive data.	Penetration testing

Table 14.1 (continued)

ID	Risk	Test Objective	Technique
X20	Developers leave debug options or backdoors that can be exploited by hackers.	Verify that all debug options and trapdoors have been removed.	Penetration testing
X21	Application or Web server code is vulnerable to buffer-overflow attacks.	Verify that all fields captured on HTML forms are validated for their length.	Penetration testing
X22	Application or Web server code has known vulnerabilities that can be exploited by hackers.	Verify that the Web server has the latest patches implemented and insecure facilities are removed or disabled.	Penetration testing
X23	Parameters passed to server-based code appear in the URL window and can be tampered with.	Verify that hackers cannot change parameters on Web pages to impersonate others, corrupt data, or subvert the security of the system.	Penetration testing
X24	An application writes user data to a file on the Web server. Hackers could discover this and view the contents of these files or put executable code in their place.	Verify that hackers cannot discover the names of or control the content of files on Web servers.	Penetration testing

The proliferation of the Internet and its global availability has opened up incredible opportunities for the security attacker community. At its heart, the Internet infrastructure was not designed with security as a high priority. A large amount of information relating to the organization and composition of a Web site is available after running a few scans using freely available tools. Just like real thieves, the attacker will case the joint, looking for unlocked doors, open windows, and intruder alarms before taking the easiest way in. Few burglars break in through the front door. In the same way, knowledgeable attackers exploit vulnerabilities in the software products you use in obscure and unusual places. Unless your system and security administrators pay close attention to the regular security-vulnerability alerts reported for all the popular networking and Web service products, the attack that cripples your company may come as a complete surprise.

Hackers, Crackers, Whackers, and Script Kiddies

The "ethical" hacking community has tried to make a distinction between hackers (those who are merely curious and enthusiastic programmers) and crackers (also known as whackers or attackers) whose aims are destructive or fraudulent. Hackers might scan and probe a site to explore its potential vulnerabilities before advising the site or the manufacturer of the vulnerable product that they have a problem. Hackers could be compared to bird watchers or train spotters. Hackers might earn their living during the day as consultants and be hackers at night, honing their skills perhaps. Pekka Himanen's book, *The Hacker Ethic* [3], sets out an interesting view of the hacker philosophy, comparing it with the Protestant, scientific, and monastic work ethics. Himanen credits several computer developments, such as the Linux operating system, to the hacker ethic and suggests that other disciplines, for example scientific research, are founded on the same hacker philosophy. We are not concerned with such matters here.

Businesses whose systems are scanned and analyzed by hackers or interfered with by crackers find it difficult to make a distinction between the two groups. Suppose, for example, a security consultant knocked on your front door offering services. He explains that he broke into your home last night and set all of the clocks in your house forward one hour (which had you wondering). If you hire him, he'll tell you how he did it and, for a fee, will make your home more secure. Is he offering a service? Or is he blackmailing you? In the context of making your home or systems secure, it seems simpler to be suspicious of all individuals that take an unusual interest in your security set up. In this chapter, we will use the term attacker to mean any individual or organization that threatens the security of your Web service.

A *script kiddie* is a derogative term coined by the more sophisticated hackers for the immature, but dangerous, exploiter of security holes on the Internet. Script kiddies use existing, easy-to-find techniques, programs, or scripts to search for and exploit weaknesses in other computers on the Internet. Their scans and attacks are often random and are executed with no regard or understanding of the potentially harmful consequences. Hackers view script kiddies with contempt because they don't advance the "art" of hacking, but bring the wrath of authority down on the entire hacker community. A hacker might take pride in the quality of an attack by leaving no trace of an intrusion, but script kiddies aim at quantity because they crave attention. Script kiddies are sometimes portrayed in the media as bored, lonely teenagers seeking recognition from their peers. Keeping a close watch on known and new vulnerabilities and promptly applying recommended countermeasures should protect you from most script kiddies because most of them are looking for easy exploits. Andrew Stephens' article, "Script Kiddies: What Are They and What Are They Doing?" [4], provides a more detailed description of script kiddies, the threats they pose, and how to stop them.

The Attacker's Methodology

Attackers do not usually attack randomly; they adopt some form of systematic attack methodology and they are extremely careful to protect themselves. The Hollywood movie characterizations of attackers make them seem unsystematic. Although it's amusing to think of them as sloppy burglars, tripping up and leaving lots of clues, this portrayal is far from accurate for the most dangerous attackers. Like successful crooks, successful attackers plan and prepare their attack thoroughly and take steps to cover their tracks after the exploit is complete. Scambray, McClure, and Kurtz's book, *Hacking Exposed* [1], provides a comprehensive overview of the vulnerabilities, methods, and tools useds by attackers and sets out a generic attack methodology. The eight common attacker activities listed in Table 14.2 provide an insight into their methods and approaches.

Denial of Service Attacks

Denial of service (DoS) attacks deserve special mention. When attackers fail to gain entry to a system, either because it is secure or, perhaps, because they are less competent, they may feel frustrated or helpless. Current or former employees who bear a grudge against their employers may have insider knowledge that could be used to gain revenge. People with political vendettas against organizations may also resort to extreme measures. With limited knowledge, incompetent attackers, frustrated employees, or criminal or terrorist gangs might all resort to DoS attacks on your installation. The following are some of the best known types of DoS attacks:

- *Bandwidth consumption:* Attackers who have more bandwidth than you, or who are able to amplify their attack using other sites on the Internet, flood your site with messages. Typically, these attacks consist of extreme volumes of ping sweeps dispatched to your hosts.

- *Resource starvation:* Attackers starve your host machines of resources, rather than your network. These attacks aim to use up all of a host's CPU, memory, disk space, or other resource until the system can no

Table 14.2
The Attacker Methodology

Footprinting	In this phase, the attacker scans the many open sources of information and Web sites for data on your organization, domain names, and the IP addresses of your servers.
Scanning	This is equivalent to rattling the windows and doors to find a vulnerable network or computer. The attacker uses tools to scan the ports on your servers looking for services and points of entry to exploit.
Enumeration	By connecting to target hosts, valid user accounts and poorly protected resource shares are enumerated.
Gaining access	The passwords of valid accounts might be guessed and the versions of software running on the host obtained. Once the vendor and version of a Web server product are known, the attacker can focus on specific techniques to exploit.
Escalating privilege	Attackers are in. Now, how do they get root or administrator privileges?
Pilfering	Attackers gain deeper insight into the environment by pilfering account details, registry contents, shares, and connections to other host machines.
Covering tracks	When total control is secured, covering their tracks is essential. Log cleaners remove all trace of attackers' activity.
Creating back doors	Altered versions of UNIX login script, netstat, and ps utilities let attackers return without leaving a trace. Network sniffers let them see and attack all interfacing systems.

After: [1].

longer provide a service or crashes. Sending large volumes of mal-formed data packets to hosts tends to consume large quantities of CPU time, for example.

- *Programming flaws:* Attackers exploit a failing in the systems running on the host to cause a system crash. Buffer overflows are a favorite technique.

- *Routing and DNS attacks:* Attackers exploit the relatively weak security of routing protocols by corrupting the routing information. The victim's Internet traffic can be redirected to any network or to a black hole—a network that does not exist. Either way, the victim's Web site can be effectively disabled.

There are few sites that can withstand so-called distributed DoS (DDoS) attacks. In this case, an attacker makes use of other sites to amplify an attack on your servers, dramatically increasing his or her ability to flood your site. There is less value in testing for these scenarios as the openness of the Web makes it easy for a determined attacker to launch attacks from third-party routers with anonymity. The most that DoS testing can do is verify that patches and configuration changes for known software vulnerabilities have been properly implemented and that certain threatening message types are rejected by your firewalls and services. Gary Kessler's article "Defenses Against Distributed Denial of Service Attacks" [5] presents an overview of the types of DDoS attacks and countermeasures.

Security Vulnerabilities

All of the major software products on the market, including browsers, client and server operating system software, networking software, and Web server and development products have security vulnerabilities. There are many books [1, 5, 6] and Web sites that describe the numerous and varied vulnerabilities of all the popular operating-system, networking, and Web server products on the market. Many Web sites publicize known security vulnerabilities, proven countermeasures, and configuration advice. For example, The CERT Coordination Center [7] studies Internet security vulnerabilities and publishes security alerts for all computer products. NTBugtraq [8] is "a mailing list for the discussion of security exploits and security bugs in Windows NT, Windows 2000, and Windows XP and related applications." We strongly recommend that (you and) your system administrators join the mailing lists of relevant services to stay up-to-date on the latest vulnerabilities and countermeasures.

It is staggering to learn how many vulnerabilities there actually are. The nature of these vulnerabilities and the tools (a large number of which are freely available) that exist to exploit them should make any system administrator very concerned. Of course, all of the published vulnerabilities have countermeasures or patches provided by the software suppliers, but it is the system administrator's responsibility to stay up-to-date and apply the patches.

In-house security testers can perform some security auditing and assessment; however, the most thorough assessments and ethical hacking require in-depth technical knowledge of the systems under attack, the tools available to assist, and the imagination and persistence to crack into systems. It is a specialized skill and, although a good system administrator or system programmer probably has the technical know-how, you normally have to hire specialists to undertake this kind of testing. A four-article series by *Internet*

Security Magazine [9] provides an excellent overview of security audit, assessment, and test approaches, as well as some advice on how to choose a security-services vendor. (See also Deborah Radcliff's article "Sizing up Security Services" [10].) Security audits tend to focus on corporate security policies and how well a site or organization adheres to them. The *InfoWorld* article "The Ins and Outs of a Network Security Audit" [11] gives guidelines on security audits. In this chapter, we will only consider the two test-oriented approaches: security assessment and penetration testing.

Security Assessment

A security assessment is a review of a site's hardware and software configuration to identify security vulnerabilities. The assessment team works with the full cooperation of the technical staff that designed, implemented, and supported the site to be assessed. Security assessments, being systematic attempts to identify all security weak points, are the most cost-effective way to address security concerns. The structure and definition of an assessment varies with the scale of the project and objectives of the organization that commission it. Assessments can be conducted from an internal or external point of view. Assessments can focus on servers, networks, or firewalls and can be technically or nontechnically oriented.

Choosing a Security Consultant

The usefulness of an assessment depends very much on the expertise of the staff that performs it. Like penetration tests, which are described later, outsourcing companies perform most assessments, so you need to be very careful whom you choose to hire. Much of the initial work involves the use of automated tools. More competent security companies have built their own scanners, rather than relying on the products of other companies.

Ask whether the company's consultants are Certification for Information System Security Professional (CISSP)–qualified [12]. CISSP reflects the qualifications of information systems security practitioners. The CISSP syllabus covers topics such as access control systems, cryptography, and security management practices and is administered by the International Information Systems Security Certification Consortium, or (ISC)2, which promotes the CISSP exam as an aid to evaluating personnel performing information-security functions.

Companies that allocate resources to perform research publish regular papers and are active in security circles. These companies are more likely to have competent staff and sophisticated assessment and reporting methodologies. We recommend that you examine the Web sites of prospective suppliers and discover how many white papers, recent exploits, and security guidelines they have published. You should also ask for sanitized sample reports of previous engagements. A site with many recent publications is a partial measure of the competence of the company and how up-to-date their approaches are. If you are trying to acquire insurance protection against hacking you might also check that the assessing company is acceptable to the underwriter.

The recommendations made in reports might include specific countermeasures to address the vulnerabilities identified. The report should also indicate the underlying reasons why specific vulnerabilities have occurred. The assessors need to go further than simply identifying system vulnerabilities against a checklist. They should identify and report on any weaknesses in organization or systems design and make recommendations as to how these weaknesses may be addressed.

Security Vulnerabilities

Security assessments comprise both technical and nontechnical activities. Nontechnical assessment might involve reviewing the technical facilities and infrastructure and examining privileged users, trust relationships, network topologies, and the roles of key personnel. Many vulnerabilities exist because security policies are not followed, not because the policies themselves are at fault. For example, weak password controls, the granting of high privileges to nontechnical staff, and excessive trusts between networked hosts are problems that this assessment might expose. Nontechnical assessment work would normally be completed before the technical work begins.

Modern (and not so modern) operating system products might have a hundred or more documented vulnerabilities. Relatively simple configuration changes, patches, or upgrades can address most vulnerabilities. Each vulnerability could be identified manually, but there are now a large number of tools that can be used to scan systems and report vulnerabilities automatically.

Security Scanning Tools

Security scanning tools are similar to antivirus products in that the scanners use a database of vulnerabilities with attributes or signatures that the tool searches for. As new vulnerabilities arise, these databases must be kept up-to-date to allow new targets to be identified. An important consideration in choosing such a tool, therefore, is the number of vulnerabilities the tool can detect. The problem is that the tool vendors may define vulnerabilities differently, so direct comparisons may be misleading. The Common Vulnerabilities and Exposures (CVE) project at http://cve.mitre.org [13] provides a dictionary of common names for publicly known information security vulnerabilities and exposures, but does not describe the vulnerabilities or provide countermeasures to them. An increasing number of vendors are making their products CVE-compliant, so it is worth checking that the products you are thinking of buying appear on the compatible products list at the CVE Web site.

Although the vendors may claim their tools scan for more vulnerabilities than their competitors', the features that differentiate them relate more to ease-of-use and the quality of results reported. Fortunately, most of the vendors allow you to download evaluation copies of their tools. Scanning tools can generate vast quantities of output, but none provides total coverage of all known vulnerabilities, so they can provide a false sense of security.

There are two styles of security scanners, which should be regarded as complementary, and together they provide a richer set of vulnerability information:

1. Network scanners report on vulnerabilities that can only be accessed across the network. They are relatively easy to set up and comprehensively report on all vulnerabilities, large or small. Reports from these tools present details of the host IP addresses, operating-system versions, Web server product details, existence of standard scripts and facilities, port numbers and the services available on those ports, and so on.

2. Host-centric scanners rely on a central controller program that communicates with scanner agents installed on the hosts to be assessed. These agents provide an insider's view of the host and obviously pose a security vulnerability in their own right! Reports from these tools present host configuration vulnerabilities and identify the exposed resources that are liable to be attacked. These cover such problems as file privileges, user-account integrity, password strength, and many others determined by user-defined parameters.

The reports produced by these tools vary dramatically from overly long textual reports to color-coded graphical displays of prioritized vulnerabilities with executive summaries, gory technical detail, and drill-downs at intermediate levels. Beyond thoroughness, an important consideration when choosing such tools is the usability and usefulness of the reports they produce. Obtaining and presenting the information on these reports are the purposes of using the tool in the first place, so make sure you examine examples of all of the output that the tools can produce.

One final reporting issue is that the severity of some vulnerabilities may be overstated in some tools. Some reported problems might take hours of research to understand before a system administrator finally decides they are too trivial and time consuming to correct. Some obscure anomalies may not be well documented by the tool and can be impossible to research elsewhere. A tool vendor who plays it safe by overstating some priorities could potentially waste a lot of your time.

In comparison with manual inspection and analysis of the reports, the setup and execution of the scans may take no time at all. Be careful to set aside enough time in your plans to read, interpret, and evaluate the reports thoroughly.

Penetration Testing

Penetration tests aim to demonstrate that within a short period an intrusion can be achieved and that a system is vulnerable to attack. Most attempted Internet attacks are performed by uninventive script kiddies. There are a wide range of capabilities between script kiddies (who know little) and determined attackers who have in-depth networking experience and programming knowledge. Somewhere in between, there are the casual hackers. These are probably the main threat to Web sites. Typically, a determined attacker will spend up to 3 days trying to crack a site [6], so penetration testers are usually given approximately 3 days to achieve an exploit. If the test does not expose a vulnerability, one can reasonably assume the site is secure from this kind of attacker (assuming your testers are as competent as the attacker, of course).

Terms of Reference

Terms of reference for a penetration test should be prepared. These define the rules of engagement or behavior for the test team. In effect, these are a contract between the client of the penetration service and the testers. The terms of reference should clearly state the limitations, constraints, liabilities, and indemnification considerations of the penetration activities of the testers. The penetration attacks may cause disruption to the client's existing infrastructure and IT services, so it is essential that the terms of reference grant permission to perform the tests and indicate that the testers are not liable for any disruptions, loss, or damages. Two articles by Nancy Simpson give useful guidance on creating penetration test rules for behavior and a sample form [14, 15].

Clearly, the testers simulate the scanning and probing that a real attacker might attempt. The testers will pursue the areas of most weakness and potential for damage and, if the client requires, will try to remain undetected. Real attackers might spend only a few days trying to crack a site, so in principle, the testers should be given at least as long (if not longer) to do their worst. Of course, this assumes your testers are as skilled as the potential attackers. Bear in mind that it is unlikely that all of the potential vulnerabilities of your site will be identified in a penetration test.

Terms of reference should define the level of knowledge the testers are allowed to have prior to the test. The three levels are typically as follows:

1. *Zero information (or blind-IP testing):* The test team starts with no information about the target environment, so the team must perform some initial information gathering to get started. Zero-information tests simulate a real attack by an outsider at a remote location.

2. *Partial information:* You provide information about the target that capable attackers might reasonably be expected to obtain for themselves. This speeds up the test by giving the testers a head start and so reduces the cost of the test. You might also provide such information to the testers if there are specific hosts you wish them to attack. You might provide the testers with security policy or network diagrams to get them started.

3. *Full information:* The test team is given access to all information it requires, making its members as well informed as internal employees. This form of test simulates attacks by internal staff having an intimate knowledge of the target.

Penetration Test Goals

The objectives of the penetration test can be defined in terms of the time required to perform an exploit. That is, the testers might be given so many hours to achieve a defined goal. If they fail to achieve that goal, the system might be deemed acceptably secure. The following are typical goals that might be set in the terms of reference:

- Gaining access to resources, which are typically restricted files or data;
- Altering restricted files or data;
- Executing system or application software programs or transactions;
- Gaining access to user accounts;
- Gaining access to root, administrator, or supervisor privileges;
- Gaining access to network management facilities;
- Demonstrating ability to control resources, such as account, operating system, or networking resources.

The goals should be defined so that if the testers fail to meet these goals, you can reasonably expect to be confident that the site is secure. Again, this assumes that the testers are competent enough to stand a realistic chance of achieving these goals on an insecure system.

Attack Methodology

There are many variations on the attack methodology summarized earlier. The test team will, however, tend to follow a standard sequence of activities, which includes footprinting, enumeration, gaining access, and exploitation. The attacks can be external (i.e., performed from a remote site, usually the testers lab) to simulate an external Internet attacker or internal to simulate an attack by an insider.

Penetration testers use the same or similar automated scanning tools as security assessors to identify points of entry visible to external Internet users. They try to penetrate the firewalls and identify vulnerabilities inside the technical infrastructure and to exploit unknown or unauthorized devices and systems on the target network, as well as on remote access servers, and so forth. Other vulnerable points are servers that run file, e-mail, Web, directory, remote access, database, and other application services. Having identified a vulnerability, the testers will then attempt to exploit it, typically by demonstrating how control over restricted resources can be obtained.

Testers should keep a log of their activities so that all vulnerabilities can be identified and, when they are remedied, rechecked to ensure that the remedial action has worked. At the end of testing, the test team provides a report presenting the results of the test and recommendations for appropriate remedial action to eliminate the vulnerabilities that have been discovered. A sample report that summarizes the specific results of a penetration test appears on the Corecom Web site [16].

The Value of Penetration Testing

Penetration tests are popular because of their obvious association with clandestine, espionage-like approaches, but these tests can only provide a partial defense against security flaws in your Web site. Because their goal is to compromise security, testers focus only on the "low hanging fruit." Their aim is not to find all of the system's vulnerabilities, and testers may not necessarily report on all of the exploits they have attempted. All a penetration test proves is that a system can be compromised in some way; it does not necessarily provide any information on other potential vulnerabilities. Penetration tests are useful when there are fears that a site is insecure, but hard evidence is required. Penetration test reports are often used to justify the addition of resources to security efforts.

If in your project you plan to perform both security assessments (or audits) and penetration tests, it is worth using different people (with different tools) to perform these two activities. If the recommendations of a security assessment are implemented, using the same staff (or company) to perform penetration testing is not likely to reveal new exposures. Different testers will approach the penetration testing from a fresh viewpoint and probably use different (or their own) scanning tools. This is much more likely to expose holes that were not considered before. If you have an adequate budget and are particularly concerned, you might consider using more than one penetration testing team. A second team may discover more or different vulnerabilities and so strengthen the coverage further.

Currently, penetration testing is probably more focused on network and host vulnerabilities. As scanning tools become more sophisticated, the emphasis of penetration testing is likely to focus more on application vulnerabilities. These vulnerabilities are caused as much by poor application-programming practices and poor user-interface and dialog design, as well as overreliance on the naiveté of end users. As e-commerce Web sites become all-pervasive, crooks and terrorists will turn to these application vulnerabilities and use the standard browser interface to steal money or bring down sites. The skills required to seek out application vulnerabilities will tend more and more to be business knowledge and application design and the ability to build crook-friendly browsers rather than deep technical insight into networking and operating system vulnerabilities.

Tools for Security Testing

Table 14.3 provides a list of scanning and attacker tools.

Table 14.3
Tools for Security Testing

Tool	URL
Scanners	
BindView	http://www.bindview.com
Chknull	http://www.nmrc.org/files/netware/chknull.zip
CyberCop Scanner by NAI	http://www.nai.com
Firewalk	http://www.packetfactory.net/firewalk/
Hping	http://www.kyuzz.org/antirez
Network Security Hotfix Checker	http://www.shavlik.com
System Scanner, Internet Scanner	http://www.iss.net
Security Analyst	http://www.intrusion.com
Nessus Port Scanner	http://www.nessus.org
Network Mapper (Nmap)	http://www.insecure.org/nmap
WinScan	http://www.prosolve.com
Solarwinds	http://www.solarwinds.net
Strobe	http://www.hack-net.com
Udpscan	http://www.technotronic.com
WebTrends Security Analyzer	http://www.webtrends.com
Tool Web Sites	
Hacking Exposed	http://www.hackingexposed.com
Hackers Club	http://www.hackersclub.com
New Order	http://neworder.box.sk
Prosolve	http://www.prosolve.com
Security Focus	http://www.securityfocus.com
Technotronic	http://www.technotronic.com

References

[1] Scambray, J., S. McClure, and G. Kurtz, *Hacking Exposed: Network Security Secrets and Solutions*, Berkeley, CA: Osborne/McGraw Hill, 2001.

[2] Sanctum, Inc., "Web Perversion Demonstration," http://www.sanctuminc.com/demo/hacking_demo_v1200.html, 2002.

[3] Himanen, P., *The Hacker Ethic*, London, UK: Secker and Warburg, 2001.

[4] Stephens, A., "Script Kiddies: What Are They and What Are They Doing?" http://www.sans.org/infosecFAQ/hackers/kiddies.htm, 2002.

[5] Kessler, G. C., "Defenses Against Distributed Denial of Service Attacks," http://www.sans.org/infosecFAQ/threats/DDoS.htm, 2002.

[6] Traxler, J. (Ed.), *Hack Proofing Your Web Applications*, Rockland, MA: Syngress, 2001.

[7] CERT Coordination Center, http://www.cert.org/, 2002.

[8] NTBugtraq, http://www.ntbugtraq.com, 2002.

[9] Winkler, I., et al., "Audits, Assessments and Tests (Oh My)," four-part article series from *Information Security Magazine*, http://www.infosecuritymag.com archives, July–October 2000.

[10] Radcliff, D., "Sizing Up Security Services," http://www.computerworld.com/cwi/story/0,1199,NAV47-81_STO54345,00.html, 2002.

[11] InfoWorld Media Group, Inc, "The Ins and Outs of a Network Security Audit," http://www.infoworld.com/cgi-bin/displayTC.pl?/980316sb3-insouts.htm, 2002.

[12] "Certification for Information System Security Professional," CISSP, http://www.cissp.com, 2002.

[13] Mitre Corporation, "Common Vulnerabilities and Exposures," http://cve.mitre.org/, 2002.

[14] Simpson, N., "Guidelines for Developing Penetration 'Rules of Behavior'," http://www.sans.org/infosecFAQ/penetration/rules.htm, 2002.

[15] Simpson, N., "Penetration Test Sample Rules of Behavior," http://rr.sans.org/penetration/Nancy_Simpson_Enclosure_GSEC.doc, 2002.

[16] Corecom, Inc., "Sample Penetration Test Report," http://hhi.corecom.com/~wg/foundstone/index.html, 2002.

Further Reading

University of Oulu, "Glossary of Vulnerability Testing Terminology," http://www.ee.oulu.fi/research/ouspg/sage/glossary/, 2002.

World Wide Web Consortium, "Security FAQ," http://www.w3.org/Security/Faq/, 2002.

SecurityFocus, http://www.securityfocus.com, 2002 (discussions and archives of security related material).

Nomad Mobile Research Center, Web FAQ, http://www.nmrc.org/faqs/www/index.html, 2002.

15

Large-Scale Integration Testing

Overview

Table 15.1 describes the risks addressed by large-scale integration (LSI) testing. Here, the term *systems* refers to the collection of integrated systems comprising the new system or systems under development, other legacy or infrastructure systems, and external systems (e.g., banks or partnering organizations). In essence, the risks associated with LSI are the same as those we tackled using transaction link testing in Chapter 11, but the interfaces we are concerned with here exist at a higher level between multiple systems and between systems and the business process. Integration is an often misunderstood concept because the integration process starts almost as soon as coding begins. You could say that integration starts when we have two lines of code: The second line of code must be integrated with the first. Integration might be said to end when we have built our system and installed it in an environment with its interfacing systems and have tested them. We suggest, however, that there is a further, final stage of integration (or at least integration testing) that aims to ensure that the systems as built integrate with the business processes of the users of those systems.

In an e-commerce application the scope of LSI testing might cover integration with external banks or credit-card processing systems, product wholesalers or distributors, as well as internal legacy systems. In a business-to-business application you might have to integrate your system to collaborating peer organizations or to an electronic marketplace where your system is one of many to be integrated with a central system. The objectives of LSI

Table 15.1

Risks Addressed by LSI

ID	Risk	Test Objective	Technique
L1	Systems are not integrated (data transfer).	Demonstrate that systems are integrated and perform data transfer correctly.	Systems integration testing (SIT)
L2	Systems are not integrated (transfer of control).	Demonstrate that systems are integrated; transfer of control with required parameters is done correctly.	SIT
L3	Interfaces fail when used for an extended period.	Demonstrate that interfaces can be continuously used for an extended period.	SIT. These checks might also be performed as part of reliability or failover testing (Chapter 12).
L4	Systems are not integrated (data does not reconcile across interfaces).	Demonstrate that systems are integrated; data transferred across interfaces is consistently used (e.g., currency, language, metrics, timings, accuracy, tolerances).	SIT
L5	Systems are not synchronized (data transfers are not triggered or are triggered at the wrong time or multiple times).	Demonstrate that data transfers are triggered correctly.	SIT
L6	Objects or entities that exist in multiple systems do not reconcile across systems.	Demonstrate that the states of business objects are accurately represented across the systems that hold data on the objects.	Business integration testing (BIT)
L7	Systems are not integrated with the business (supply-chain) process.	Demonstrate that the systems integrate with business processes and support the supply-chain process.	BIT

Table 15.1 (continued)

ID	Risk	Test Objective	Technique
L8	Planned back-end business processes do not support the Web front-end.	Demonstrate that the supply-chain processes are workable and support the business objective.	BIT
L9	Integrated systems used by the same staff have inconsistent user interfaces or behavior for similar or related tasks.	Demonstrate that users experience consistent behavior across systems while performing similar or related tasks.	BIT These checks might also be performed during collaborative usability inspections (Chapter 13).

testing remain consistent even though the technologies and application areas vary considerably. Sometimes, the term *interoperability testing* is used in place of LSI testing. Interoperability describes how well systems must collaborate to deliver functionality to support a business process; however, we will use the term *LSI testing* in this chapter.

The notion of *fit* is appropriate for component-to-component integration, system-to-system integration and system(s)-to-business-process integration. We have conducted business integration testing (BIT) on many client projects where user acceptance was (at least partially) based on the results of these tests. Using the same integration framework for user acceptance makes test planning easier, and business management will support this activity because they can understand how it will give them confidence that the delivered service will work.

We are not suggesting that BIT is the same as user acceptance testing. Rather, we expect that in many organizations, the final stages of LSI testing provide some confidence to users that the system will work as they require. If you are asked to plan an acceptance test for your users, we expect that the techniques we describe in BIT in particular will play some part in your planning.

We separate LSI testing into two stages because the risks and test objectives differ. Systems integration testing (SIT) is more technically oriented because it is at this point that the physical connections between systems are established and used for the first time. The tests are somewhat more white-box-oriented in that the physical interfaces between systems must be understood enough to allow test designers to prepare tests that cover them. BIT is more focused on the paths through business processes to ensure that the integrated systems provide seamless support to the user activity throughout.

Integration Knowledge Is Critical To Success

In larger projects, the lack of integration knowledge is the first major barrier to conducting LSI tests. (The second major barrier, of course, is the difficulty in building LSI test environments.) Integration knowledge can be difficult to obtain because the information is usually (1) buried in huge documentation sets for custom-built systems; (2) not available for off-the-shelf components; and (3) undocumented and residing in the heads of experienced staff that maintain legacy systems. The dispersed nature of this knowledge makes it very difficult to define the scope of the testing to be done for coverage purposes. It also makes it difficult or impossible to specify tests that exercise the interfaces of concern. Although many organizations face the challenge of LSI in most of their projects, LSI testing is not well documented in the testing literature, unfortunately.

An Example of LSI

As an example where a systematic approach to LSI was required, consider a recent project where LSI testing was a major challenge. An Internet-banking application being built by a major European bank had 10 major interfaces to new and legacy systems. The development of the core functionality was outsourced. The supplier, working with a customer test team was responsible for all testing up to and including system testing. Subsystem and system testing were performed on the supplier site with all interfaces to other, external systems stubbed out. The customer had to perform LSI testing in their own test environment where interfaces to the bank's legacy test environment and other newly developed support systems could be installed. LSI required its own separate stage because of the complexity of the overall technical architecture. It took a lot of planning and preparation, as well as a significant investment in technical infrastructure, to implement.

You would imagine that in mature organizations, the systems and the interfaces between them would be well understood and documented. In this project, the information existed, but much of the knowledge relating to the legacy systems and their interfaces was all in the heads of the developers who maintained the systems to be integrated. (Most banks have hundreds of systems to maintain so this was no surprise.) The technical designers who specified the interfaces to the new system relied heavily on the undocumented knowledge of key staff. Developers on the project obtained the information they needed at a working level by liaising closely with these key staff. (Typically, they wrote code, but did not document their findings.) When it came to preparing LSI tests, the testers had to reinterview these people to track down the information required.

The financial value of the transactions that the system would process was huge, and the accurate reporting of a customer's current account balance was critical. The summary information presented to end users in their browsers was derived from detailed data drawn from several legacy systems, some having different processing cycles (24-hour batch, 2-hour batch, and real-time). Because of this, there was concern that the final figures presented to end users in their browsers might not reconcile with the raw data held in the legacy banking systems, and compliance with these reconciliation rules became acceptance criteria for the system as a whole. This was expected to be a difficult challenge for the testers, and so it turned out to be. A systematic approach to LSI testing was essential.

Integration Analysis

Over the last 10 years, we have been involved in many LSI projects. In this time, we have developed our own systems integration analysis methodology called SIAM [1], for dealing with large, complex technical environments where our client's need was to integrate and test systems, including packages, custom-built systems, and legacy systems. In this section, we describe a simplified version of this methodology and present three techniques that we use in an activity called integration analysis. In complex environments where a large number of interfaces are to be tested, a systematic approach to the identification of interfaces and the transactions that exercise them was essential. Because the integration knowledge is extracted from many sources, it is a good idea to get your integration inventories reviewed by the development project teams. There are three techniques for documenting integration knowledge:

1. Identification of systems and system-to-system interfaces and the compilation of integration inventories;

2. Identification and documentation of high-level business transactions that are dependent on these interfaces or trigger their execution;

3. Analysis of the use of data across multiple systems for the purpose of tracking data flows and reconciliation.

Planning and preparing an LSI test that addresses the risks of concern normally require information from all three dimensions: interfaces, transactions, and reconciliations. The integration analysis takes two views of systems and interfaces:

1. A technical or system view (to prepare for SIT).
2. A business view (to prepare for BIT).

The system view and the business view are similar in approach: The system view captures interfaces and transactions in terms of physical connections (files or messages) and system transactions; the business view captures interfaces in terms of business entities being transferred between applications via business transactions.

Inventories

The inventories stage is primarily concerned with data gathering. The first objective is to identify the systems that are in scope. From the information provided by technical staff, we can build a picture of how the systems interact and derive an inventory of the interfaces or connections between the systems. Assembling information on the systems from the business perspective allows us to build up knowledge about how they are used within the business process. The specific inventories we normally prepare are listed in Table 15.2.

A sample application interface inventory is shown in Table 15.3. Each interface appears only once, but identifies two systems. Clearly, in a tabular representation, every interface could be described in two ways, with the systems appearing as either A or B and the direction reversed for the alternate representation. Conventionally, we would designate the system that initiates the transfer across each interface as System A. This does not affect the overall content of the table, of course.

Transaction Analysis

This stage has two sets of objectives, depending on whether a business- or systems-oriented view is required:

1. *Systems perspective:* From the systems point of view, the objective is to derive a set of system transactions that use or cause the

Table 15.2

Deliverables from the Inventories Stage of the Integration Analysis

System inventory	This is the list of systems in scope for LSI testing. This may include manual procedures or departmental systems to which there are manual interfaces.
Direct interfaces (the system view)	This is the set of system-to-system interfaces in scope. Normally, we collect the system names, the nature of the interface, the data items transferred, the quantity transferred, the frequency of transfer, and the trigger that causes it to occur. These interfaces are subject to coverage in SIT.
Application interfaces (the business view)	Whereas the direct interfaces reflect the technical transfers of physical data between systems, application interfaces reflect the logical business entities or objects that are moved between systems. One application interface may represent multiple direct Interfaces. These interfaces are subject to coverage in BIT.
Manual rekeys	We record all manual data transfers between systems: The source and target systems, the data rekeyed, the format of the data received, who performs the rekeying, and when it is performed are captured.
Other deliverables	Context diagrams show each system and its interfaces (direct or application) with its neighboring systems. A systems interconnections diagram presents the entire application architecture. It is based on the combination of all context diagrams.

Table 15.3

Sample Application Interface Inventory (A Partial Listing)

System A	Direction	System B	Data	Trigger Process
Web front end	Both	Stores	Stock check request	Stock check
Web front end	Both	Card processor	Credit check	Credit check
Web front end	A → B	Card processor	Payment request	Confirm order
Web front end	B → A	Card processor	Payment confirmation	Confirm order
Web front end	A → B	Stores	Order details	Confirm order
Web front end	A → B	Sales ledger	Order details	Confirm order
Web front end	A → B	User mailbox	Order confirmation	Confirm order
Sales ledger	A → B	General ledger	Payment journal	Confirm order
Stores	A → B	Work orders	Stock allocation	Fill order

movement of data across an interface. Knowing which transactions trigger the movement of data will ultimately allow us to identify the physical interfaces being used when business transactions are performed.

2. *Business perspective:* From the business view the objective is to derive a set of business transactions that can be used to describe the processes that exercise the application interfaces. Business transaction–flow diagrams document how the business makes use of its integrated systems and identifies the business transactions that depend on specific systems integration (or are affected by integration failures).

Transaction flows describe the paths of linked activities, systems, and events involved with business processes. The method is very similar to the transaction-flow testing approach documented by Beizer in his books [2, 3], but in this context, we focus on transactions that depend on system-to-system interfaces. Beizer suggests that a transaction is a unit of work seen from the system's point of view. In the context of SIT, a transaction is a unit of work seen from the point of view of multiple systems and causes data flows between those systems. In the context of BIT, a transaction is a unit of work seen through the eyes of one or more users and represents a path through the business process that involves the use of multiple, interfacing systems to complete. A business-oriented transaction flow typically covers multiple system transactions, user activities, and possibly manual processes also.

Figure 15.1 shows a sample transaction-flow diagram with a series of two decisions and four processes that invoke the data flows indicated on the right of the figure. Each of these data flows would have been documented in an application interface inventory.

The flows can be documented as simple flowcharts with decisions and processes as normal. People or systems can make decisions and execute processes. Each element on the transaction-flow diagram may have associated data flows:

- Users might perform a system transaction that causes a data flow to occur, or they might execute a query on the system to obtain the data required to make a business decision. The query might cause a data flow.

- If the system executes a process or makes a decision, this may cause data flows in just the same way.

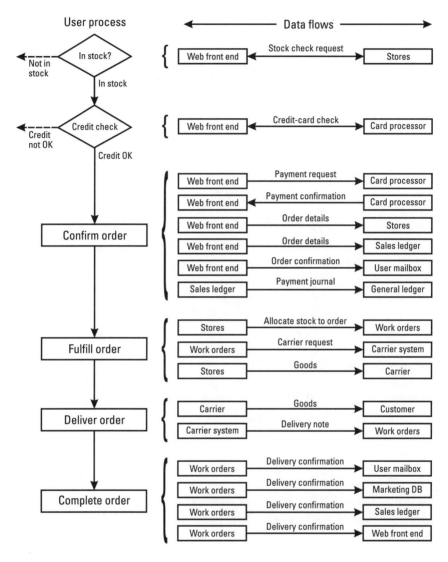

Figure 15.1 Sample transaction-flow diagram.

Each decision or process may therefore invoke data flows between systems or people. The diagrams relate data flows to the decisions or processes that cause them and can be prepared at either the system or business level.

There are two useful coverage targets we can define:

1. Data-flow coverage (we need to exercise each data flow at least once).
2. Transaction branch coverage (we need to exercise each decision outcome at least once).

Transaction branch coverage subsumes data-flow coverage in the same way that branch coverage subsumes statement coverage in path testing. We can sensitize the transaction-flow diagrams by tracing paths through them. These business scenarios identify events and decisions to be made and the test data required to implement them. Single-shot tests may be prepared to exercise single data flows, but it is more common to trace paths through the diagram. These paths represent end-to-end business scenarios that might involve different groups of users accessing different systems in sequence.

Transaction-flow diagrams can and should be prepared early in projects. Because they are based on relatively high-level business requirements and very specific interface information, it should be possible to prepare them as soon as a technical architecture is documented. The diagrams are very useful in the early stages of a project as they allow users (and technical staff) to understand the relationship between business transactions and the system interfaces. They can therefore be very useful when reviewing the technical architecture and the design of business processes being changed or developed for the new system.

Business Object Definition

For BIT planning, the purpose of business object definition is to derive meaningful definitions of objects that reflect the real-world entities of interest to business users. A business object might be a product, a person, an invoice, an airline flight, or a theater booking, for example. The analysis for SIT is similar, but some of the objects you identify may have no meaning to the system's users. System objects are like the objects designed and implemented by developers in an object-oriented system that are reused or recreated in multiple systems.

Real-world objects are either moved around the business literally, or information about the object is passed around between data stores and systems. Figure 15.1 identifies flows of data between systems, but also includes the delivery of the ordered goods by a carrier as a data flow. Objects are important because they allow the business to visualize movements of data between systems in terms of the objects described by the data. Business documentation will tend to describe processes, events, and data in terms of these objects.

When the business objects are defined, these can be related back to the transaction-flow diagram. The flow of object data through systems can now be traced and sets of test cases that cover the entire life cycle of these objects can now be derived. The full definition of a real-world object might include many data attributes. When an object is first created in one system, only a subset of those attributes might be set. As data relating to that object is transferred to another system, this system might use (read) or update existing attributes, or create new attributes for that object. The full set of data that describes that object will reside in multiple systems, and some data will be duplicated.

Table 15.4 shows an example of business object definition. The table resembles a create, read, update, and delete (CRUD) matrix for a table in a database where different functions can perform different actions on data in a table. A business object definition enhances this to span multiple systems at the level of each object attribute.

Table 15.4
Sample Business Object Definition

Object: Customer Order	System				
Attribute	Web Front End	Stores	Card Processor	Sales Ledger	Words Order
OrderID	C*	R†		R	R
CustomerID	C	R		R	R
Value	C			R	R
OrderDate	C	R		R	R
ScheduledDeliveryDate	C	R			U‡
ActualDeliveryDate	R			R	C
Status	C				U
DiscountApplied	C			R	

*Create
†Read
‡Update

Optionally, the cells in the business object definition can contain the processes that create, read, update, or delete the data attribute. We can use these tables to help prepare business object life cycles that represent the flow of data related to an object through the various systems. A life cycle describes the normal sequence of events from the birth of the object to its death. There are always variations on these normal life cycles, however. For example, an order can be placed, but not confirmed, or an order could be cancelled before delivery, and so forth. Using these normal and alternative life cycles, we can define a set of covering paths through the systems to give users confidence that the flow of data through systems is consistent, and we can prepare tests and reconciliations accordingly.

Some business objects represent quantities of money or assets that exist in various systems. Examples would be items of stock, invoices, and payments. In these cases, the aggregate values of orders, invoices, and payments across the multiple systems should reconcile. Where such reconciliations are required, we usually execute a number of transactions that cover the various life cycles of the objects to be reconciled, then derive formulas and procedures to create both detailed and summary reports on the contents of systems both before and after the test transactions are executed.

In the most general case, the tests that are implemented follow three stages:

1. Reports that extract the values for selected objects are produced for all of the systems in scope. The data on these reports should reconcile with one another.

2. Transactions that create objects, transfer object data, and manipulate objects are executed. These tests might cover the entire life cycle of objects or just one stage.

3. The same reports that extract the object data are produced and reconciled to each other and to the pretest reports.

It is usually simpler to execute these three stages during selected phases of an object's life cycle and to run the tests in a series of cycles that execute transactions, produce reports, and reconcile. Whether these tests are executed for SIT or BIT, the same procedure is used, although for SIT, some of the reports might be direct printouts of the contents of database tables or interface files. Often, you need to involve technical support staff or developers to extract this data for you or to write custom reports to your specifications.

SIT

To plan SIT, the tester needs to know quite a lot about the physical interfaces between systems. Only by knowing the following about the internals can the tester design tests that will exercise these interfaces adequately:

- The details of the internals of the interface;
- The nature of the system-to-system dialogs;
- How to exercise the interface from the application user interface or batch processes;
- How to create test data to exercise the interface;
- How to find evidence that the interface works.

We said earlier that one of the problems of LSI testing is that it can be difficult to find details of interfaces. It's not just the interface details that cause problems. It may be that there is no documentation available at all for the legacy systems. In our experience, the LSI test team often has to write documentation describing a system's interfaces (at least in summary), as well as the test plan to exercise them. Once the integration inventories are prepared, the tester follows a simple process to define the integration test:

- For each interface, identify the dialogs between systems and which business or system events trigger them to work.
- Derive test cases for success and failure to negotiate each step in the dialog.
- Derive test cases from the interface data validation and use descriptions to ensure that valid data is transmitted, invalid data is rejected, and the storage and use of data in each interfacing system reconcile.
- Define your test environment and infrastructure needs early, so they are met in good time.

Integration tests tend to fall into one of two types: They are either very simple (and easily automated) or they are very complicated and have to be executed manually. When the tests are executed, early tests focus on the correctness of the interface calls. Later tests (usually automated) focus on memory leaks, loss of synchronization between systems, and failure and recovery of clients, servers, or the network. These automated tests that run for an extended period are similar to those performed in the reliability/failover tests described in Chapter 12. In some situations, it might be possible to merge these tests and run them in one stage.

BIT[1]

The primary aim of BIT is to provide final confirmation that systems, processes, and people work as an integrated whole to meet an organization's objectives and provide a sophisticated, efficient service to its customers. BIT takes a process- and people-oriented view of the entire system. It is possible to define specific test objectives for BIT at a somewhat lower level than those listed in Table 15.1. Table 15.5 summarizes the key aspects of a total business solution that should be validated in testing.

BIT objectives can span a large range of issues. For example, some of the objectives listed in Table 15.5 overlap with the usability and service test objectives in Chapters 12 and 13. The problems encountered during BIT can relate, however, to aspects other than the software system. Typically, the business process itself might need adjustment. Perhaps a new process needs to have rough edges removed; perhaps an existing process needs changing to reflect a new way of doing business. Alternatively, the training provided to end users might be the problem: perhaps users need more detailed instruction in how to use particular aspects of the system. BIT is a more rounded approach to finding faults in system implementations, not just the software.

BIT differs from SIT in that it is more likely to be associated with user acceptance. Assuming that the technical testers have demonstrated that the interfaces between the new system and other systems work in SIT, the imperative for a business wishing to deploy the new system is to ensure the system supports the intended business activity. For example, if a system supports the on-line purchase and delivery of books, the following questions must be addressed:

- Can a customer search for a book, add it to a shopping basket, and place an order?
- Can a customer's credit card be validated and can payment be authorized and processed successfully?

---

1. This section is partially derived from a paper on business simulation testing [4] available on the Web at http://www.evolutif.co.uk.

Table 15.5
BIT Objectives

Category	Test Objective
Processes	• The business processes define the logical, step-by-step activities of the desired tasks. • For each stage in the process, the inputs (information, resources) are available at the right time in the right place to complete the task. • The outputs (documents, events) are sufficiently well defined that they may be produced reliably, completely, and consistently. • Paths to be taken through the business process are efficient (i.e., there are no repeated tasks or convoluted paths). • The tasks in the business process are sufficiently well defined to enable people to perform the tasks consistently. • The process can accommodate both common and unusual variations in inputs to enable tasks to be completed.
People	• People are familiar with the processes such that they can perform the tasks consistently, correctly, and without supervision or assistance. • People can cope with the variety of circumstances that arise while performing the tasks. • People feel comfortable with the processes (i.e, they don't need assistance, support or direction in performing their tasks). • Customers perceive the operation and processes as being slick, effective, and efficient. • The training given to users provides them with adequate preparation for the task in hand.
Systems	• The system provides guidance through the business process and leads them through the tasks correctly. • The system is consistent with the business process in terms of information required and provided. • The level of prompting within the system is about right (i.e., it provides sufficient prompting without treating experienced users like first-time users). • Response times for system transactions are compatible with the tasks that the system supports (i.e., response times are fast where task durations are short). • The users' perception is that the system helps them to do their job, rather than hindering them. • Users experience consistent behavior across systems while performing similar or related tasks.

Derived from [4].

- Does the legacy order processing system receive the on-line order accurately?
- Is the book in stock, located in the warehouse, packed, labeled, and dispatched correctly?
- Are order confirmation, progress notification, and thank-you e-mail messages sent at the right time? Do they reliably reach the customer?
- Are payments processed promptly, accurately, and reliably?

Ultimately, the sponsors of the system want to know whether the new system meets the cardinal business objectives of the project. Testers must develop and execute selected business scenarios that will exercise the integrated systems to provide evidence that they support the business process in its entirety.

Compared with SIT testing, BIT may take a smaller number of test cases to give confidence that the system works correctly because the number of tests should be limited to a finite number of business scenarios. However, BIT alone may not provide enough information on which to base acceptance of a system. Users will certainly want to see many more system transactions executed to ensure that the core functionality of the new Web system works. Acceptance is discussed further in Chapter 19.

Challenges

A major difficulty in staging LSI tests is that they tend to require the entire technical architecture and coherent data to be set up in the interfacing systems. In large organizations, the legacy systems may be very large and complex and undergoing enhancements and bug-fixing activity in their own right. In large development programs, multiple project teams may be delivering separate applications to be integrated and tested by a program integration test team. The development and maintenance teams may be extremely busy. When you ask for support in the implementation of LSI tests requiring interfaces between your test system and theirs, the effort and time required to do this may be significant. You need the data in their system to be consistent with the data in your own databases, but you may be limited to only one or two of the following options:

- They provide you with an empty database that you have to populate yourself (a task that may be beyond your capabilities or resource).

- They provide you with their own, self-consistent test data that does not match yours (and so could be unusable).

- They provide an extract from production data that may not match selections from other interfacing systems.

- They provide a full copy of production data that is so large it is unwieldy to use for testing.

Negotiation for access to and interfaces with legacy systems, coherent test data, and technical support may be difficult. Consequently, it is essential that these requirements be identified as early as possible in your project so that the plans of other groups and projects can be synchronized with your own. Of course, it is very likely that your plan will have to change to adapt to the pre-existing plans of these other groups. Because of the codependency of multiple projects on scarce technical resources, slippage in any of these projects is likely to cause problems. LSI testing often consists of periods of high-intensity test execution separated by long waits for environments or technical support to become available. For this reason, LSI testing in large environments benefits from thorough planning and preparation. If your test plans are comprehensive and flexible, you will be better able to cope with untimely nonavailability of environments and technical staff.

When a new system is written and system tested, the interfaces with other newly developed systems, legacy systems, and external systems might all be stubbed out. The system designers would design stubs to simulate these interfaces because interfacing systems might not be available in time for the system test. This is common when development (and system testing) is outsourced. If the system test will take place on the supplier's site, it might be impossible to set up the system-to-system interfaces on their site. Later LSI testing might be conducted in an incremental way as interfaces become available. The system designers need to think through the build and integration sequence so that (1) they have stubs for all interfaces that need them, and (2) they can refine the stubs to do more than make an identical, simple response again and again. If interfaces are not going to be available until very late in the project, it might be worth building stubs that can simulate an interface in a more realistic way to allow the test designers to prepare more thorough LSI tests. Designers, developers, and testers should liaise closely to work out how the build and integration process will work and what level of sophistication needs to built into the stubs.

References

[1]   Systeme Evolutif, "SIAM: System Integration Analysis Methodology," Internal methodology document, 1995.

[2]   Beizer, B., *Software System Testing and Quality Assurance*, New York: Van Nostrand Reinhold, 1984.

[3]   Beizer, B., *Black Box Testing*, New York: John Wiley & Sons, 1995.

[4]   Gerrard, P., "Business Simulation Testing," http://www.evolutif.co.uk, 2002.

16

Postdeployment Monitoring

Suppose you were browsing an e-commerce site and thinking about using it to buy an airline ticket for the first time, but it failed while you were searching for a flight. It's not likely that you would report a problem to the company running the site. After all, it's not your problem—it's theirs. If a store is closed or service is slow or difficult to use, you just walk away and visit the next store on the street. It's the same with Web sites. Search engines and portals offer you a multitude of Web sites matching your search criteria, so it is easy to use the back button and click on a different link. With some e-business sites, this is less likely. If your on-line bank account fails, you probably would report the fault and complain, too: The bank has your money, and you want access to it now. For the most part, however, we cannot rely on users of our Web site to report problems.

With this background, it is sensible to monitor your site in production so that you are alerted to problems on your Web site before your customers encounter them. You might not think this is a testing issue, but monitoring a live site involves much the same technology, approach, and software tools. Some of our clients adopt what has been called a continuous testing approach. In these companies, one of the test manager's roles is to oversee the continuous monitoring of the tested service in production. One could look at the role of testers as a continuous monitoring activity, from requirements through development, deployment, and production. In some organizations, this arrangement might make sense. Under any circumstance, where a dedicated team takes ownership of a Web site to provide technical support, the monitoring tools would be a key part of their service. This short chapter outlines the main options for monitoring your live production Web site. The main decision to make is whether you monitor your live site yourself or you outsource the task.

In theory, you could reuse the automated tests that you prepared during the development stage and execute these from a remote site to execute test transactions on your live servers. You probably want to base this test tool host machine on a site connected through a different ISP to ensure ISP problems don't affect the monitoring system too. There are quite a few tools and services designed to perform monitoring tasks now available. Most sites use their internal network and system management tools to perform monitoring on their networks and servers internally and use remote monitoring services to do the rest. Your system and network administrators may already have tools that perform these monitoring functions on your infrastructure. This chapter is mainly concerned with remote monitoring tools and services, which are listed at the end of the chapter.

Remote Monitoring Services

There are now many companies offering continuous site monitoring. Some of the companies that previously offered HTML validation and download speed checking portals now offer simple availability and performance monitoring facilities. Most of the proprietary performance test tool vendors now offer more sophisticated availability- and performance monitoring by both simulating real-user activity and monitoring much of your technical infrastructure remotely.

For the simple services, prices can be free or as low as a few dollars per month to monitor a site or specific pages. Large sites requiring a comprehensive service may pay thousands of dollars per month. Most offerings include regular (e.g., 15-minute) checks and alerts in the form of SMS, e-mail, fax, or pager messages.

Types of Monitoring

Link and Page Download Speed Checking

The tools and services that perform these checks and assessments have already been described in Chapters 9, 10, and 13 and will not be described further. Refer to the references in those chapters for tool offerings.

Availability and Performance Monitoring

Availability and performance are most commonly monitored using remote tools and services. Although your system-management software might keep track of the status of your internal network and servers (and alert you to any failures), remote monitoring services are often used to detect availability or performance problems that a real user might encounter. Broadly, the remote monitoring services detect problems in four ways:

1. Remote servers can ping your Web servers across the Internet. A ping request is a message sent to a host simply requesting an acknowledgement. By tracking the ping responses (if your server responds at all), the remote server can report whether your servers are up and running and how quickly they respond.

2. Remote servers can send HTTP requests to tell whether the Web service is running on your Web servers.

3. Simple HTTP GETs of selected Web pages can tell whether pages are downloadable, and the download speed can be monitored over time.

4. Calls to server-based components or CGI programs can execute selected test transactions to ensure that connections to back-end systems are also operating properly. In this case, prepared test transactions are executed, and the response times are recorded and plotted over time.

The NetMechanic tool was used to produce the report extract shown in Table 16.1, which is based on an analysis of the Evolutif Web site. This example is typical of the reports that site monitoring services produce when they use simple ping and HTTP requests. The results are compared with NetMechanic's own internally calculated averages to give an indication of your site's relative speed.

Some monitoring services have remote agents based in many locations to provide comparative timings. Measurements may be taken from cities across the United States, Europe, and the Far East for example. Weekly and monthly trend reports may also be offered as part of the service.

More sophisticated tools can execute prepared test CGI transactions whose response times can be recorded and analyzed. Figure 16.1 shows a daily response time report for a Web transaction that seems to be getting slower day by day. If response times are gradually increasing in this way, it might indicate one of several problems:

Table 16.1
Sample Site Monitoring Report

Report for: http://www.evolutif.co.uk
Date: Thursday, September 28
Time: 6:00–13:00 USA Eastern Time
Server type: Microsoft-IIS/4.0
Overall rating: Fair

Performance Summary			
Event	**Your Server's Average**	**NetMechanic's Average**	**Percentile**
Host ping	190.34 msec	277.26 msec	27
DNS look up	0.18 sec	0.13 sec	9
Connect time	0.09 sec	1.11 sec	62
Download time (10K file)	0.50 sec	1.10 sec	37
Timeouts	0	—	—

Host ping:	Indicates the network speed between your server and ours
DNS look up:	Indicates the time required to look up your server's address in the DNS database
Connect time:	The time required to open a network connection to your server
Download time (10K file):	The time required to download a 10K file from your server
Number of timeouts:	The number of times your server failed to respond within 30 seconds

Produced using NetMechanic.com facility (with permission).

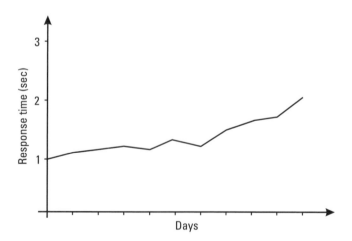

Figure 16.1 Daily response times getting worse over time.

- There is a memory leak somewhere in your system. Eventually, the software (or the server) will crash when all of the available memory is used up. Check the available memory of servers that have been up without a reboot for the period of the report, and monitor the process memory usage to identify the problem process or component.

- The number of simultaneous users of your service is increasing. The resources used by the users of your system may be consistent with previously run performance tests. If, however, the growth in usage or the demand on your system resources is greater than planned, you may have to perform some system optimization, upgrading, or redesign. If these options are impractical, you may have to restrict the number of users allowed on your systems.

- As databases grow in size with usage, the speed of updates and queries may slow. If the impact of database growth on response times is dramatic, this may indicate, for example, that some indexes have not been created or that the initial storage allocation or extent size of key tables are too small.

There are myriad possible causes of increasing response times. Even if you have performed a thorough performance test, it is possible that the system configuration as deployed does not match your test set up and, therefore, performs worse than expected. Especially in the early days after deployment, you should monitor response times very closely indeed.

Security Monitoring

When your system goes live, bug fixes and other maintenance activities may cause your technical infrastructure to undergo many changes. As your system configuration changes, the security precautions you have previously taken may be compromised. Further, new security vulnerabilities in popular software products on the market are appearing almost daily, and attackers become aware of them at the same time you do. Because Web sites are under constant threat from script kiddies and other attackers, critical Web sites are often monitored by remote monitoring services and alarmed by internally or externally run intruder detection systems.

Most security experts recommend that you redo security assessments regularly, perhaps every 3 months or so. It is also sensible to do spot checks (or continuous monitoring) on products you use to ensure you are not exposed when new vulnerabilities are publicized. Even if you register with one of the popular security vulnerability mailing lists, of course, the attackers are on the same e-mail lists as you are. When a new vulnerability alert is published, the attackers have a window of opportunity to exploit it before the affected sites install the patch or make the required configuration changes to eliminate it. If you choose a remote security monitoring service, choose one that appears to update its vulnerability database promptly so that your exposure is minimized.

One such service is the Security Space facility (http://www.security-space.com). The report extract in Table 16.2 is derived from a sample advanced

Table 16.2
Sample Security Monitoring Report Extract

Vulnerability Category Summary

The vulnerability category summary shows how the various issues that were reported are distributed across the different test categories.

Category	High	Med	Low	Other
CGI abuses				
DoS	1			
Windows	1	1	2	
Gain root remotely				
General			1	
Miscellaneous				1
RPC				
Remote file access				
FTP				
Backdoors				
Gain a shell remotely				
SMTP problems				
Firewalls				
Useless services				
Finger abuses				
SNMP				
NIS				
Total:	2	1	3	1

Vulnerability Title Summary

High-risk vulnerabilities
10394   SMB log-in
10204   rfpoison

Medium-risk vulnerabilities
10150   Using NetBIOS to retrieve information from a Windows host

Low-risk vulnerabilities
10398   SMB get domain SID
10397   SMB LanMan pipe server browse listing
10201   Relative IP identification number change

Other Items to be Considered
10287   Traceroute

From: Security Space, www.securityspace.com.

security audit report available from their Web site. Sophisticated services cover more vulnerabilities and provide detailed descriptions of both the vulnerabilities found and how the exposure may be eliminated or minimized. Less sophisticated services might only provide summary reports on a limited set of vulnerabilities.

Remote Monitoring Services and Tool Web Sites

The Web sites listed in Tables 16.3 and 16.4 provide information on the many remote Web site monitoring services and tools that are now available. In some cases, the vendors offer services using their own proprietary tools, some of which might also be marketed as stand-alone products. Included in the security monitoring services are some of the main vendors of managed security services that usually include vulnerability and intruder alarm systems. Many of these companies also offer security audit and configuration services.

Table 16.3
Available Security Monitoring Services

Service	URL
FoundScan Monitoring service	http://www.activis.com
Security Protection service	http://www.assessmentandrepair.com
Outsmart Services	http://www.coradiant.com
Managed Security Monitoring service	http://www.counterpane.com
Intrusion Detection Systems tools	http://www.cybersafe.com
Several Managed Security services	http://www.iss.net
SiteMonitoring service	http://www.mfn.com
Intrusion Detection Systems	http://www.nfr.com
Real-Time Security Monitoring service	http://www.riptech.com
ISensor Intrusion Detection/Prevention tools	http://www.secureworks.com
Network monitoring tool	http://www.securityspace.com
OnlineGuardian Monitoring service	http://www.ubizen.com
Intrusion Monitoring, Vigilance service	http://www.veritect.com
Vigilinx Monitoring service	http://www.vigilinx.com

Table 16.4
Availability and Performance Monitoring Services and Tools

Service or Tool Name	URL
Availability and performance monitoring service	http://www.1stwarning.com
247 SiteWatch Web site monitoring service	http://www.247sitewatch.com
AlertSite Web site monitoring service	http://www.alertsite.com
Web Performance Management service	http://www.appliant.com
Server, database, and Web page monitoring service	http://www.assessmentandrepair.com
Netsys network and service level management tool	http://www.cisco.com
WebMaster Pro Web site monitoring tool	http://www.coast.com
EcoSystems and PointForward, tools, and Web site monitoring service	http://www.compuware.com
OutSmart Web Performance Monitoring service	http://www.coradiant.com
Resolve network monitoring tool	http://www.crosskeys.com
AreYouThere Web site monitoring program	http://www.cyberspyder.com
Dotcom-Monitor Web site monitoring service	http://www.dotcom-monitor.com
FarSight, E-Monitor Web site monitoring service	http://www.empirix.com
SiteReliance, SiteSeer, SiteScope application and Web site monitoring	http://www.freshwater.com
Enterprise Perspective, Red Alert application and Web site monitoring service	http://www.keynote.com
LinkAlarm HTML link checking service	http://www.linkalarm.com
VitalSuite network monitoring tool	http://www.lucent.com
Topaz, ActiveWatch Web site performance and monitoring service	http://www.merc-int.com
SiteMonitoring application and Web site monitoring	http://www.mfn.com
Site Monitoring Service	http://www.netmechanic.com
NOCPulse Command Center application, network, system, and transaction monitoring software	http://www.nocpulse.com
Foglight application monitoring tool	http://www.quest.com
QoEtient performance, availability, reliability, and security monitoring service	http://www.qoetient.com
ReliAgility Web site monitoring service	http://www.reliagility.com
Care Services availability and performance monitoring service	http://www.siterock.com
TeamQuest Alert system performance monitoring tool	http://www.teamquest.com

Table 16.4 (continued)

Service or Tool Name	URL
Tivoli availability and performance management tool	http://www.tivoli.com
Uptimetools Web site monitoring service	http://www.uptimetools.com
Visual Uptime network monitoring tool	http://www.visualnetworks.com
AppMonitor, SiteMonitor application and Web site monitoring service	http://www.webmastersolutions.com
WebSite Availability Web site monitoring service	http://www.websiteavailability.com
Web site monitoring service	http://www.wspecialists.com

17

Tools for E-Business Testing

In Chapters 9 through 15, we discussed the techniques for testing Web-based systems and, at the end of each chapter, provided references to Web sites where further information about tools can be obtained. Of the 24 test types listed in Table 7.2, no less than 22 either must be done using a tool or, at least, there is tool support available. Some tools can be used for more than one type of testing, the most flexible being browser test execution tools as these can run (or at least support) nine of the test types. The following key categories of test tool are now available (previously listed in Chapter 7, page 115):

- Spelling and grammar checkers (SC);
- HTML validators (HV);
- Web accessibility checkers (WA);
- Browser compatibility checkers (BC);
- Link checkers (LC);
- Browser test execution tools (TE);
- Test drivers for server-based code (TD);
- Load and performance test tools (LP);
- Security scanning tools (SS).

Some proprietary tools combine more than one of the tool types. A common combination is test execution and link checking in a single tool, for example.

The functionality of many vendors' test execution tools is reused in their load and performance test tool offerings. Expect to see more sophisticated combinations in time. External site monitors haven't been included in the list because they are really services supported by the same tools above. The more sophisticated of these services might use several of the following: HTML validation, link checking, test execution, performance monitoring, and security scanning.

In this chapter we look at how browser test execution tools work because they are probably the most useful. They are also the most complex to implement effectively. We also discuss three potential sources for tools: proprietary, shareware, and freeware. Appendix B shows how dummy Web pages and simple self-built test execution tools can be a viable alternative to the proprietary tools in some situations.

Proprietary Test Execution Tools

Proprietary test execution tools for browser-based applications are widely available. Given the predominance of Microsoft Windows in both corporate and home environments, virtually all of these tools work on the Windows platforms. The test execution tools that drive browser applications work somewhat differently from the pre-existing GUI tools that drive VB or C++ applications. If you were to use an older GUI test tool to test a Web application through a browser, the test tool would see a browser window as just another Windows application, of course. The tool could see the browser menu options and command buttons, and mouse clicks on them would be captured without a problem. The links, buttons, graphics, and other visible objects inside the browser window would be invisible to the GUI test tool, however. The GUI test tools would see the browser window content as a simple bit map with no objects or controls on it at all, so you cannot use existing GUI test tools to drive browser-based Web applications.

The modern browser-based test execution tools have several refinements as compared with the GUI test tools:

- They recognize standard browser window objects and navigation controls.

- They can identify and follow HTML links.

- They recognize images, video clips, and other media objects and their attributes.

- They can manipulate HTML forms, fields, buttons, check boxes, and so on.

- They can recognize and manipulate browser plug-ins and embedded objects, such as Java applets, ActiveX components, and so on.

- They can better deal with scrolling content in browser windows (many HTML pages are longer than standard screen sizes and need to be scrolled).

For most of the tools that were available a few years ago, these refinements were applied to existing GUI test tool engines, so migrating skills from the old tools to the new was relatively painless. Over the last year or two, several of the tool vendors have rebuilt their browser-based test tools from the ground up and left their legacy technology behind. Although the new tools have slicker user interfaces and many new facilities, the principles of test automation (insofar as they have been documented) are hardly changed. The best-known books on test automation [1, 2] hardly mention Web testing at all, but this does not detract from the good advice provided in them.

Tool selection and implementation ought to follow a systematic process, and the decision to purchase a license (costing perhaps $5,000 per seat) should not be taken lightly. It is a sad fact that there is huge dissatisfaction with test execution tools and that of those purchased, many are never used or are used only briefly, then discarded [3, 4]. The biggest threat to success with test execution tools is that of over-expectation. Fewster and Graham make the following points in their book [2]:

- Tools do not eliminate manual testing.

- Tools find fewer faults than manual tests.

- Automated tests need to be more reliable than manual tests.

- Tools do not improve test effectiveness.

- Automated test maintenance may prove to be a barrier to change.

- Tools have no imagination.

Essentially you must determine what exactly you are trying to do with these tools and be realistic about your expectations before you promise huge savings in your testing. See [1–3, 5–7] for sound advice on the essential thinking, planning, and preparation required to select and implement tools.

In some ways, the technical issues to consider are straightforward. The following questions address some of the most important considerations when reviewing browser test execution tools:

- Does the tool work on the browser versions you require? Do you want to test just Microsoft Internet Explorer, or do you need to cover Netscape Navigator too? Do you want to test the latest versions or perform configuration tests on older versions too?

- Will you be testing on multiple operating system platforms? Do you want to test Windows 2000, NT4, 98, and 95? Are you interested in porting tests to Unix/Linux too?

- Does the tool interact with all of the features of the browser? Are you using obscure features or features that are browser-specific? Can the tool deal with large pages, frames, and small windows?

- Does the tool interact correctly with the plug-ins and embedded objects on pages? Can the tool drive Java applets or ActiveX components, for example?

- Does the tool have the features you need? (This sounds obvious, but in our experience, test developers usually need many extra functions to achieve the desired end. Most test automation projects depend on reliable test architectures and large amounts of scaffolding script code to be successful.)

- Is the tool easy to use? (The user interface is important, but the underlying scripting language itself must be accessible. Some tools offer visual facilities to record and maintain scripts, but at the expense of flexibility. Others use C++ or Java as their scripting language. These tools might provide complete flexibility, but demand considerable programming skill and experience to use effectively.)

Above all, set out your key objectives, requirements, and constraints before embarking on the selection process, and take the time to perform a realistic evaluation by using the tools to do some real work. If you can get some hands-on experience, your opinion of a particular tool (or all tools) may be changed.

Justifying Automation

Automating test execution is normally justified based on the need to conduct functional regression tests. In organizations currently performing regression testing manually, this case is easy to make: The tool will save testers time. Most organizations, however, do not conduct formal regression tests, so buying a tool to perform regression tests will not save time, because no time is being spent on regression testing in the first place. In organizations where development is chaotic, regression testing is difficult to implement at all; software products may never be stable enough for a regression test to mature and be of value. Usually, the cost of developing and maintaining automated tests exceeds the value of finding regression faults (which are a minority of all faults anyway).

The use of tools during development is often justified by saying they allow you to execute tests much faster. If you need to execute tests 5 or 10 times before they are passed (and several times again for regression purposes), test automation pays because automated test execution is cheaper than manually performing the tests, or so the calculation goes. The set up and maintenance costs of automated tools, however, is far higher than those for manual tests. Also, less information is gleaned from automated tests because the tester is not involved. Test automation should be justified by using the tool in a very focused way to do things a manual tester could never do. Some simple guidelines for selecting tests to automate are given later.

How Test Execution Tools Work

In this section we will briefly describe the technical architecture of the functional test execution tools used to capture and replay automated test scripts. Most of the proprietary tools are stand-alone products that drive the application through a separate Internet browser. A variation on this is where the tool itself incorporates a built-in browser. Most test execution tools adopt a video-recorder metaphor with the record and play buttons on the tool menus representing the capture and replay functions. The capture-replay metaphor is oversold, however. The capture facility may seem like a valuable asset, but most test scripts are developed from scratch or copied from existing scripts. Initially, some scripts will be captured, but these will rarely be usable before they have been customized to make them data-driven, repeatable, capable of trapping failures, and so on. The vast majority of the tester's time is spent writing script code, testing the test scripts, and debugging them.

The skills required to develop and test automated test scripts are programmer skills, not testing skills. The test tools are badly named, really. They are software development environments used to develop special-purpose programs that drive applications under test. One of the major pitfalls associated with these tools is that nontechnical testers believe capture and replay (nontechnical tasks) are all that is required to make the tools successful.

In the section that follows, we describe how the capture facility works, but you should note that most testers use capture mode to record short sections of script code that they immediately customize. It is usually faster to copy and amend existing scripts to get what you want, so the capture mode is only used to get hold of the perfectly formed script commands that access the fields on a Web page. We describe the script capture activity here to introduce the various components of the tool.

Capturing Test Scripts

Figure 17.1 presents a schematic that represents how the test execution tools can be used to capture an automated test script. Normally, the test tool is started first; then clicking on the tool's record button sets it to capture mode. The tool will record all the user activity until the browser session is terminated, or the tool's stop button is clicked.

There are six data flows that occur during script capture (numbered paragraphs refer to the arrows in Figure 17.1):

1. The tester starts the browser and opens the home page of the system under test. The user executes the prepared test case manually and (unless a bug is encountered) sees the system under test behave normally.

2. The browser communicates with the Web server sending and receiving the HTTP messages and responses. These messages are not normally visible to the test tool.

3. The test tool intercepts all of the user inputs, including mouse clicks and character and function key presses.

4. The user inputs are codified and transformed into test script code. The test script code is usually a programming language dialect that the tool understands. The raw input data is embedded in code that indicates whether the user has clicked on a link or a button or has entered data into a form field, for example.

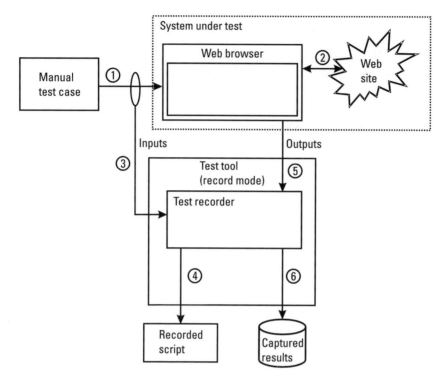

Figure 17.1 Capturing a test script using a tool.

5. As the system under test responds and the browser displays the new HTML pages, this output is also intercepted by the test tool. All of the HTML, images, and other objects are logged when the user signals that a test-case check should be recorded.

6. The intercepted outputs from the system under test are written to the tool's repository and stored for later use as an expected result.

As the user executes transactions, the inputs are recorded exactly in the script. When a check of the actual output needs to be made in the test, the user would normally click on a button that signals a test case is being checked. Depending on what the user requires, the tool will take an exact snapshot of the entire browser window, a small item of data, or perhaps just a calculated value. This is stored in a captured-results repository and given a name for future reference. The user continues through the test, capturing test cases as required. At the end of the test, the user stops the tool's recording, and the test is captured.

Customizing Test Scripts to Make Them Data-Driven

Although a test script represents a perfect copy of a user interaction with the system under test, if the user interaction changed the database when it was recorded, the recorded scripts are unlikely to work if rerun on the same system unless the test database is restored to its original state when the recording was done. Rather than restore the database before running every test script (which is probably impractical), we usually edit the script to make it repeatable. We do this by replacing the literal data values entered by the tester with parameters in the test script code. If we can read some prepared data into these parameters at run time, we can replicate the test, and we can change the data used by the test, rather than restoring the database each time. The script is further amended to allow it to read prepared data (and expected results) and to use the recorded procedure in the script as many times as there are rows of test data in the data source.

When we separate the procedural parts of the script and test data in this way, we say the test is data-driven. Most automated testing depends on this process to make the tests repeatable. The other obvious benefit is that we can create a script once, but use it to execute as many tests as we like, the only limit being the number of test cases we create in our external data source.

Replaying Test Scripts

Figure 17.2 presents a schematic that represents how the test execution tools can be used to execute a data-driven, automated test script. Normally, the test tool is started; then, clicking on the play button of the tool sets it to replay mode. The tool will replay the recorded user actions and execute all of the prepared test cases in the external data source.

The flow of data in automated test execution is more complicated than script capture (numbered paragraphs refer to the arrows in Figure 17.2):

1. Using the tool, the user indicates the script to be executed. The tool opens the test script and processes it, just like a software program, then follows the script steps precisely. The test driver is the part of the tool that reads the script, interprets it, and executes the commands it contains.

2. Because some user activities are repeated many times and may occur in more than one test session, these activities might have their own miniscript that is used again and again. Login and logout procedures are obvious examples. These reusable scripts are stored in a script library, referenced by the script we want to run. Much of the

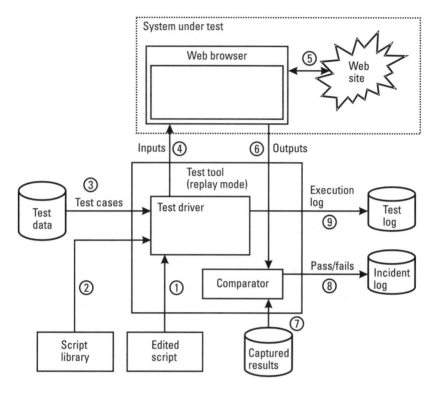

Figure 17.2 Replaying an automated test script.

script development effort goes into the preparation of these script libraries.

3. When the tool encounters a script step to read in a new test case, the tool accesses the prepared test data and reads in the next test case. Typically, this would include all the variable data to be entered in a screen and may include an expected result, perhaps a calculation or expected message, for example.

4. The test script will contain commands to input data to the system under test, and the test script provides all the detail required to access and click buttons, enter data into fields, click check boxes, and so forth. The test driver executes these commands and enters the prepared data precisely as a user might have done.

5. As the system under test executes under the control of the test tool, the browser continues to exchange messages with the Web server and back-end application.

6. As the system under test responds, the browser displays the new HTML pages.

7. When the test script indicates a test case should be checked, the script may do one of two things. Either it reads the previously captured result for the test case or the tool might already have a copy of the expected result read directly from the prepared test data. Either way, the tool makes a comparison of the actual result with the expected one.

8. If the comparison for the test case indicates a failure, the tool writes a record of the test case, its reference, the nature of the failure, and a date and time stamp into the incident log. The incident log provides valuable information to the test manager and developers: It indicates which tests have failed and drives the remedial action required to correct the failure.

9. As the test progresses, the tool logs progress through the script and each test case. In this way a permanent record of the test execution is retained for the project.

The tool will continue executing the test script until it runs out of test cases and the script terminates. Normally, at the end of execution, the tool will provide a summary report of progress through the test and indicate whether the test passed in all respects or there were failures. The incident log will provide sufficient information to track down the failed test cases so that the developers can diagnose the failures.

See [1], [2], and [8] for broad advice on how to plan, design, and implement automated test regimes.

Tools with Built-In Browsers

One variation on the standard test execution tool architecture is the eValid™ product (available from Software Research at http://www.soft.com). eValid incorporates a fully functional Internet Explorer–compatible browser. The tool requires you to install Internet Explorer on your test machine. When eValid starts up, it appears just like Internet Explorer but has an additional menu option that has all the eValid features behind it. There are also the familiar record, playback, and stop buttons on an additional button bar.

Figure 17.3 shows the eValid technical-architecture schematic for comparison with the more standard architectures used by most of the other tools.

eValid eliminates the need for a separate browser application and simplifies the playback process a little. Of course, the tool cannot test other

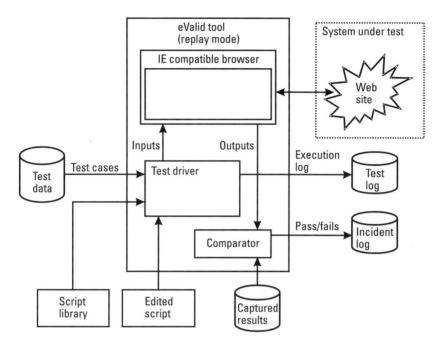

Figure 17.3 The eValid test tool architecture.

browsers, but is limited to testing your Web site's functionality as implemented through the eValid browser. For all practical purposes, however, it is a perfectly usable test tool for the version of the Internet Explorer you have installed on your test machines.

Selecting Tests to Automate

The various test types described in Chapters 9 through 15 focus on specific risk-based test objectives. Because the tests have specific objectives, we will be in a better position to make successful choices as to whether we automate or execute them manually. Many tests are better done manually; automation is likely to take more time than it is worth. We offer some general recommendations concerning test automation in Table 17.1.

Proprietary, Shareware, and Freeware Tools

Building your own tools might be fun for some and, in some environments, may be economical (see Appendix B for more information). Most companies

Table 17.1
General Guidance for Test Tools

Pareto law	• Expect 80% of the benefit to derive from the automation of 20% of the tests. • Don't waste time scripting low-volume complex scripts at the expense of high-volume simple ones.
Hybrid approach	• Consider using the tools to perform navigation and data entry prior to manual test execution. • Consider using the tool for test running, but perform comparisons manually or off-line.
Coded scripts	• These work best for navigation- and checklist-type scripts. • Use these where loops and case statements in code leverage simple scripts. • These are relatively easy to maintain as regression tests.
Recorded scripts	• These need to be customized to make them repeatable. • These are sensitive to changes in the user interface.
Test integration	• Automated scripts need to be integrated into a test harness. • Proprietary test harnesses are usually crude, so custom-built harnesses are often required.
Migrating manual test scripts	• Manual scripts can document the automated scripts. • Delay migration of manual scripts until the software is stable, then reuse them for regression tests.
Nonfunctional tests	• Any script can be reused for soak tests, but they must exercise the functionality of concern. • Tests of interfaces to server-based components are high on the list of tests to automate. • Instrument these scripts to take response time measurements and reuse them for performance testing.

acquire off-the-shelf tools from specialized tool vendors. Proprietary tools are popular and very sophisticated, but can be expensive. If your budget does not run to many thousands of dollars, you might consider shareware or even freeware sources as an alternative. In this section we briefly set out the merits (and demerits) of these three sources of ready-built tools.

Proprietary Tools

Browser-based test execution tools are only available from specialized tool vendors. These are all proprietary, and they are all large, complex pieces of software. They tend to be relatively expensive, costing up to $5,000 for a license. Most of the vendors of these tools also offer performance testing tools based on the same technology. These are also expensive products that can cost tens of thousands of dollars.

With proprietary tools, you get high-quality, sophisticated, functionally rich products. They are generally more user friendly, and easy to implement, and you typically get high-quality technical support. You also get high prices, and when it comes to performance test tools in particular, getting tools from other sources may be your only option if you have a limited budget.

Shareware Tools

Shareware is software that is distributed for free on a trial basis with the understanding that the user may need or want to pay for it later. Some software developers offer a shareware version of their products with a built-in expiration date (after 30 days, the user can no longer access the program). Other shareware (sometimes called liteware) is offered with certain capabilities disabled as an enticement to buy the complete version of the program. Tools offered as shareware are likely to be HTML validators, browser-compatibility checkers, link checkers, and some security scanners. Typically, these tools cost less than $100.

Shareware tools tend to have a fairly narrow focus. In terms of complexity, these tools are not likely to be huge pieces of software, hence the low prices. They tend not to integrate with other tools, documentation is less comprehensive and slick, and support can be scarce. You might get support directly from the developers, however, and your bug fixes and suggestions for improvements might be implemented very quickly indeed if the developers see your suggestions as useful. Low prices do not necessarily indicate low quality, and you might find that shareware is a viable alternative to some of the offerings of the larger vendors. Bear in mind that some of the expensive products offered by the larger vendors actually started life as shareware—the big vendor simply bought the shareware and the company that wrote it and integrated the software into its existing product set.

Freeware Tools

Freeware is software offered at no cost. Freeware may have a huge or a tiny user base. You might possibly get personal support by the programmer who wrote the tool. You use freeware tools completely at your own risk without warranty or support. Even so, there are a large number of useful tools and utilities available. There are completely free versions of all of the test tool types, except browser-based test execution tools (at least, I have never found one that worked). Most notable in this category are the performance test tools. Many are Unix-oriented, written in Perl, perhaps, and tricky to set up unless you are a programmer. There are also Windows-based products, the most usable of which are Microsoft's Web Application Stress Tool (available at http://webtool.rte.microsoft.com) and the OpenSTA product (available at http://www.opensta.org). These and other free performance test tools are listed at the end of Chapter 12.

Don't dismiss free tools because they are free; free does not necessarily mean low-quality. You might find a little gem of a utility that saves you many hours of work if you just take some time to research what is freely available on the Web.

Sources of Tool Information

Table 17.2 lists several of our favorite Web sites and directories offering tools listings and, in some cases, reviews of a limited number of tools.

Table 17.2
Sources for E-Business Testing Tools

Tool Directories and Listings	URL
Rick Hower's Software QA/Test Resource Center Web test tools listing	http://www.softwareqatest.com/qatweb1.html
Danny Faught's Frequently Asked Questions site for testers	http://www.testingfaqs.org/tools.htm
StickyMinds, resources for testers and QA staff	http://www.stickyminds.com
Cigital Labs tools list	http://www.cigitallabs.com/resources/hotlist/comm-test.html
Test Tool Evaluations and Reports	**URL**
Ovum Evaluates Software Testing Tools	http://www.ovum.com/go/product/flyer/tst.htm
Testing FAQs list of published tool reviews	http://www.testingfaqs.org/tools.htm

References

[1]   Dustin, E., J. Rashka, and J. Paul, *Automated Software Testing*, Boston, MA: Addison-Wesley, 1999.

[2]   Fewster, M., and D. Graham, *Software Test Automation*, Harlow, UK: Addison-Wesley, 1999.

[3]   Gerrard, P., "CAST Tools Past, Present and Future," *Proc. 6th EuroSTAR Conf.*, Munich, Germany, November 30–December 4, 1998.

[4]   Grove Consultants, "Software Testing Tool Use Survey," http://www.grove.co.uk, 2002.

[5]   Gerrard, P., "Selecting and Implementing CAST Tools," http://www.evolutif.co.uk, 2002.

[6]   Hendriksen, E., "Making the Right Choice: The Features You Need in a GUI Test Automation Tool," http://www.qualitytree.com, 2002.

[7]   Hendriksen, E., "Evaluating Tools," http://www.qualitytree.com, 2002.

[8]   Gerrard, P., "Testing GUI Applications," http://www.evolutif.co.uk, 2002.

Further Reading

Bach, J., "Test Automation Snake Oil," http://www.satisfice.com/articles/test_automation_snake_oil.pdf, 2002.

Kaner, C., "Architectures of Test Automation," http://www.kaner.com/testarch.html, 2002.

Kaner, C., J. Bach, and B. Pettichord, *Lessons Learned in Software Testing*, New York: John Wiley & Sons, 2002.

Kaner, C., "Improving the Maintainability of Automated Tests," http://ww.kaner.com/lawst1.htm, 2002.

Kit, E., "Integrated, Effective Test Design and Automation," http://www.sdmagazine.com/breakrm/features/s992f2.shtml, 2002.

Pettichord, B., "Seven Steps to Test Automation Success," http://www.pettichord.com, 2002.

Zambelich, K., "Totally Data-Driven Automated Testing," http://www.sqa-test.com/w_paper1.html, 2002.

Part IV
Making E-Business Testing Happen

18

The Context of E-Business Testing

E-business does not change everything. Testing of Web applications is not fundamentally different from traditional testing, and (despite what you may read) most of the old methods and rules still apply in a modified form. E-business systems and evolving development methods bring new paradigms, such as statelessness and object orientation, and new pressures to projects, but in most cases, these just are amplified versions of all the old pressures. New technical approaches and testing techniques may well be appropriate, but a sound testing process, managed well, is still an asset, not a liability [1].

The risk-based method of this book enhances the W-model and builds on existing testing methods; it does not replace them. Whether the project is large or small (and of longer or shorter duration) will influence the degree of detail we go into and rigor we apply. Further, the amount of "ceremony" [2] surrounding processes and products may also vary, and this is influenced greatly by organizational culture. All the same, some basic testing disciplines are always necessary to prevent chaos:

- Testing needs a baseline against which to test. The baseline is used to identify things to test and to predict expected behavior.

- Development methods have evolved over the years, modern examples being eXtreme Programming (XP) and the Rational Unified Process (RUP). Although these can be thought of as being at opposite ends of the agility spectrum (and may be intended for different project sizes and cultures), both are applicable to e-business systems, both are strong on testing, and both can be enhanced by using the methods of risk-based testing.

- Whatever the method, tests still need to be specified and stored in an orderly manner.

- Test specifications should be refined stepwise (just as systems specifications are, from requirements and by way of designs). Even during test execution, testers learn more and see new testing opportunities.

- The testing process still needs effective management.

- Testing makes the key information contribution to the acceptance process for a new system.

This chapter sets out some of the challenges which modern methods and paradigms present to these basic principles. Chapter 19 describes the resulting test planning and organizational considerations, and Chapter 20 presents some of the key test management issues related to test execution.

Methods and Requirements Formats

Functional and nonfunctional requirements, designs, and specifications are the baselines against which we test. Some projects seem to regard the absence of specifications as something of a virtue. Rapid application development (RAD) and other agile methods, such as XP, attempt to harness the speed and flexibility of lightweight specifications. Other projects (using a variety of methodologies) rely on heavyweight specifications, the most widely promoted of which is the UML. Figure 18.1 compares the two very different specification styles of XP and UML.

On the left side of Figure 18.1, XP has minimal documentation and maximum emphasis on the responsive use of technology with a very collaborative approach. Here, our main problem as testers (including the developers who do their own testing) is likely to be too little documentation on which to base tests. On the right side of the figure, UML challenges testers to make the best use of the many diverse (often optional) documentation products. In the following paragraphs we look in more detail at these two contrasting specification formats and the methods associated with them.

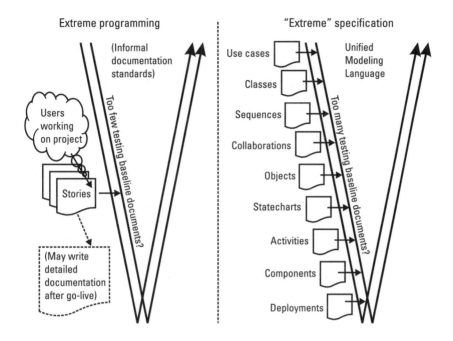

Figure 18.1 Two extremes of specification detail.

XP

The lack of specifications (at least initially) is a deliberate policy of XP [3], so this might be seen to present a problem for testing. But XP is strongly in favor of testing, making it a key element of the philosophy, and extreme in its frequency and intensity. Test specification is done early, ideally before programming. Tester is an explicit role on the team, although published material on how to do testing in the XP world is only just emerging. Development in XP is done pairwise, providing immediate and ongoing review of design decisions, coding, and test design.

XP's scope extends from the earliest development stages into live use and maintenance. Typically, the system is documented just before release when the requirements and design are (at last) stable. So, until then, testing is against "stories" written on pieces of card. XP advocates two levels of testing (rather than the traditional four or five), but then, XP is normally aimed at small systems of limited scope. XP testing is founded on the two viewpoints of developers and users.

Developers write tests to demonstrate that the code they have written performs the way that they expect—the baseline is their own expectation and knowledge of the code. The tests are retained indefinitely and exist primarily as regression tests that continuously confirm that the latest code changes have not disrupted previously existing code. A major benefit of these tests is that they bolster the developer's confidence, but they don't really help anyone else to believe the code does what it should do. Perhaps the greatest benefit, therefore, is that the tests are designed before coding begins. Thinking about testing before coding helps developers to expose uncertainties in their understanding of a requirement.

User tests are more focused on the requirement itself and aim to demonstrate that a requirement as stated in a user story is met. The user thinks through examples of usage that would provide evidence that a story has been implemented completely and correctly. Tests focus on each feature and situation described by the story. Test failures could indicate a fault in software or the story itself.

XP does not prescribe that developers, users, or testers perform any particular types of test. Rather, it suggests that only tests that have potential value are created. Tests that "pay off" include either of the following:

- You expect them to pass, but if they fail, you will learn something.
- You expect them to fail, but if they pass, you will learn something.

If you knew in advance all the tests that would pay off, would there be any need to test at all? Would you also know in advance what it is that you will learn? XP promotes the idea that you learn through experience which tests are the best. This notion fits easily into the exploratory testing approach promoted by James Bach and others [4]. The difficulty for test managers is managing the testing process under these circumstances. We suggest that the early risk analysis is as appropriate for an XP project as any other. The risks and test objectives identified in the MTP process can be used in just the same way as more traditional, "staged testing" projects because they can influence the selection of tests. In a risk-based testing regime, the tests that pay off are those that provide information about the existence or nonexistence of faults that can be related to a risk (or those which expose new risks). When enough tests have been prepared, executed, and passed to convince the risk-owners that the risk has been addressed, enough testing has been done.

As a tester in an XP project, you might feel a little uncomfortable with this rather laissez-faire approach to testing. But there is no need to feel unwelcome: XP values testing, but values only tests that could pay off. Preaching test coverage of features that are either unlikely to fail or of little consequence if they do is not an approach that fits. An experienced tester may feel some culture shock, as XP values can seem very different from those of a traditional project, and much of the baseline information to test against will need to be obtained and remembered from conversations and informal meetings. He or she will need to be agile to cope with rapid and perhaps repeated change and refinement (refactoring) of the system's design. Because XP makes developers responsible for the bulk of the testing, they may want to control it all, and they may not think independent testers (other than customer representatives) add much value. Independent testers add most value when they have an instinct for faults and can support users and help them organize their ideas for interesting scenarios into tests.

Testers who work within the XP framework have a key responsibility to question the following:

- The completeness and consistency of customers' stories;

- The developers' understanding of those stories.

They do this by continually suggesting test scenarios that explore the boundaries of the requirements and asking how each risk relevant to a story can be better explored by such tests. Test management should encourage testers to behave in this way and help developers and users to understand that this is how testers add the most value to an XP project.

UML and Unified Process

UML [5] is promoted as the most appropriate specification medium for incremental (and other iterative) developments. It is founded on the object-oriented approach. UML consists of several (complementary) specification formats, which include graphical representations. Not all of these diagrams need to be used on every project, and UML allows for this flexibility. UML is a language rather than a methodology, so it does not imply that each product needs to be produced in a particular sequence in a particular way. But readers of UML are naturally tempted to define a process for its use, and the inventors of UML have offered the Unified Software Development Process (USDP) [6], supported by the specific extensions of RUP [7]. Table 18.1 summarizes the key UML diagram types. Behavioral diagrams are representations of the requirements for the external behavior of the system; structural diagrams are representations of the internal structure, design, or implementation of the system.

Table 18.1
Key UML Diagram Types

Diagram Type	Characteristic	Description
Use case	Behavioral	A set of use cases and actors and their relationships
Class	Structural	A set of classes, interfaces, and collaborations and their relationships
Sequence	Behavioral	An interaction emphasizing the time-ordering of messages
Collaboration	Behavioral	An interaction emphasizing the structural organization of the objects that send and receive messages
Object	Structural	A set of objects and their relationships
Statechart	Behavioral	A state machine emphasizing the event-ordered behavior of an object
Activity	Behavioral	A state machine emphasizing the flow from activity to activity
Component	Structural	A set of components and their relationships
Deployment	Structural	A set of nodes and their relationships

In its full form, UML could be seen as "extreme specification" and as different as can be from XP's minimalist documentation. The challenge for UML users is to plot a course through the mass of documentation in diverse formats. There is also the possibility that testers and developers need training in UML, but UML (unlike XP) does not insist on an all-or-nothing approach. UML is still valid with some of its diagrams omitted from the development process. Arguably, therefore, it is permissible for testing to ignore some of the diagrams that are produced, in which case the extra risk of doing so should be acknowledged. As an aside, not all agile methods insist on every element of the method being present.

In UML, it is the use cases that are most often set as baselines for testing, but testers instinctively seek to use any products that exist. If someone has used them as a basis for development, then it should be possible (and it is indeed recommended) to write tests against them. Acceptance testing against use cases is the most obvious pairing, but use cases can be the baseline for other levels of testing too. The test manager must, however, resist the desire to use only the use cases at every level of testing. These different levels of testing seek different faults, and there must be a limit to how many tests can be derived from the same baseline and still pay off. Testers should consider using other documentation products as baselines for subsystem and system testing. It is relatively easy to define some form of coverage targets from the diagrams, so these could be used as exit criteria for earlier test stages. This will force the developers and system testers to read these documents.

Each test stage could have a primary baseline and, where appropriate, one or more secondary baselines. The primary baseline provides the main structure of the tests, and the secondary baselines give additional behaviors to test against. Thought is needed where an individual testing stage uses more than one UML product, however. It is tempting to use the multiple products together to specify the tests overall, but this would make test coverage difficult to monitor. It is usually easier to structure different tests around each product's specification format. Other than the use cases, the most useful UML products for testing are the sequence and statechart diagrams. Even the structural diagrams are testable, however, and not doing so could miss some important fault types.

One of the claimed strengths of UML is its ability to extend itself as required by circumstances: The framework for extension is an intrinsic part of the language. Specific extensions have been proposed for the particular characteristics of Web-based systems and these are presented in [8]. Binder's book [9] gives a thorough and detailed treatment of testing against UML products.

Architectures, Objects, Components, and Middleware

One challenge for e-business testers is the diversity of technologies with which they have to deal. In the past, programmers and testers tended to specialize in mainframes, probably those of a single vendor, or in one or more brands of minicomputer. In the client/server age, things got more complex, but still manageable. Now, anyone seeking to understand an e-business system end-to-end may need to know mainframe plus a good selection of Unix and Windows, and potentially different versions of them. An acquaintance with (or at least exposure to) HTML, XML, HTTP, SSL, TCP/IP, Java, scripting languages, and database technologies and query languages is also called for.

E-business testing managers may survive as adaptable, intelligent, and energetic generalists, but they must know which specialists they need to bring in and when. They need to know enough to source, interview, and select them. Subsystem testers will also almost certainly need to understand the technical architecture in use and most of the principles concerned with object orientation, component-based development, and middleware.

All of the above have an associated set of characteristics and risk areas that the informed tester should take into account. System testers will also need to understand these subjects when, for instance, integration testing has been less than perfect and there are still complex interaction problems to be diagnosed. Even at the LSI test level and above, a broad understanding is helpful, and ignorance will damage credibility in the eyes of the developers. There is not space here to describe these subjects further, but there are many relevant books available, for example [9–12].

Coping with Iterative and Incremental Methods

Systems are increasingly built using iterative and incremental methods, and of course, these pose a challenge for testers. An iterative method is one where a system is developed in a single project, but where there may be two, three, or more iterations of development and testing before a system is deemed acceptable. An incremental method is where functionality is built up in a series of projects or project stages, and each increment adds to the functionality developed in previous stages. In effect, incremental is merely a special case of iterative. If increments are added without disturbing the basic architecture, then regression testing should be relatively trouble-free (the main work being in testing the new functions), but iterations of design can give testers a surprising amount of work. We will therefore discuss the issues below as they apply to iterative methods in general.

The emerging agile methods and the already established Dynamic Systems Development Method (DSDM), an early formalization of RAD, propose that testing, including acceptance, is performed perhaps several times throughout a project [13, 14]. There are other iterative methods, the best-known currently being USDP and its extension, RUP, both of which we have already mentioned. Web systems are naturally developed in an iterative way because of the pressure to get something out there as quickly as possible, then build on it as needs dictate and resources allow.

In an iterative method, the stages of testing often run in parallel, rather than in series (they are sometimes termed levels, partly for this reason). It is not uncommon to start the next stage before the previous stage is completely finished; late deliveries combined with project time and budget pressures often dictate this.

Larger projects are often organized to deliver testable subsystems into integration and system testing. The theory goes that by delivering partial builds, much of the higher level testing can be performed in parallel with the later stages of development, reducing the elapsed time to final acceptance and release. It is possible to plan and perform most integration testing in this way, but the build and integration sequence must be synchronized to the integration test sequence. Some system testing might be possible on partial builds or subsystems, but typically, a substantial amount of system testing requires that most of the system be available. Lack of even a small number of subsystems might make a large proportion of system tests impractical.

Serious problems, such as the following, can arise when integration and system tests on partial systems detect faults:

- Many of the tests in the plan might be impossible to perform because key functionality is missing, which is very frustrating for the testers trying to execute tests that are blocked midway. Blocked tests do not provide full information and have to be repeated later anyway.

- The faults that are reported might relate to functionality that has not yet been built. Superficially, a system build might appear to the testers to include certain functionality, which could actually have been stubbed out. It is possible that the faults that testers report are due to the fact the stubs provide a partial simulation of the missing functionality. Do the developers ignore the fault, or do they change their plans and build a refined stub (which might be thrown away later)?

- Some of the faulty code might be undergoing change for the next delivery of new functionality. Either the old version of the code must be changed and rereleased, or the bug fix has to be retrofitted into the new version of code under development. The bug fix might have to be undone later because subsequent releases make that fix redundant or incorrect. A temporary source code variant might have to be released simply to eliminate the problems from the current test phase.

- The developers will be focusing on development of the new, outstanding functionality. They may not appreciate the disruption of being asked to debug and fix faulty code at irregular intervals.

All these situations cost the testers and developers extra time, and they are certainly frustrating to all involved. Further, there is a risk that things will be forgotten when developing and testing partial builds. Tests that are assumed to have been run may never actually be completed. Fixes that should have been removed when later functionality became available may accidentally remain and cause later failures. If management believes that by testing partial deliveries they will save time, they should be advised of the following:

- Management of the incremental build and test strategy will be more complicated and difficult.
- The complications may introduce faults that cause problems later.
- Developers and testers may get frustrated.
- The time that will be saved will always be less than that calculated on paper.

One overhead of an iterative approach is that the parts that are ready early (and work) might be tested multiple times to little effect, while the most important testing is not feasible until the last iteration is available. Automation tools might help by reducing the effort spent on this repetitive testing, but automated scripts are time-consuming to maintain in line with changing user interfaces, so there is often a delay in getting the automated scripts stable again.

Finally, we do not want to waste time attempting to test a partial system that is extremely buggy or untestable in its current state. Regardless of how well your entry criteria for, say, system testing are defined, it is likely that thorough system testing of a delivery is impaired by the fact that key components might be missing from that build. In general, it is better to have comprehensive exit criteria defined for a test stage than entry criteria for a subsequent stage. This puts the onus on developers or test teams to ensure their testing is complete, rather than handing it off to a later team who have difficulty performing their testing tasks and then complain about the earlier team's failings. Exit criteria should therefore be negotiated between, say, the subsystem testers (usually the developers) and system testers. System testers should be allowed to include specific tests they would like to see performed in the earlier stage to give them confidence that the following objectives have been met:

- The build is complete (according to pre-existing plans or designs).
- Certain specified core transactions can be executed successfully.

These two requirements can be defined as a single, simple exit criterion that requires that a small number of tests, specified by the system testers, be performed successfully. To minimize the burden on the earlier subsystem testers, these tests should be highly focused and simple to run. They should be defined in such a way that they demonstrate that the objectives above have been met. Some of these tests comprise checks that all the screens, components, and reports specified exist in the build. Others will exercise some core transactions that simply must work with normal data, so that later testers can be confident they are working on software that is stable enough. System testers might define these tests for their own use as a basic integrity check to be performed very early in their test plan. The same tests would be given to earlier subsystem testers to use in their own environment.

When fixes to code are implemented, they first need to be unit tested; then, subsequent regression testing is influenced by when the fault was originally detected. If a fault were reported in acceptance testing, then the best practice would be to repeat all unit, integration, and system regression tests before resubmission to acceptance. Each change should be regression tested through the earlier test stages, but it is normally unrealistic to expect this. Iterative methods make even a partial attempt to repeat earlier regression tests very difficult unless a high degree of test automation has been employed and the scripts are maintained throughout the project.

One of the underlying principles of XP is that developer tests are maintained forever; they are executed in their entirety (and faults detected are fixed) possibly daily and certainly prior to every release to later testing. This discipline is fundamental to the XP approach in which regression tests provide confidence that software functionality remains stable in projects where change is rapid and continuous.

Many iterative projects do not have this disciplined regime of automated regression testing. The usual compromise is to retain some proportion of regression tests from one test stage (commonly system or acceptance tests) and use those to ensure stability between releases.

References

[1]   Marshall, S., and R. Szarkowski, *Making E-Business Work: A Guide to Software Testing in the Internet Age*, Barnstable, MA: Newport Press Publications, 2000.

[2]   Herzlich, P., "Graduating Ceremony," http://www.evolutif.co.uk, 2002.

[3]   Beck, K., *Extreme Programming Explained—Embrace Change*, Boston, MA: Addison-Wesley, 2000.

[4]   Bach, J., "What Is Exploratory Testing?" http://www.satisfice.com, 2002.

[5]   Booch, G., J. Rumbaugh, and I. Jacobsen, *The Unified Modeling Language User Guide*, Boston, MA: Addison-Wesley, 1999.

[6]   Booch, G., J. Rumbaugh, and I. Jacobsen, *The Unified Software Development Process*, Boston, MA: Addison-Wesley, 1999.

[7]   Kruchten, P., *The Rational Unified Process—An Introduction*, 2nd ed., Boston, MA: Addison-Wesley, 2000.

[8]   Conallen, J., *Building Web Applications with UML*, Boston, MA: Addison-Wesley, 1999.

[9]   Binder, R.V., *Testing Object-Oriented Systems: Models, Patterns & Tools*, Boston, MA: Addison-Wesley, 1999.

[10] McGregor, J. D., and D. A. Sykes, *A Practical Guide to Testing Object-Oriented Software*, Boston, MA: Addison-Wesley, 2001.

[11] Shan,Y.-P., and R. H. Earle, *Enterprise Computing with Objects: From Client/Server Environments to the Internet*, Boston, MA: Addison-Wesley, 1998.

[12] Serain, D., *Middleware*, London, UK: Springer-Verlag, 1999.

[13] Stapleton, J., *DSDM: Dynamic Systems Development Method*, Harlow, UK: Pearson (Addison-Wesley), 1997.

[14] DSDM Consortium, http://www.dsdm.org, 2002.

19

E-Business Test Organization, Planning, and Specification

Theory does not always work in reality as originally envisaged. Textbook methods tend to work better in corporate information systems departments where there is continuity in staff, methods, tools, and management across projects. In organizations where the culture is to form and disband separate projects when needed (and in organizations that specialize in single projects for diverse clients), the success of each individual project is often paramount. In such regimes, the trade-offs between time, quality, cost, and scope cause tensions, conflict, and fatigue. Because lessons are not properly learned from previous projects, each new project starts all over again with an almost clean slate, and then goes on to encounter the usual timescale panic. Getting the project live is seen as far more important than adherence to best practices and process improvement.

These two distinct organizational styles (corporate and by-project) endure partly because people tend to pursue whole careers working in one type of environment or the other. The corporate types may move from one permanent job to another every few years, but their career is stable over long periods of time; their real-life practice probably comes closest to the theory. By-project types also tend to remain such throughout their careers, typically working for one or more consultancy organizations or as freelancers. Of course, professionals do cross over to the other side occasionally, but may find it uncomfortable.

In our experience on small and large projects in both corporate and by-project cultures, e-business systems are increasingly being integrated with legacy systems, and large projects in particular may be performed in the corporate environment with legacy-type controls. But e-business is fast moving; rapid difficult projects require energetic, can-do people, so where there are potential conflicts between styles, compromises must be made. In this chapter, therefore, we set out some advice about conscientious pragmatism based on some of the discord we have encountered on recent projects, and the solutions we have come up with.

Testing's Place in the Project

One of the first things to decide is whether testing is responsible only for finding and logging problems, or also for getting them fixed. The conventional position, which is still maintained in RUP [1], is the former, but some perceive the latter [2, 3]. The testing manager needs to agree with project management and stakeholders on which it is to be and state this in the MTP.

We recommend that the testers not assume responsibility for getting faults fixed, although they should facilitate that process (e.g., by providing the highest-quality information on incidents and giving clear priorities for when fixes are needed to retest). If the testers are independent, they have no power over the developers anyway. Testers' main job is to provide responsive information on residual risk.

Independent or Codependent?

Queries about responsibilities can occur not only between testers and others, but also between development testers and the independent testers who run the later stages. System and acceptance testers sometimes attempt to compensate for less-than-thorough unit and integration testing, and this is one example of what has been likened, by Lee Copeland [4], to the psychological disorder codependency. Copeland isn't suggesting that all testers have some kind of group psychological disorder, but there are some parallel patterns of behavior in testers, which could be explained by that theory. An example of the original usage is where a codependent parent might compensate for a child's antisocial behavior rather than prohibit it and reprimand the child.

There are other opportunities for testers to practice codependency, such as taking on additional responsibilities in areas like quality management

(QM) and configuration management (CM). We will examine these areas a little later in this chapter.

Testing Manager as a Role

We are assuming in this book that the testing manager actually exists as a separate role, but is this always the case? Some project management methods, such as PRINCE [5] and the USDP/RUP, do not explicitly require such a role. Because the risk-based-testing method spans almost the entire project life cycle, and because testing requires an increasing amount of specialization, our view is that all medium-sized or larger projects should have a separate test management role defined, and that the testing manager should work closely with the quality manager (if there is a separate quality manager).

QM and CM

If there is no separate quality manager then the testing manager may have to fill that role, although in theory, it is the project manager who should take responsibility for quality along with the other main variables of time, cost, and scope. QM tends to require a different personality type than project management, and the objectives of a quality manager are broader than those of the test manager. If you are asked, as a test manager, to take on QM also, be sure you have clear (and achievable) terms of reference and the authority to enforce process changes, should these be necessary.

The testing manager might also be asked to perform CM. This is an essential responsibility in all projects, but if the project manager does not value CM highly or cannot afford to hire a dedicated resource, the test manager might find him- or herself "volunteered" for the role. It is good news when a test manager is appointed early, but not such good news if project management assumes that the (often perceived as lesser) roles of QM and CM can be readily accommodated within the test management role. Not all projects have big budgets, but it could be seen as codependent to take on three jobs at once unthinkingly. A big project would require the roles to be filled by separate people.

Organization and Control

The organization of testing is of course influenced by the structure of the development project (or program of projects). Figure 19.1 depicts a management structure that was in place on a large e-business program in which we

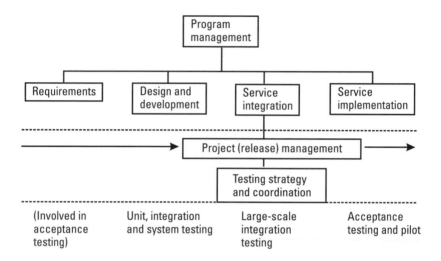

Figure 19.1 Sample project and testing-team structure.

were (successfully) involved. Each release of the application was delivered by a grouping of program staff, which constituted, in some ways, a separate project.

In this organization there were two alternating release managers (manager A was responsible for releases 1, 3, 5, and manager B for releases 2, 4, 6). At any one time, however, the testing manager was dealing with test execution for one release while planning the testing for the next release. This is more difficult than might be expected; it takes great determination to take time away from the urgencies of the current tests to plan the work on the relatively distant matter of the next release.

Another challenge with such an organization is the effort involved in achieving adequate horizontal control. Management responsibility is vertical, so each manager tends to look after his/her own team's interests first. Communication is more through management (perhaps involving skirmishing at meetings) than through team synergy. The problem gets worse if development and other teams are at different sites, and it could get more serious still if teams are dispersed widely across the country or even abroad. If development is outsourced or otherwise subject to tight contractual arrangements, it is common to get into increasingly time-consuming arguments over faults (which must be fixed) and variations of scope (which are usually deferred to some future date).

It is possible to imagine process reengineering such an organization into horizontal team structures, and to a certain extent this was done in the program that we are citing (by having release-specific development teams, for example). There is, however, no escaping the fact that business analysts, developers, and testers are all specialists, and that in the end the problem comes down to matrix management or some similar scheme.

Another challenge is in the area of project control: There can be tensions between the fast, responsive culture of the typical Web developer and the traditional corporate project culture of high ceremony, project control overheads, and multiple reporting requirements. The smaller the project, the more likely the former is to work; for big projects, there is no escaping some kind of formal management framework, and the best we can do is to negotiate against any bureaucracy that seems unnecessary.

Credibility of Testing

Many testers suffer the management and developer perception that testers are second-class citizens of software projects. The credibility of testing is particularly threatened in some e-business projects. As technology changes happen even faster, and hardware and software become obsolete within perhaps a year or two, staff with an in-depth understanding of the latest techniques are scarce and valuable. One effect of this is that the value of independent testing (which is self-evident to testers) might be questioned by others, and questioned harshly, with the following misconceptions:

- Only the developers understand the technology, so they must be the best people to test it.
- These testers dress up what they do.
- What value do these testers add? They just ask stupid questions and slow things down.

It is true that the designers and developers of a system understand it before the testers do. This may be because the testers get involved at a later stage. Even if independent testers get involved early, they can absorb information only when that information is available: typically requirements first, then design. If the design is not well-documented, the testers can be forgiven for not immediately knowing its details, but the main value of independence in testing is in the fresh view taken.

Technical experts in the latest technologies tend to be young, and because the Internet is as much a media phenomenon as a computing one, the developers are often new to the information systems business and may not have been trained in development methods or project disciplines. Furthermore, in fast-moving clicks-no-bricks companies, management tends to be made up of risk takers, and these incautious attitudes filter down.

The tester's response to this should be a development of the basic discipline principles put forward at the beginning of Chapter 18 in defense of the W-model. Testers may have to justify their existence and the resources required to do their job. The (almost) philosophical argument to use is based on the differing viewpoints of developers and testers:

- Whereas developers need to focus on their own technical challenges, testers must look outward to the context of their project, act like customers or users, and provide information to management for them to make decisions.

- Developers focus on delivery; testers must focus on product risk and, by so doing, build confidence that the product actually works.

- Whereas developers have intimate knowledge of the internals of the software and, in principle, could test a system as thoroughly as could ever be required, they become immersed in their own work and therefore will miss some of the faults that need to be detected.

Testers also have a valuable role to play before the technical people start to implement a system. This is because testers view requirements in a different way from developers. A tester (at least initially) regards a requirement as a fixed point of reference to identify features to be tested and situations of interest to be explored and as an oracle to predict the behavior of the system in all testable situations. Using what might be called skepticism and pedantry, testers will question the accuracy, completeness, nonambiguity, and consistency of a requirement before they can accept it as a usable baseline for testing. On the other hand, developers might regard a requirement as simply a starting point for development, a guideline that need not be fully detailed because the developers, in discussion with users, will fine tune the requirement as they build the code. Involving testers in either early requirements review or in discussions with users to refine requirements leads to the finding of faults in requirements: It can clarify uncertainties in their meaning and can therefore eliminate many inappropriate assumptions developers might make. A good tester will insist that the needs of users, the understanding of developers, and the testable behavior of a system are congruent. One could argue that the greatest contribution a tester makes to a project is the improvement in requirements, and consequently improved communications between users and developers. This improved communication should continue during test execution, as the testers facilitate incident review.

The different viewpoints of the development and testing roles (segregation of duties, as in the accounting field) are not the only argument for valuing independent testers. Let's accept reality and use people for what they are good at. Some developers simply do not want to test; rather, they do not want to document. Whether developers really ought to test more thoroughly or not, testers protect a project from many of the faults that developers do not find, so they act as extra insurance against faults surviving into live use.

Explaining Testing to Other Managers

A testing manager will write test plans and will typically publish them through the project library process. But, it would be dangerous merely to assume that other managers will, by that means alone, understand the testing process and content. As with any document, and particularly with comprehensive or detailed publications, there is the problem that people tend not to read them. Either they do not like reading as a means of communication, or they have been exposed to too many unhelpful or tedious documents in the past, or perhaps they are genuinely too busy. This is a real problem in documentation-heavy projects, even if the documents are well-structured and illustrated. No matter how hard one tries, the documents just get the rubber stamp of unthinking approval, or they are ignored entirely.

A good way of getting your message across is first to summarize your key points in a set of presentation slides: pictures, tables, and bullet points. Use a meeting or workshop to walk your immediate audience through these, and you will pick up the main areas which need amending. Only then need you write some text to fill out the message. And the slides should be kept for future use in refresher sessions, when new staff members join, or when senior management asks what's going on.

One of the key features of the risk-based testing approach is the initial risk workshop, a series of formal events that involve the project stakeholders. Once the set of risks in scope have been defined, these same people will look out for the risks of greatest concern and review documents with a view to ensuring that their concerns are being addressed. In particular, the overall test strategy or MTP and the documents that specify in overview the tests to be performed in system and acceptance testing should get the review time and attention they deserve. These documents scope the tests that will address the risks. Once the testers start producing test scripts and data, however, it is unlikely that they will get any useful feedback from senior managers. Review of these materials is a technical activity. It is therefore important to get the right level of documentation to the right level of management at the right time.

Another communication challenge is explaining the role of testers to the nontesters in a project, particularly those who have influence or budget authority. Again, the risk-based testing approach helps focus the objectives: Testers aim to provide information to make a risk-based release decision. There may still be senior and not-so-senior project staff who expect perfection or think that testing can inject quality into a project at a late stage. In dealing with these colleagues, you should try to be as informative as possible, without being patronizing, about why testing is so expensive, complicated, and difficult to estimate. Even better, invite your colleagues to think through the testing challenge themselves (perhaps assisted by some hints from you). When presented with some recent project history, with indications of what testing was (or wasn't) done, most of your colleagues will reach common-sense conclusions. If managers ask you to reduce the amount of testing resources or to squeeze the testing into a shorter time, respond positively. It can be done, but this will increase the risk that faults will be left in the product or that there will be gaps in the knowledge of what the product can and cannot do. The release decision would then be made with less data and, therefore, less confidence. The impact of lateness may be greater than the impact of faults, and this is a choice to be made by the project stakeholders.

Estimation in a Vacuum

Very early in the project life cycle, the prospective or actual testing manager will probably be called upon to estimate the duration and cost of testing. The typical response is, That's impossible! We have no requirements yet! We don't know the risks! We don't know how many faults the developers are going to leave in there. We don't know how severe the faults will be. We don't know how long the developers will take to fix them. And so on. Strictly speaking, the time required to plan and execute all tests is indeterminate. The following are some of the challenges of estimating in a vacuum:

- To estimate the time required to plan all tests, you need to have defined and agreed on the types of testing required, as well as some target levels of black-box and white-box coverage. These coverage targets cannot be used to prepare estimates until you have some idea of the size and complexity of the requirements and the software that will be built to meet those requirements. You then need to know what levels of productivity your (not yet recruited) testers can achieve.

- To estimate the time required to implement and execute tests, you need to know what technical test environments will be required and what levels of technical support will be required. Of course, you then need to know how long it will take to build test databases and configure your test environment. Beyond that, test execution would be easy to estimate if all tests were going to pass, but of course they will not. How many faults will be found? How will the faults affect your test execution plan? How severe will the faults be? How long will it take for the developers to fix them and for your testers to retest and regression test? And so on....

Even with previous experience on similar projects or when using reliable metrics, you will still probably apply a significant contingency figure to be on the safe side.

We described in Part I of this book an approach to risk-based master test planning by consensus, but you may be pressed to provide estimates before having the opportunity to follow such a process. Although the risk analysis will later help you refine your estimates, you need some initial figures so that the project manager can prepare a budget for the overall project. Of course, the project still might not yet have the full go-ahead. The proposed budget will be used to help the senior management make that decision.

A major problem with estimates made at a very high level is that, because they are unsubstantiated by lower-level detail, management often adds a dose of optimism into the mix, and your estimates may be pruned or your contingency removed if it sticks out too much. Estimates that are not properly justified will be challenged or simply thrown out. Yet, management tends to set time targets based on pride or on real or imagined pressure from above, and managers lose credibility if dates are not met. The project may not even get off the ground if the estimates are unacceptable.

Table 19.1 presents some guidelines for setting estimates. The steps in estimates 1 to 4 are linked because the best estimating includes a bottom-up estimate, a top-down estimate, and one or more sanity checks; however, the estimates you can actually make depend on what data you have. For example, if there are no detailed requirements, the development estimates will probably be as good as anything else to base the testing estimates on. At least then the development and testing estimates will have some consistent basis! And, of course, our suggestions are somewhat arbitrary at the detailed level. Where numbers or percentages are presented, use your experience to adjust them—use our numbers with caution and as an initial guesstimate. Imagine you heard someone in a bar quote them to you (if that helps you not to take them too literally). Put them up on a whiteboard in front of your team and discuss them. The guesstimates will stimulate a valuable discussion and lead you to a better estimate.

Table 19.1
Guidelines for Setting Estimates

Estimate 1	• This estimate is based on the idea that it takes as long to test a product as it takes to design and build it.
	• Take the estimate for technical design and documentation plus development (excluding any testing at all) and match that number. Call it FUNCTESTBUDGET.
	• Ask the developers what proportion of FUNCTESTBUDGET their unit and integration testing should take up. Call that DEVTESTBUDGET.
	• Subtract DEVTESTBUDGET from FUNCTESTBUDGET to leave INDEPTESTBUDGET. Document an important assumption: that your team will have sign-off authority on the developers' unit and especially integration test plans. This may seem overbearing, but if testing is neglected at any stage, the price will be paid (with interest!) later.
	• Divide INDEPTESTBUDGET into 75% allocated for functional system test (SYSTESTBUDGET) and 25% for user acceptance test (USERTESTBUDGET).
	• If you believe that there will be a substantial amount of nonfunctional testing, provide for up to 25% of FUNCTESTBUDGET in addition. (If you need stringent performance testing, use the maximum 25%; otherwise, choose some lower figure, such as 15%.)
	• The total test budget for staff resources is therefore FUNCTESTBUDGET + 25% (or whatever uplift you choose for nonfunctional testing).
	• Then add a figure for the cost of test tool licenses that you believe you will incur. If you do not know what tools you need, ask one or more vendors what to budget. If they exaggerate the figure, they risk losing the business! Tools can cost up to $100,000, or even $150,000, depending on the complexity and scale of your technical environment. Cheap tools can be used with care.
	• Finally, ask your technical architect to estimate the cost and effort required to build three independent functional test environments (say, for unit plus integration plus system testing overlapped for most of the functional testing period) and one production scale performance test environment available for 2 months. Add that to your total estimate.

Table 19.1 (continued)

Estimate 2	• If you have detailed requirements (or designs) that you believe will allow you to specify system tests in enough detail, estimate how many test conditions can be found on each page by scanning a few typical pages of the requirement, then multiply the average number of conditions per page by the number of requirements pages. Then divide this number by the number of test conditions a typical tester can identify and document per day (we suggest 50 test conditions per day for this). Call the resulting effort (number of person-days) required to document test conditions N.
	• Then add $2N$ for the effort required to prepare test scripts, test data, and expected results. If finding or preparing test data is hard in your case, or if audit requirements necessitate very detailed scripts, use $3N$ (or even $4N$ in extreme cases).
	• Then, add another $3N$ for the effort required to execute the tests, as prepared. This assumes a typical level of trauma during system testing: environment difficulties, plus retests.
	• If you need a full clean regression test run thereafter, add a further N.
	• The total cost of system testing will then be between $7N$ and $9N$.
	• Compare this with the estimate for system testing derived from Estimate 1 above; take the more realistic figure, or the greater figure if you are unsure.
	• Allocate an additional budget of one-third of the system test budget for user-acceptance testing.
	• For other parts of the testing effort, you may still use the figures from Estimate 1 above.
Estimate 3	• If you have a list of software risks, convert each into a test objective. Estimate costs for meeting each test objective in turn. Allocate each test objective to a test stage. Assume no optimization of test objectives or testing. Assume all risks are in scope. Publish the risks, test objectives, and estimates in detail, and publish costs for each test stage. Compare these with the figures above.
Estimate 4	• If you have done the risk analysis and have consensus on the scope of testing, estimate as you would in estimate 3, but only on the risks in scope. Do not optimize further.

The scheme outlined above is, of course, somewhat arbitrary, but it is based on our experience. Who is to say this is enough testing? At least you have a "straw man" that you can discuss with other management. For the purpose of setting an initial testing budget, you can start with some numbers and explain how you calculated them; if these formulas give estimates which you do not believe, then use your own assumptions (and, ideally, data from previous comparable projects).

Inversion of the Tester's Role

We described earlier how and why testing often suffers a credibility problem, and how to address that. But there are risks in going too far in the other direction: The developers may come to believe that the testers are responsible for all testing. Even worse: If testing is so good, then developers might take less responsibility themselves for producing quality products in the first place. Also, testers could be burdened by extra responsibilities that they may not be able to perform properly with the time and resources available.

Externally imposed testing late in the life cycle is less effective and more expensive than earlier quality and testing discipline self-imposed by the developers. It is therefore important for testers to explain the importance of the developer's role in the overall test process. If system and acceptance testers try to please other groups too much, a codependent relationship can develop. This is one example of a situation we call inversion because instead of testers being dependent on things to test and baselines to test against, other groups try to make themselves dependent on testers. This is codependency indeed. Expressions that spring to mind include the tail wagging the dog or putting the cart before the horse. This may be caused either accidentally (through a lack of understanding of the tester's proper role) or deliberately (by taking advantage of the tester's desire to add value, or even by trying to divert attention from problems elsewhere in the project)!

Test managers must be wary of being pulled into situations such as the following:

- System specifiers and designers want to know how their products will be used in testing before they refine the requirements.

- Developers want to phase development in increments, but cannot decide how until the testers tell them in what sequence and on what dates they want to test things.

- Business analysts prioritize requirements only after system tests generate incidents.

- Trainers cannot decide on a training schedule for the users until the testers tell them exactly which user individuals will be testing on which days.

- The project manager relies on the testers to tell them what really is going on (rather than believing official progress reports).

- The project manager relies wholly on the testing manager to decide when to release or go live (rather than taking responsibility for the decision based on information from not only test management, but also business and technical managers).

We have seen all of the above on recent projects. The last two are not inversion as such, but represent excessive reliance on testers, and we have suggested the proper alternative in parentheses. For the inversion situations, the remedy must be to explain the reality of the project life cycle to those who seek to distort it. Testers are not there to take over everyone else's job or to take the blame for every imperfection on the project. Where they can add value within their capabilities and available time, they should be happy to do so. Each testing manager needs to position the testing function carefully within the project's organization and culture by deciding how much to take on, being clear with others about the scope of the role, being consistent, and not promising more than can be delivered.

Testing Stages, Teams, and Environments

The risk-based testing method described in this book helps us to produce an MTP that allocates risks and the techniques that address them to stages of testing. The first step in taking the work forward from the MTP is to fit the desired stages to manageable teams of people and to test environments that are available or procurable. Figure 19.2 shows a typical staged test process based on the W-model approach (which we introduced in Chapter 4). In addition, we need to consider the need for acceptance of the system by users and their management. This is typically done by a specific stage of acceptance testing, which is needed on e-business projects just as it is on any other. Acceptance testing mitigates a different set of risks to the previous test stages up to and including LSI testing. During these earlier stages, the risks relate to whether the system and its interfaces contain undetected faults, whereas acceptance testing is more concerned with the risk of the business being unable to implement a system that purportedly meets a set of specifications. There is also an element of confidence building to acceptance testing in that it demonstrates that the risks have already been mitigated.

Often, we have to recruit a separate test team for system testing, although that same test team could then be retained to carry out LSI and/or acceptance testing (the latter under user/business management). Typically, the development team is responsible for both unit and integration testing. Each team will ideally have its own testing environment, but it may be

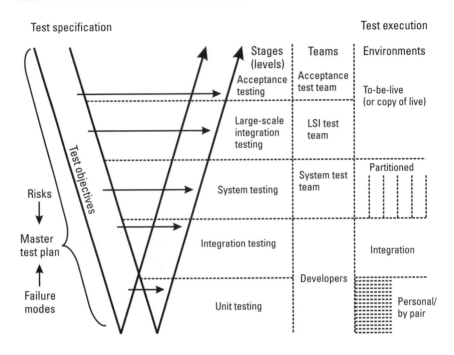

Figure 19.2 Risk-based testing stages in the W-model.

possible (and perhaps necessary) to share an environment: for example, acceptance testing may use the same environment as LSI testing.

Getting, Organizing, and Keeping Resources

In recent years, the term *resources* has tended to refer to human resources. We favor the original, broader definition that includes all human, technical, physical, and equipment resources required by a test manager to achieve the test objectives. Testing resources includes all of the peripheral essentials like office space, furniture, stationery, and, of course, test environments. The first three may be surprisingly difficult to obtain and retain, but the primary resource with which we are most often concerned is the test environment.

Environments

Since the client/server architecture first appeared, test environments have become more complicated. Nowadays, a large e-business test environment might include legacy test beds, PC labs for browser-compatibility testing, and a large assortment of Web servers, application servers, other specialized servers, firewalls, and load balancers. The servers can at various times be used either in their complete configuration or in subdivided groups, and with single or multiple instances of software and database components.

The need for multiple test environments (to support multiple stages of testing) hasn't changed, and the only ways to reduce this requirement are either to reduce the number of testing stages or to increase the overall testing time. So, the MTP must balance the number of stages of overlapping testing with the environments you think you have a chance of obtaining. The more environments you obtain, the more leverage you can (in theory) acquire by promoting deliveries of software early into new fault-detection arenas. One might think that overlapping stages of testing would tend to detect and be held up by the same software failures, but in reality, the different viewpoints and objectives of each test stage for the most part tend to expose different faults. The main difficulty with multiple test environments (other than the cost of them and of staffing multiple testing teams to use them) is the CM overhead, or more commonly, the threat of chaos if CM is insufficiently sophisticated and responsive.

Environment availability and usage should be planned out in a Gantt chart or similar diagram, just as human resources usually are. Figure 19.3 shows an example from a recent project. In the situation depicted, there were four environments. We had the luxury of testing Release 1 on the hardware

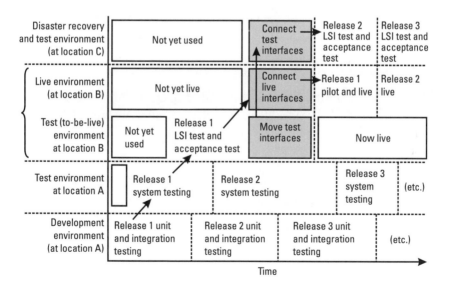

Figure 19.3 Sample usage of environments.

that was to become the live environment. There was, however, the complication of sharing parts of that environment with another e-business project in the same organization (which was going live at about the same time). We were fortunate to be able to test Release 2 onwards on an environment almost identical to live, this being the disaster recovery environment. Obviously, we would need to relinquish it immediately in the event of a disaster, but for the remainder of the time we could use different parts of it for different levels of testing (including performance testing, which took place in a near-live-scale environment). This overall scheme of environments worked very well, though we recognize that many projects will be more constrained and will have to make compromises.

Rex Black's book, *Managing the Testing Process* [6], offers some guidance on stocking a test lab, although it focuses mainly on the office and workstation environments. The literature on test environments in general is sparse, although some conference papers are helpful.

Staffing

The usual challenges of getting human resources are worse than ever in the e-business world. The latest skills are scarce, and although you can train people, they may then leave for more money. The cynical view is, of course, to lure people ready-trained from other organizations. The virtuous approach is to provide training, then to make people so happy they won't want to leave. We believe, however, that the skills crisis is exaggerated and is partly caused by the cynicism just mentioned. There are plenty of skilled testers around who are willing (and usually able) to learn new skills. The depth of knowledge required for Web technologies and toolkits is not too high and can therefore be learned relatively easily, although it does seem that old-world testers have more difficulty with object orientation (OO). This is just as much a problem with old-world developers, however, and is caused by a genuine paradigm shift. The skills can be learned, but not always just by reading a book; the language of OO is unashamedly and pervasively different from what has gone before, and it is necessary to work through examples and exercise the OO thinking end-to-end.

The day-to-day problem is, however, that there is rarely the time (or justification) to train people within an individual project, so the usual approach is to find informed users from within the business and technically qualified external consultants or freelancers to fill the more specialized testing roles. This presents a real challenge when it comes to recruiting nonfunctional testers: Usability, performance, and security testing are specialized areas where skilled people can be hard to find, and the best ones are nearly always busy. Prospective hires may present impressive-sounding résumés. Do not be fooled into believing that anyone who has used an automated tool knows how to do automated regression or performance testing. A tester who has conducted usability or security tests may have no idea how to plan such tests. When you meet with specialized testers, be sure to involve someone with experience in that area in the interviews to ensure that you probe the right areas of prospective testers' backgrounds.

It is often difficult to justify full-time nonfunctional testers. Management may expect nonfunctional tests to be done in short, cost-efficient bursts at a late stage in the testing. When software is delivered late or turns out to be unstable, however, the testers you have hired to conduct these short, sharp tests may not be available to you. It may be difficult to reschedule the testers' involvement and you may have to pay them whether they test or not.

These problems are magnified for security testing, which is a fast-moving and arcane discipline. A security expert may not always be a very practical tester, be keen on writing progress reports, or be able to communicate in very accessible language, but he or she is likely to be in high demand and so will not see these matters as such a problem. Security testing is particularly susceptible to regression problems; the smallest change in functionality or configuration can be enough to expose a vulnerability, and in theory, all security tests need to be run again. It would be awkward, to say the least, if it turned out that the vulnerabilities that could not be rechecked (perhaps because the security testing budget ran out just before deployment) were to be exposed in a live security breach.

You may be lucky in resource selection, perhaps finding, for example, a functional tester who can also design and lead a performance test, or a technically oriented integration tester who also knows security. The chances are, however, that you'll need individual specialists, and so, you must schedule carefully. Although they charge high daily rates, specialized consultancies are probably the most reliable and flexible source of targeted nonfunctional testing skills (especially for performance, security, usability, and configuration testing). One approach that the testing consultancies will be delighted to discuss with you is outsourcing a specific part (perhaps an entire stage) of the testing, although only system testing and LSI testing are really suitable for this.

Integration testers tend to need technical skills. System testers theoretically do not need to be so technical because black-box testing requires only testing expertise and the ability to read the system's specifications. Given the large number of test methods presented in Part III of this book, however, system tests might include functional-, nonfunctional-, and black- and white-box-oriented methods. If the system still does not work smoothly at the system testing stage, and project management cannot wait for another integration testing cycle, then the system testers may need enhanced diagnostic powers to report faults effectively and enhanced flexibility to make much progress at all! Also, in an incremental environment, system testers will need to specify or custom-build test utilities, stubs, and drivers—a technically oriented task. So, the reality is that your system test team will benefit if it includes at least some technically competent staff who can provide technical support to the rest of the team, rather than having the team rely on the developers.

Retention

Getting resources is one thing, retaining them is another, and you must pay attention to this. For example, after you have gone live, the folks who set up and supported your test environments may assume that you don't need them any more. In an incremental project, however, you may need to have another test bed set up because you now have to test bug fixes to the live system, in addition to supporting all the stages of testing on the next release. If timescales and system stability allow, you may be able to merge two stages of testing together to compensate for the extra environment. It may also be that you have done enough nonfunctional testing to relinquish an environment.

Keeping staff can also be a challenge. Managers from the business (especially the best ones) may be drawn away to the next big project. Permanent staff seconded to your project may get bored, see opportunities elsewhere within the company, or simply feel that to leave for another project would do their career more good than staying on. Business users might simply wish to return to their normal jobs because they prefer line management to project work, or they might be forced to do so because their departments are struggling without them.

Freelance consultants or contractors are often mobile and flexible, but this can work both ways. The best ones are in demand and can justify high fees, and thus, might leave for better offers. When people commute long distances to work or spend long periods away from home, personal pressures may cause them to leave your project for an easier life. Contracts are sometimes written to the advantage of the employer, so that the project can terminate before the contract term, but the contractor cannot. It is unwise to tie contracts to the original planned end dates of pieces of work, because projects often slip. What happens then is that contractors might be leaving at a crucial time when it is not feasible to replace them. The obvious pressure on you puts them in a commanding position when negotiating a new rate! Setting up annual or six-month contracts that start with a few weeks' probationary period and stipulate one month's notice from either side is probably the simplest solution. There is still the risk of losing a good contractor at an inconvenient time, but this will encourage team leaders to hone their motivational skills and not take people's loyalty for granted.

Specifying Tests

Having agreed on an organizational structure, planned the testing effort overall, and obtained some resources, you can get on with specifying tests in more detail. An early consideration here is terminology. If your organization has standards, you should adhere to them, unless you can justify good reasons not to. If you have no agreed-on in-house set of testing terms, however, the next best alternative is to use the industry standards [7–9]. These will cover most of the terms you need, although you can supplement them with you own project-specific definitions. You might even use the glossary presented at the end of this book. Terminology in such a complex and precise discipline as testing can be problematic, however.

The more sophisticated the testing strategy, the more time and energy are needed to explain terms and persuade people to stick to them. Writing a glossary is a good starting point (an appendix to the MTP is an obvious place to put it), but is not by itself sufficient: You cannot expect project staff and stakeholders to read it in bed every night. Once people start using a term, they will tend to remember it and will not appreciate being asked to change. So, as soon as possible, define your working terminology and adhere to it. Be relentlessly consistent without appearing pedantic. In this way, the terms will become ingrained in the project team's vocabulary.

In many projects, the terms that give rise to the most contention are those that define the actual stages of testing. Component, unit, module, program, and object testing might all refer to the first stage of testing, which is performed by programmers on their own software. Link, or integration testing (in the small), refers to subsystem testing that aims to ensure that assembled components are consistent. Functional system testing aims at demonstrating that the functionality of the system as a whole meets its functional requirements. Nonfunctional system testing addresses the variety of nonfunctional attributes of a system: performance, security, usability, and so on. Acceptance testing is associated with contractual handover, whether internal or external to the organization. LSI testing covers the consistency and interoperability of multiple integrated systems.

Although the above definitions are commonly understood, they are not sacrosanct, and it is important that everyone understands each stage in terms of the test objectives it addresses. The true definition of each test stage is how it unambiguously contributes to the overall test objectives without omissions or unnecessary overlap.

Having decided which stages of testing will use which document(s) as a baseline (and communicated this in the MTP), each team can then get on to specifying its own tests. The test specification process must allow for stepwise refinement of the tests, so that the testers can initially set out what they want to test and the constraints on doing so (test design). Then, they prepare test cases, procedures, data, and expected results in enough detail for them to be executed (test preparation). It is worth highlighting some guidance concerning the test materials to be prepared.

Stage Test Plans

The test plan for a testing stage should set out not just the intended scope of the tests, but also their priorities. The test objectives set out the overall ambition in a stage, and all tests should reference one or more test objectives. Each objective relates to a single risk, and the risk prioritizations set out the highest-level priorities for the testing. There are, in effect, two levels of coverage to be achieved in a test plan:

1. The test objectives themselves must be covered by sufficient tests to provide enough evidence and confidence that the risks have been addressed.

2. The features and functionality described in a baseline document or the structural aspects of the software itself must be covered by sufficient tests to meet the coverage target in the plan.

Typically, coverage matrices (cross-references of coverage items to tests) are used to ensure that the coverage targets are clear and that they are met. Coverage matrices are a good format for review by stakeholders, perhaps represented by business analysts, who should be encouraged to specify where they recommend that more (or perhaps fewer) tests be specified. This review should be done before committing a significant effort to test design so as to minimize the rework required to address review comments.

Test Design

Test design is the most difficult and important step in test specification. We think of it as distributing all the items from the structured shopping list of the test plan (the scope and priority of what is to be tested) onto the available resources (environments and people). This takes us from a logical list into a physical structure of specific tests, or at least groups of tests. The core of the test design is a table of tests plotted against time and resources, acting as a framework for the next step, test case specification (which defines each test case and expands it into as much detail as necessary).

A test design is already, in effect, an outline test execution schedule because it shows what can be run in parallel and what must be run serially, and it sets out a physical sequence. When test procedures (or scripts) are prepared, some tests may expand or contract in scope or complexity, and inter-test dependencies may change. So, this is the time to fine-tune and confirm an explicit test execution schedule, showing which testers should be doing what tests in which environments on which dates. If this is not done, then it is a leap of faith to assume that we can ever get through all the tests in time (and it will be a struggle to present accurate and credible progress reports).

Expected Results

A policy decision is needed for each test stage on whether to specify explicit or implicit expected results. Explicit expected results are easier to check against at execution time, but they are, of course, directly affected by the actual test data values. They, therefore, require much more amendment when anything changes. If the scripts allow testers to choose data values at test execution time, typically according to some stated guiding framework, then the corresponding expected results must be implicit (and the test procedures must provide guidance on how and when to translate implicit expected results into explicit ones).

Where test data is taken or converted from existing systems, perhaps for the deliberate aim of realism, it is easier to go for the implicit option. This situation is likely to be part of acceptance testing, where the scripts should be guiding the business users in doing their jobs, not spoon-feeding them with explicit test steps. The most suitable place for explicit expected results is in system testing, which should include some test data contrived specifically to exercise unusual conditions. If the data is being written explicitly, it is convenient and sensible to make the expected results explicit.

Stage-Specific Considerations

In the remainder of this chapter, we describe some particular considerations that apply to the late stages of testing:

- Testing interfaces with other systems (in LSI testing);
- Acceptance testing viewpoints.

These stages are worth special attention because they are very visible and important to stakeholders as the go-live date approaches.

Testing Interfaces with Other Systems

The difference between a Web site and an e-business application is that the Web site is simply the front-end to the application. The Web site part is like the tip of an iceberg: the part you see, the part that attracts all the attention. The whole system is much bigger, however. The complexities of end-to-end processing based on a fragile front-end, potentially offered to an unlimited number of customers (with no user training), are many times those of a simple Web site. We must take this into account when we plan e-business testing. This is one reason we don't throw away all the old rules; we are testing large, sophisticated systems on which businesses are highly dependent.

Developers may tend to think only about the new front end and immediate interfaces. But back-end legacy systems may need enhancements to cope with the new usage, and even if they do not, different legacy systems could be used in ways that have not been exercised before. Legacy systems (being impossible or at least expensive to replace, and perhaps difficult to modify safely) are often front-ended. The new functionality, and most developer attention, is focused on the new front-end. Much of the complexity lies, however, in the existing systems, in interfacing robustly with them, and in the coherence of modified business processes end-to-end, so the overall testing job is much larger and more challenging than that for just the new functionality.

These risks must be given enough time, attention, and clarity in the risk workshops. Then, for each interface, test conditions must be derived using specific knowledge of how the interface works or is supposed to work. The usual suspects for potential faults are data validation mismatches, null messages, empty batch files, undetected missed runs, interfaces being exercised erroneously more than once, daily cut-off times, and so forth.

Although it is technically correct to test first with stubs and drivers, then to exercise the built interface, the principle of earliest-possible risk reduction suggests that a test version of each interface should be set up as soon as possible. It may be helpful for unit and integration testing to use test interfaces, then for system testing to revert temporarily to stubs and drivers to get the most flexible exercising of the application itself.

The most common pitfall with interfaces is obvious, yet not trivial: It is that of incorrect assumptions (examples of which we have already listed), typically exacerbated by distant or infrequent communications between the teams involved, and perhaps also by a degree of complacency. Despite apparent simplicity, interfaces nearly always, in our experience, throw up at least one late scare on a project, often something unbelievably glaring and basic. Our advice to LSI testers is broadly as follows:

- Be particularly persistent in chasing and checking specification documentation of interfaces. Don't accept the common excuses like there isn't any documentation, there never has been, or here's the documentation, but it might be a bit out of date. If necessary, tabulate the message flows for yourself, and query anything that isn't clear.

- Keep talking. Much of the problem with interfaces is that the people responsible for different systems may not meet regularly, may not speak the same language (for example, Unix as distinct from legacy mainframe), and may be organizationally, even geographically, distant.

- Take advantage of any opportunity to test, even in the production environment just before go-live (and even after that, if feasible!). It may be difficult to check some interfaces properly in anything other than the live environment. Finding a fault after deployment might be embarrassing, but not as embarrassing as having a customer find it for you.

Acceptance Testing Viewpoints

When planning acceptance testing, we seek to merge (economically) the different viewpoints that each needs to build confidence in the system and in its fit with business and operational processes. In an incremental project life cycle, acceptance testing spans the transition from multiple, partial subsystems to accepting the complete system (or group of systems). The acceptance viewpoints to be considered are typically those of the following:

- Business users (will the staff who actually use the system day-to-day accept it?);

- Business operational management (will the staff who manage and depend on the system as part of their business operations accept it?);

- Technical operations (will the staff who provide operations support, monitor performance, perform backups, and the like accept it?);

- Technical support (will the staff who provide first-line support of the system in production accept it?).

In an e-commerce project, user acceptance is more complex than it is for, say, an intranet project because the real customers are out in the public domain, spread around one or more countries. Also, the customers did not directly specify the system. This is not a problem peculiar to e-business systems of course. Vendors of mass-market software products and other software packages have always had to test on behalf of their end-users. Software houses often make use of beta programs as an alternative to formal acceptance testing. It is possible to implement partial releases of Web services to selected customers, but there is the obvious risk that a beta site deployed on the net is also accessible (unless specific precautions are built in) to noncustomers, competitors, and hackers or crackers.

Business acceptance testing (including user and business operations acceptance) applies to both Internet and intranet systems because management will want to ensure that they get what they want. Typical tests here will focus on usability and supply-chain issues. Business acceptance tests might be derived from system-level tests that demonstrate that the key functionality operates effectively. LSI tests are often based on the need for business management to see that the flow of business from enquiries through sales orders, delivery, and billing are working correctly.

Technical operations acceptance testing is the concern of the staff who manage and maintain the e-business system as part of the overall technical architecture. Typical operations tests relate to the ease by which the system can be shut down, restarted, backed up, restored, and made secure, so these tests tend to be oriented towards nonfunctional risks. Further, the operations activities may need to take place without disrupting the availability of either the service to its users or of other systems that share the same technical infrastructure, in addition to complying with technical standards and procedures.

In summary, acceptance testing needs to cater to both the customer-business and technical operations support viewpoints. The most effective and efficient way is to combine these into a single set of realistic scenarios that simulate the interaction of supply-chain transactions while performing both operations and technical support activities. Typically, these tests need the entire technical infrastructure and a significant level of coordination between the various test teams.

First of all, all the acceptance viewpoints need to be represented at the risk workshops. When it comes to test planning and execution, we strongly recommend that the acceptance tests be rehearsed during earlier stages, most likely as part of system testing and LSI testing. Part of the reason for this is acceptance testing's role in building confidence: We want to minimize the occurrence of any new functional bugs at this stage. As long as the appropriate business or operations teams specify the tests, this does not compromise their independence unduly. The acceptance test process should still provide the necessary assurance that the systems will work in production. Rehearsing the acceptance test conditions finds problems earlier, allowing a clean run of acceptance testing proper (or at least a cleaner run than would otherwise have occurred).

A variation on this theme is needed if the project life cycle is incremental. Ideally, we would wait until the system is finished before taking the valuable time of business people, but we want to minimize the risk of unpleasant surprises too near to the go-live date. So, in addition to the rehearsal of acceptance tests in LSI testing, we can have the acceptance team witness some of these tests and perhaps participate in them too. The acceptance tests proper are not run until all the functionality is complete and the major faults have been eliminated from the system. The acceptance team will see each new delivery of functionality soon after it becomes available, increasing their confidence early and building it up incrementally. This has the obvious benefit of ensuring their involvement and buy-in throughout the project, not just at the end.

References

[1]   Kruchten, P., *The Rational Unified Process—An Introduction,* 2nd ed., Boston, MA: Addison-Wesley, 2000.

[2]   Lewis, W. L., *Software Testing and Continuous Quality Improvement,* Boca Raton, FL: Auerbach, 2000.

[3]   Patton, R., *Software Testing*, Indianapolis, IN: Sams, 2001.

[4]   Copeland, L., "When Helping Doesn't Help: Software Testing As Co-Dependent Behavior," *Proc. 6th EuroSTAR Conf.*, Munich, Germany, November 30–December 4, 1998.

[5]   Bradley, K., *PRINCE: A Practical Handbook*, Oxford, UK: Butterworth-Heinemann, 1993.

[6]   Black, R., *Managing the Testing Process*, Redmond, WA: Microsoft Press, 1999.

[7]   Institute of Electrical and Electronics Engineers, *Standard for Software Test Documentation IEEE Std 829-1998*, New York: IEEE, 1998.

[8]   British Standards Institute, *Software Testing—Part 1: Vocabulary BS 7925-1:1998*, London, UK: BSI, 1998.

[9]   Institute of Electrical and Electronics Engineers, *IEEE Standard for Software Engineering Terminology ANSI/IEEE Std 0610.12-1990*, New York: IEEE, 1990.

20

E-Business Test Execution

Setting an appropriate test coverage target is a difficult part of test specification, but it is even harder to meet that target overall to the end of test execution. There are several factors that contribute to the erosion of coverage. *Erosion* is a sensible choice of terms as the word truly reflects the little-by-little reduction of the scope of planned tests and the inevitable realization that not all of the planned tests can be executed in the time available.

The erosion of test planning coverage occurs in several stages between the MTP's preparation and the start of test execution:

- The MTP identifies the risks to be addressed and the approach to be used in addressing them. The MTP also presents the testing budget available (already a compromise) to conduct the tests in the plan.

- Poor, unstable, or unfinished system requirements, designs, and specifications make test specification harder. Typically, the planned coverage of the system is somewhat compromised by the lack of detail in the specifications or by the apparent expense of some features.

- Technical constraints, such as the late availability or inadequacy of test environments, make certain planned tests impractical or unmeaningful. LSI tests, for example, may be impossible to execute as planned because not all interfaces required can be made available simultaneously. Performance testing might be a waste of time because only a small-scale environment is available for testing.

- Late delivery of software into test environments means that, when deadlines remain fixed, the amount of testing "in scope" is diminished. (The perennial optimists in most projects vainly believe the project won't suffer the fate of most others; they think, we have a mitigation plan to claw back the slippage, or that activity is noncritical path, and so forth.)

The erosion of test execution coverage then takes place in several stages after the software has become available for test:

- If the quality of the software to be tested is poor on entry to a test stage, running tests can be particularly frustrating. The most basic tests might fail, and the faults found could be so fundamental that the developers need more time to fix them than anyone anticipated. If testing is suspended because the software quality is too poor, the test execution schedule will run over deadline (or tests will be descoped if a deadline is fixed).

- Where more faults occur than were anticipated, the fix-and-retest cycle will take more time, reducing the time available to complete the test plan.

- When time runs out and the decision to release is made, not all of the test plan may have been executed: Either some tests were never reached in the plan or some faults that remain outstanding block the completion of the failed tests. Where the go-live date has not moved, this is the classic squeeze of testing.

Dealing with test coverage erosion is one of the challenges the test manager faces in all projects. Things never go smoothly, and where the testing is under pressure, reducing coverage is usually the only option for keeping the project on track. We have said before that it is not wrong to reduce the amount of testing; it is only wrong to reduce the testing arbitrarily. Consequently, when making choices on which tests to cut, the impact on the test objectives (and risks) needs to be assessed and the stakeholders who originally identified the risks need to be informed. Where the impact is significant, the test manager ought to convene a meeting of those who are asking for the cuts (typically, project management) and those whose interests might be affected by the cuts (the stakeholders). As usual, the test manager should facilitate the subsequent discussions.

Incident Management

Once the project moves into the system and acceptance testing stages, it is largely driven by the incidents created during test execution. These incidents trigger activities in the remainder of the project, and the statistics about them provide good insight into the status of the project at any moment. When categorizing incidents, we need to think ahead about how that information will later be used. We will discuss decision making later, but first we need to decide on a scheme for incident severity and priority.

An incident is broadly defined as an event that occurs during testing that has a bearing on its success. This is a broader definition than most testers adopt because it includes events that might never result in a change to a system or its documentation. An incident is raised when the software fails to exhibit the behavior predicted by a test. Events that are outside the control of the testers, however, like machine crashes, loss of the network, or even a lack of testing resources, might also be logged as incidents. Whether you adopt this definition or limit incidents to test failures only is up to you (although we would strongly recommend that you log nontest failure events in a diary at least). Incident management is about logging and managing the response to these events. Whatever incident management process you adopt, we advocate assigning both a priority and a severity code, defined as follows, to all of your incidents:

- Priority is assigned from a testing viewpoint and is the main influence on when the fault will get fixed. The tester should decide whether an incident is of high or low (or whichever intermediate degree is allowed) priority. The priority indicates the urgency of this fault to the testers themselves and is based on the impact that the test failure has on the rest of testing.

- Severity is assigned from a user's viewpoint and indicates the acceptability of the fault found. The end users or their management should assign severity, or be able to override the testers' initial view. The severity reflects the impact of that fault on the business were the fault not to be fixed before go-live. Typically, a severe fault makes the system unacceptable. If a fault is of low severity, it might be deemed too trivial to fix before go-live, but could be fixed in a later release.

A high priority incident, by definition, stops all testing. If no further testing can be done and (at that point in the project) testing is on the critical path, then, in effect, the whole project stops. If a failed script stops some, but not all, testing, then it might be considered a medium-priority incident. An incident might be considered low-priority if all other tests can proceed. Table 20.1 presents a scheme for assigning incident priority. Table 20.2 presents a scheme for assigning incident severity.

It is important to bear in mind with the classification schemes set forth in Tables 20.1 and 20.2 that not every urgent incident is severe and not every severe incident is urgent. In this particular sample set of codes, we have also

Table 20.1
Incident Priority Codes

Incident Priority	Priority Description
0	*Critical:* All streams of testing for this stage (e.g., system testing) are halted
1	*Urgent:* One or more streams of testing are halted for this stage, but testing can continue in other streams
2	*Nonurgent:* No streams of testing for this stage are halted, but modifications or compromises to other tests may be necessary
3	*Minimal:* There is no effect on test execution, other than incorrect results
4	*Improvement:* The testware is to be corrected or extended for future runs

Table 20.2
Incident Severity Codes

Incident Severity	Severity Description
0	*Not negotiable (or worth evaluating further):* The problem absolutely must be fixed
1	*Major:* The problem affects a large or particularly important part of the functionality or nonfunctional characteristics; the release overall could not be allowed to go live with this incident outstanding
2	*Significant:* The problem affects enough of the functionality or non-functional characteristics to have an adverse effect on the business, but could be worked around, and release overall could go live provided that workarounds are adequate
3	*Minor:* The application does not conform to its specification, but the release overall could go live without unacceptable adverse effects
4	*Enhancement:* The application does conform to its specification, but still may not meet business needs

embedded the distinction between "fails to conform to specification" and "specification needs changing," although in a contractual situation, the latter might necessitate a separate change request.

Incident management is about logging test failure events and using that information to control progress through the debugging, fixing, and retesting activity. When testing closes, the incident log will provide the data on outstanding incidents required to make the release decision. Incidents are usually formally logged during system and acceptance testing, when independent teams of testers are involved.

Much has been written on incident management (see, for example, [1]), but one source of potential conflict that arises in larger projects is worth mentioning. Where multiple outsourced development companies are involved in a project, it can be difficult to agree on ownership of resolution. The developers may believe the tests are invalid, the database vendor may blame the application software and vice versa, the smart-card-interface programmers may blame the browser plug-in, and so on. The causes of problems may be controversial, and in a few cases they may be genuinely shared and require a team effort to resolve. Do not underestimate the degree of flexibility required in your incident-management process or the amount of senior-management involvement needed to agree on responsibility. Large sums of money might be at stake, and some suppliers' professional reputations might also take a dent.

Testing in a Live Environment

You might think, initially, that testing in a live environment is one of those taboos so basic that it should never even be contemplated. Conducting any test activity in a live environment is risky and ought to be very strictly controlled, but there are some specific areas where testing crosses the boundary into live operation. In some circumstances, very careful testing in a live environment might be of some benefit in that it addresses risks not adequately testable before. We have given names to these areas of testing, but these names are nonstandard. We have used one or more of the following activities on some of our own projects and suggest you consider what value they might have for you before you dismiss them:

- *Prelive testing:* towards the end of acceptance testing, where we might try out aspects of the live environment before we deploy our live production system;

- *Pseudolive testing:* at and immediately after the go-live point, when we test that the installation into live has been done correctly, and we run confidence tests as part of live operation;

- *Pilot:* where we try out the system with a limited number of customers (if possible and useful), collecting information on user experiences while carefully monitoring the system's performance;

- *Postdeployment monitoring:* a routine part of e-business operations already discussed in Chapter 16.

Prelive Testing

Before deploying the system live, we want to know not just that it works in the test environment, but that the links from the live Internet will work and the system works fully end-to-end. The dilemma here is to balance the risk of the testing missing some factor against the risk of exposing the system to harm before it is ready. We do not want attackers to practice their exploits on our test environment. Neither do we want customers and potential customers to see the system until we are ready. One of the most important parts of prelive testing is to check very carefully the scope and results of all security testing to date before fully connecting to the Internet.

Pseudolive Testing

After the deployment installation is complete, you might check that the full installation is in place and works before customers start to access the system. In essence, a check is made that all of the installation components are in place and then a few selected user-oriented system transactions are executed to make sure a user would not find an obvious problem.

Pilot

Another option for a risk-managed implementation is a pilot, during which (if we can engineer controlled access to the system) a small number of customers are gradually introduced. As this happens, the performance, availability, and stability of the system are carefully monitored. If the system depends on smart cards for access, this control is relatively easy. If your system is open to the public, you might disable new registrations, but allow logins of prepared accounts that you have set up for your pilot customers. One can consider a pilot as a beta test of sorts, but really, it is a very limited rollout of the system to allow you to monitor the vital signs of your systems for problems.

Managing the End Game

The ultimate objectives of our e-business project are to deploy a live e-business solution with known risk and to continue this risk management after deployment. We call the final stages in our test process the end game because the management of the test activities during these final, possibly frantic and stressful days requires a different discipline from the earlier, seemingly much more relaxed period of test planning.

Many years ago C. Northcote Parkinson stated the law [2] that has since borne his name: that work expands to fill the time available for its completion. This implicitly assumes that the time available is more than adequate. But software projects are not like that, particularly e-business projects. Many software projects are underestimated, and they often overrun because arbitrary, sometimes political, deadlines are set and then not moved, or at least not moved enough, even when it has been recognized that the project is bigger (or its difficulties more real) than management planned for.

Someone has probably already produced an alternative law to Parkinson's more suited to today: that work does not contract to fit the time allowed for its completion. To a small extent, work can be squeezed into shorter timescales with fewer resources: Humans are very adaptable, and the right degree of stress (and other motivations) can take advantage of a degree of elasticity. There are limits, however, and the result is often more haste, less speed.

One of the values of the risk-based test approach is that where testing is squeezed late in a project, we use the residual risk to make the argument for continuing to test or even adding more testing. Where management insists on squeezing the testing, testers should simply present the risks that are the trade-offs. This is much easier when an early risk assessment has been performed, used to steer the test activities, and monitored throughout the project. When management is continually aware of the residual risks, it is less likely that they will squeeze testing in the first place.

People need deadlines to focus on, and if a deadline is too far away then people tend to relax somewhat. Deadlines based on realistic estimations of the small activities that make up an overall task are the answer, but all too often, deadlines are set without reference to detailed estimates. The information required to estimate a project may simply not be available at the time the plan needs to be set. Getting the balance right between commercial pressures and achievable reality is the biggest challenge of all. Commercial pressures necessitate ambitious plans, to give our business managers a chance to excel (or at least to survive). Reality means planning to take account of risk.

The role of the testers in a software project is to identify the product risks of concern and focus attention on managing those.

Whatever the size of the project or the prevailing culture, we plan for risks, we measure them throughout the project, and we use residual risk to decide when to go live. E-business projects want to get as close as possible to their target dates while taking on an acceptable level of risk. The two keys to success are (1) for testers to know what the risk is at all times, and (2) for testers to contribute to a consensus decision. The first requires responsive and accessible management information systems within and around the project. The second requires a suitable forum facilitated by testers throughout the project.

References

[1]   Kaner, C, J. Faulk, and H. Q. Nguyen, *Testing Computer Software,* 2nd ed., New York: Van Nostrand Reinhold, 1993.

[2]   Parkinson, C. N., *Parkinson's Law, or The Pursuit of Progress,* New York: Penguin, 1957.

Further Reading

Schaefer, H., "Strategies for Prioritizing Tests Against Deadlines," http://home.c2i.net/schaefer/testing/risktest.doc, 2002.

Appendix A:
Essential Web Technologies for Testers

HTTP	The Hypertext Transfer Protocol (HTTP) is the set of rules for exchanging files (text, graphics, sound, video, and other multimedia files) on the World Wide Web. HTTP is an application protocol compared to TCP/IP, which is a lower-level networking protocol.
URL	A uniform resource locator (URL) is the address of a file or resource accessible on the Internet. The type of resource depends on the Internet application protocol. Using HTTP, the resource can be an HTML Web page, an image file, a program such as a CGI script, a Java applet, or any other file supported by HTTP. The URL contains the name of the protocol required to access the resource (usually HTTP), a domain name that identifies a specific computer on the Internet, and a hierarchical description of a file location on the computer (e.g., http://www.evolutif.co.uk/subdir/index.html).
HTML	Hypertext markup language (HTML) is the set of markup symbols or codes inserted into a file intended for display on a browser page. The markup tells the Web browser how to display a Web page's words and images for the user. Each markup code is called a tag. Most tags come in pairs that indicate when some display effect is to begin and when it is to end. The HTML standard is managed by the World Wide Web Consortium (http://www.w3c.org) and is generally adhered to by the major browsers.

CGI	The common gateway interface (CGI) is a standard way for a Web server to pass a Web user's request to an application program and to transmit data back to the user. When the user requests a Web page (for example, by clicking on a highlighted word or entering a Web site address), the server sends back the requested page. When a user fills out a form on a Web page and sends it in, however, a server-based program usually processes it. The Web server typically passes the form information to a small application program that processes the data and may send back a confirmation message.
	This method or convention for passing data back and forth between the server and the application is the CGI. It is part of the Web's HTTP protocol. CGI scripts are Perl, C++, or other programs that execute on the server. ASP (see below) is simply a special implementation of the CGI mechanism.
Cookies	Cookies are small amounts of data stored by a browser on the user's hard drive at the invitation of a Web site. Cookie data is sent with every HTTP request and response for that Web site. Cookies normally contain information about a user.
	A transient cookie, sometimes called a session cookie, disappears when the user's browser is closed. Unlike a persistent cookie, a transient cookie is not stored on your hard drive, but only in temporary memory that is erased when the browser is closed. A transient cookie is created by simply not setting a date in the set-cookie option when an application creates the cookie. To create a persistent cookie, an expiration date is set and the cookie is stored on the user's hard drive until the expiration date or until the user deletes it. Transient cookies are often used to enable a site to track the pages that a user has visited during a session so that information can be customized for the user in some way.
How a Web page works	You select a target URL in your browser by using the URL window or clicking on a link. The browser sends an HTTP request for the HTML file to the site defined by the URL. If there is a cookie stored on your computer for this Web site, the cookie accompanies the HTTP request. The server processes the request; sets up a connection, sends the HTML file in a HTTP message back to the client browser and closes the connection. The Web server includes the cookie information as part of the HTTP message. The browser interprets the HTML information in the HTTP message and displays it according to HTML standards.
JavaScript, VBScript	These are programming languages (somewhat similar to Java and Visual Basic) used to provide functionality within a Web page on the client or on servers. Typically, these scripts are used to perform automatic page formatting, change a formatted date on a Web page, create and manipulate new windows for links to appear in, and cause text or a graphic image to change during a mouse rollover.

ASP and JSP	Both Microsoft's Active Server Pages (ASP) and Sun's Java Server Pages (JSP) are types of scripted Web pages that can display dynamic content requested by a Web browser. Both technologies use HTML to determine page layout. For generating content and querying databases or other applications, ASPs rely on programs written in embedded Microsoft scripting languages (VBScript or JavaScript), while JSPs use Java programs.
Applets	Written in Java, an applet is a small program that can be referenced within a Web page and downloaded to a client's browser. Java applets can perform interactive animations, immediate calculations, or other simple tasks without having to send a user request back to the server.
Servlets	Similar to CGI scripts, Servlets are programs written in Java that usually execute more quickly than CGI scripts because they require fewer server resources.
Statelessness of the Web	After processing an HTTP request, the server forgets everything about the transaction. Developers need to maintain context through business transactions and use cookies or hidden form fields to do this. Testers should ask how developers maintain the context of business transactions and design tests of this mechanism.

Appendix B:
Web Testing Using Home-Brew Tools

Nontechnical testers might think that building your own test tool is impossible or too ambitious to consider. Developers might think building a test tool is an interesting challenge that provides temporary casual programming recreation, then just write it on the fly. A sensible attitude is at least to consider what home-brew tools could do and how sensible it would really be to build your own tool. This section describes some potential opportunities for building your own tools, but you should seriously consider whether it is a sensible option before proceeding. Elisabeth Hendriksen's article "Build It or Buy It" [1] provides a broader discussion of two myths: we can build that and just go buy something. What follows is a description of the potential of dummy pages and test drivers that require a relatively small amount of programming knowledge to implement.

Using Dummy HTML Forms to Test Components

If the user interface is not yet available or stable, it can be easier to implement tests of Web server–based components using dummy Web pages. Although more appropriate for developers performing component-level testing, there are advantages to later testers adopting such methods to speed up their system or acceptance testing. Using dummy Web pages to drive tests can save a lot of time. Figure B.1 shows an example of using a dummy Web page to drive server-based forms handlers. On the left-hand side is a window displaying a dummy page. Clicking on one of the links on the left-hand window

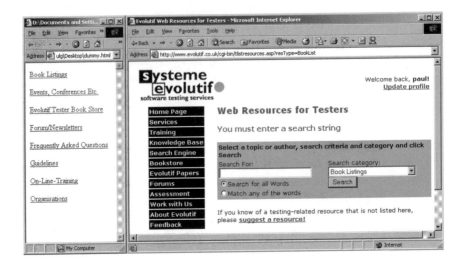

Figure B.1 Using a dummy page to test server-based code.

sends the HTTP message to the Web server, and the browser displays the results in the new browser window on the right. When a new link is clicked, the window on the right is created and displays the results of the transaction initiated.

The HTML source code for the dummy page on the left is shown below. The anchor tags (the <A> </A> pairs) implement HTTP GETs of the URL identified in the HREF attribute. The component under test is an Active Server Page called tlistresources.asp in the cgi-bin directory of the Evolutif Web site.

```
<a href="http://www.evolutif.co.uk/cgi-bin/tlistresources.asp?resType=BookList"
target="_test">Book Listings</a>
<p><a href="http://www.evolutif.co.uk/cgi-bin/tlistresources.asp?resType=Event"
target="_test">Events, Conferences Etc.</a>
<p><a href="http://www.evolutif.co.uk/cgi-bin/tlistbooks.asp?resType=BookStore"
target="_test">Evolutif Tester Book Store</a>
<p><a href="http://www.evolutif.co.uk/cgi-bin/tlistresources.asp?resType=Forum"
target="_test">Forum/Newsletters</a>
<p><a href="http://www.evolutif.co.uk/cgi-bin/tlistresources.asp?resType=FAQ"
target="_test">Frequently Asked Questions</a>
<p><a href="http://www.evolutif.co.uk/cgi-bin/tlistresources.asp?
resType=Guideline" target="_test">Guidelines</a>
<p><a href="http://www.evolutif.co.uk/cgi-bin/tlistresources.asp?resType=
OnLineTraining" target="_test">On-Line-Training</a>
<p><a href="http://www.evolutif.co.uk/cgi-bin/tlistresources.asp?resType=
Organisation" target="_test">Organizations</a>
```

If you look closely at the first line of HTML above, you will see that it generates the underlined link labeled Book Listings in the left-hand window. When you click on this link, the browser sends an HTTP GET message, referencing the following URL: http://www.evolutif.co.uk/cgi-bin/tlistresources.asp?resType=BookList. The resulting page generated by the ASP file is displayed in the window on the right. The HTML allows you to do this with the target attribute in the anchor <A> tag. The target="_test" attribute tells the browser to open a new window labeled _test and display the results in that window. If the window already exists, it will be reused. Moving and resizing windows on the desktop can make for a convenient layout.

It is easy to click on each link in turn and verify that the correct page listing appears in the window on the right. Consider how you might generate this HTML from a simple database containing just two columns of data: URL and parameter resType. We have used the Word mail-merge function to generate large HTML dummy pages with dozens of links to execute test cases from template files and prepared test data.

Alternative techniques involve the generation of dummy forms rather than simple links. Many, many forms can be displayed serially on the same Web page. Each form contains the fields that would have been supplied using the real Web page in the application, but is generated by a database. With forms you can implement both HTTP GETs and POSTS, and in this way, simulate both types of transaction in a realistic, but simple way. There are some issues relating to the set up of cookies and potentially to application and session variables on the Web server, but your developers should be able to create simple server-based scripts to ensure these are correctly set up. This is a more advanced topic, outside the scope of this book.

Clearly, to implement such facilities you need some detailed knowledge of HTML and the way forms, GETs, and POSTs work. However, if you can get the help of your developers or bring a developer into the test team, it should be a simple task to build some very effective dummy forms for your server-based code.

Using Test Drivers to Test Components

This section is slightly more technical, but we suggest that you read it even if you are a nonprogrammer. Our aim is to explain how simple it can be to create a simple test driver and provide some reference information for programmers to take advantage of.

In our own projects, we at Evolutif have built simple automated test drivers using Visual Basic and Access databases. The drivers simulate a real browser sending HTTP requests to retrieve Web pages and execute server-based code. In this way, we have run functional tests that execute 40,000 transactions in a single test run.

Creating and running a manual test of 40,000 transactions are probably impractical. Creating and running such large tests using proprietary test execution tools that drive the browsers could also pose a significant challenge if the user interface is complex. Homegrown drivers that use the application programming interface (API) may be an economic alternative, particularly if large numbers of similar transactions need to be tested.

Proprietary tools driving the user interface are expensive, but easy to use. They generate complex GUI scripts and force the tester to navigate perhaps slow, complex application scenarios to reach the server-based component under test.

Home-brew test driver tools that simulate the HTTP messages transmitted by a browser and drive server-based code can be cheap and easy to use and eliminate slow navigation through complex application scenarios. They are less good at verifying actual results against expected results because you would have to write quite complicated comparison code for your test driver. One way of making results checking easier is to get component developers to add extra instrumentation code to their component. This would write execution results into comments embedded in the HTML that is returned to the browser (or test driver). By searching for HTML comments, the test driver might be able to perform some simple results checking. For example, a comment in the HTML page written on output from the server component might say

```
<!- TESTRUN: 9999 MESSAGE: Successful Completion ->
```

The driver could be programmed to search for the comment and TESTRUN string in the returned HTML and then to search for the MESSAGE: text within the HTML comment. A few lines of Visual Basic, Perl, or C++ would be sufficient to enhance the driver into a quite capable test tool. When the component has been tested, the debug feature in the component code under test could be removed or commented out.

We strongly suggest that you investigate the use of test drivers for at least the higher volume functional test transactions because this approach may save you a lot of time. Also, because the drivers avoid the need to write complex scripting code to handle the user interface, your scripts will require minimal maintenance if (when) the user interface changes. If developers write such drivers, the burden of functionally testing server-based components may shift to the developers (a good thing!) System testers could perhaps reuse the developers' test drivers to explore more complex and higher volume scenarios.

The Simplest of Test Drivers

Figure B.2 shows a very simple test driver written in Visual Basic. It consists of a single window that allows you to enter a URL address and execute an HTTP GET request to fetch a Web page. The HTML code in the Web page

Figure B.2 The simplest of test drivers.

is displayed in the larger scrolling text field. At the bottom of the window, the lower text field contains the status of the HTTP request. You enter a URL (I used http://www.microsoft.com) and click the GO button. The HTML code for the Microsoft home page is displayed. How simple is that?

The Visual Basic code for the driver is listed below:

```
Private Sub Command1_Click()
   Inet1.URL = Text1.Text
   Text2.Text = Inet1.OpenURL(, icString)
End Sub

Private Sub Inet1_StateChanged(ByVal State As Integer)
   Text3.Text = GetState(State)
End Sub

Function GetState(s As Integer) As String
Select Case s
   Case 0
      GetState = "No state information is available."
   Case 1
      GetState = "Looking up the IP address for the
      remote server."
   Case 2
      GetState = "Found the IP address for the remote
      server."
   Case 3
      GetState = "Connecting to the remote server."
   Case 4
      GetState = "Connected to the remote server."
   Case 5
      GetState = "Requesting information from the remote
      server."
   Case 6
      GetState = "The request was sent successfully to
      the remote server."
   Case 7
      GetState = "Receiving a response from remote
      server."
   Case 8
      GetState = "The response was received successfully
      from the remote server."
   Case 9
      GetState = "Disconnecting from the remote server."
```

```
Case 10
    GetState = "Disconnected from the remote server."
Case 11
    GetState = "An error has occurred while
    communicating with the remote server."
Case 12
    GetState = "The request was completed, all data
    has been received."
Case Else
    GetState = "Unknown state: " & FormatNumber
    (State, 0)
End Select
End Function
```

The driver uses the Internet transfer control (INET control). The INET control is simply a piece of software, freely available from Microsoft, that handles all of the complexity of setting up the Internet connection, sending and receiving HTTP messages, and synchronizing the responses. The control can perform both HTTP GETs and POSTs, and you can supply parameters (as if entered on an HTML form) to simulate completely the interactions a user might experience when using Internet Explorer to access a Web application. The INET control is very easy to use.

There are only three functions required for the simplest of drivers. One function executes the HTTP request. The other two functions deal with the text in the status field (and this isn't essential to the testing, really). Table B.1 describes each of the three functions.

Table B.1
Descriptions of the Simplest of Test Driver Functions

Function	Description
Command1_Click()	Called when the user clicks the GO button. First, it sets the control's target URL. Then, it calls the control and sends the HTML response to the larger scrollable text field.
Inet1_StateChanged	Because the HTTP request can take some time to complete, this routine is called when the state of the INET control changes. The control goes through a series of states as the request progresses. It displays the states in the lower text field. The state is obtained from the function GetState.
GetState	GetState provides a translation of the state code to a piece of text.

As I hope you can see, the programming effort to create the simplest of test drivers is tiny. (It only took me 10 minutes to create it.) It takes only two Visual Basic statements to execute the simplest HTTP transaction. The reason for presenting this in this book is to demonstrate the ease with which the most trivial test driver can be built. Show this to your developers and then ask them how long it would take to enhance the test driver to do the following:

1. Read a prepared set of test data values and expected results from an external file or database;

2. Make the program loop and repeatedly read parameters defining the HTTP verb to use (GET or POST) from the external file and to construct the call to the INET control;

3. Capture the HTML from the system under test and append it to an actual results file (that could be opened and read by your browser);

4. Get the developers to identify a set of actual outputs and embed them within an HTML comment on the Web server output to be interpreted by the test driver.

5. Scan the returned HTML looking for the result embedded in an HTML comment, compare it with the expected result in the prepared test data, and write a pass/fail record in a test log.

These requirements for a test driver identify most of the facilities required to execute a potentially very large number of tests of a single, server-based component with a large number of potential data input combinations. Work out what facilities are the most important and the variations on these requirements that have most value to you as a tester.

On more than one occasion, we have built simple Microsoft Access databases for technical testers to manage their testware. Using the databases, testers could build up template scripts, parameter definitions, test data, and expected results. The database could generate test scripts written in a very simple scripting language. The test driver we wrote parsed and interpreted these scripts and executed tests according to the script. In this way, we separated the nontechnical testers from the detailed technicalities of the test driver. The effort required to build these tools was less than 1 month, but over a period of 6 months, the tool was used to execute hundreds of thousands of tests.

Personally, I use Visual Basic and Access to build my tools. In the Unix community, Perl, C, C++, and Java are popular programming languages capable of being used to build your own test tools. There are thousands of freeware utilities and tools available for download off the Web. Downloading and amending existing tools is a fast way to get your own customized versions, but this method is only for experienced programmers. One source of reusable code that I have found useful in the past is the SourceForge.Net Web site. Searching for "test tool" at http://www.sourceforge.net brings up over 100 projects that are building and supporting test tools. Many are still under development, but there are plenty of other products to investigate.

Reference

[1]   Hendriksen, E., "Build It or Buy It," http://www.qualitytree.com, 2002.

Further Reading

Sweeney, M. R., *Visual Basic for Testers*, Berkeley, CA: Apress, 2001.

List of Acronyms and Abbreviations

ADSL   asymmetric digital subscriber line

API   application programmers' interface

ASP   active server pages

BIT   business integration testing

BVA   boundary value analysis

CAST   computer-aided software testing

CGI   common gateway interface

CM   configuration management

CRM   customer relationship management

CSS   cascading style sheets

DDOS   distributed denial of service (attack)

DNS   domain name system

DOS   denial of service (attack)

DSDM   Dynamic Systems Development Method

DTD   document type definition

EJB   Enterprise Java Beans

EP   equivalence partitioning

ET   exploratory testing

FAQ   frequently asked questions

FMEA   failure mode and effects analysis

FTA   fault tree analysis

FTP   file transfer protocol

GUI   graphical user interface

HTML   hypertext markup language

HTTP   hypertext transfer protocol

IE   (Microsoft) Internet Explorer

IIS   (Microsoft) Internet Information Server

ISP   Internet service provider

JSP   Java Server Pages

LSI   large-scale integration (testing)

MTP   master test plan

PDA   personal digital assistant

PDF (Adobe) portable document format

PHP personal home page (tools)

PID project initiation document

QA quality assurance

RAD rapid application development

RUP Rational Unified Process

SIAM Systeme (Evolutif) integration analysis methodology

SIT systems integration testing

SSL secure sockets layer

SUMI software usability measurement inventory

UML Unified Modeling Language

URI uniform resource identifier

URL uniform resource locator

USDP Unified Software Development Process

TPN test priority number

TPW test process worksheet

VB (Microsoft) Visual Basic

WAI Web Accessibility Initiative

WAP wireless application protocol

WML wireless markup language

XML   extensible markup language

XP   extreme programming

Glossary

Acceptance criteria A set of targets to be met by a test stage to plan when to stop testing

Acceptance testing Formal testing conducted to enable a user, customer, or other authorized entity to determine whether to accept a system (or, less commonly, a component or subsystem where external suppliers are involved)

Accessibility The ease by which users with disabilities can use a system

Ad hoc testing Unplanned, undocumented testing

Alpha testing Simulated or actual operational testing at an in-house site not otherwise involved with the software developers

Applet An application embedded in a Web page, written in Java

Application system testing The process of testing an integrated system to verify that it meets specified requirements

Attacker (hacker, cracker) An individual or organization that threatens the security of your Web service

Availability A measure of the time a system is up and running, normally expressed as a percentage

Backup and recovery testing Testing of the procedures used to make backups and perform recovery from failures

Baseline A document that describes the behavior of a system: a requirement, specification, or design to test against; strictly, the specific version (and date) of each such document that is to be used

Behavior The combination of input values and preconditions and the required response for a function of a system

Beta testing Operational testing at an external site not otherwise involved with the software developers

Black-box testing (functional testing) Test case selection that is based on an analysis of the specification of software without reference to its internal structure

Boundary value analysis A test case design technique in which test cases are designed to include boundary values

Browser page testing Testing of the functionality available within a Web page that does not exercise server-based components

Browser syntax compatibility checking Verification (normally automated) that HTML is compatible with a browser type

Business integration testing Tests that provide confirmation that the systems, processes, and people work as an integrated whole to meet an organization's objectives

Business object A real-world entity of interest to business users

Business volumes Quantities of business transactions used to size a database or plan a performance test

Candidate risk A potential risk identified and added to the risk register, not yet analyzed

Cardinal business objectives A principal (business) aim of a project

Cascading style sheet A separate file on a Web server containing reusable style definitions, referenced by Web pages

Common gateway interface The mechanism that enables a Web page to invoke functionality residing on a Web server and to receive output from it

Cognitive walkthrough A detailed review of a sequence of steps that an interface requires a user to perform in order to accomplish some task

Collaborative usability inspection A systematic examination of a finished product, design, or prototype from the point of view of its usability by intended end users

Compatibility tests Testing whether the system is compatible with other systems with which it should collaborate

Component A minimal software item for which a separate specification is available

Component (unit) testing The testing of individual software components

Condition A Boolean expression containing no Boolean operators; for instance, A<B is a condition but A and B is not

Configuration testing Tests that aim to demonstrate that Web applications will operate correctly on a range of client hardware, operating system, and browser combinations

Content checking Checking of the content of Web pages for accuracy, completeness, consistency, and correct spelling

Context testing Tests whether weird paths through the application and irregular network connectivity do not disturb the workings of a Web site

Continuous testing Continuity of testing and monitoring of systems into production

Control flow graph The diagrammatic representation of the possible alternative control flow paths through software

Cookie   Small amounts of data stored by a browser on the user's hard drive at the invitation of a Web site

Coverage   The degree to which a test case suite has exercised a specified coverage item, expressed as a percentage

Debugging   The process of finding and removing the causes of failures in software

Denial of service attack   Attempt by an attacker to disrupt or disable your Web service

Distributed denial of service attack   Where an attacker makes use of other sites to amplify an attack on your servers

Dynamic testing   Testing that involves the dynamic execution of tests of software

E-business   The conduct of business on the Internet

E-commerce   The buying and selling of goods and services on the Internet

Equivalence class/partition   A portion of the component's input or output domains for which the component's behavior is assumed to be the same from the component's specification

Error   A human action that produces an incorrect result

Error guessing   A test technique where the experience of the tester is used to postulate what faults might occur and to design tests specifically to expose them

Expected outcome   The behavior predicted by the specification of an object under specified conditions

Exploratory testing   Test design and test execution at the same time; a systematic approach to error guessing

Extranet   A private network that uses the Internet to share part of a business's information or operations securely with suppliers, vendors, partners, customers, or other businesses

Extreme programming   A pragmatic approach to program development that emphasizes business results first and takes an incremental, get-something-started approach to building the product, using continual testing and revision

Failover testing   Tests that aim to verify that designed-in recovery features maintain the service for end-users when failures occur

Failure   Deviation of the software from its expected delivery or service

Failure mode   A way in which a system can fail (that gives cause for concern)

Failure mode and effects analysis   A systematic way of identifying modes of failure and preventing their occurrence

Fault (bug, defect)   A manifestation of an error in software; a fault, if encountered may cause a failure

Fault tree analysis   A method used to analyze the cause of hazards

Firewall   A set of related programs, located at a network gateway server that protects the resources of a private network from users from other networks

Freeware   Software that is offered at no cost

Good enough   A set of criteria for deeming a product or system as acceptable, which acknowledges that products need not be perfect at the moment of release

Hazard   A state or set of conditions of a system that, together with other conditions in its environment, will lead to a failure

Heuristic evaluation   A systematic examination of a user interface to judge its compliance with recognized usability principles (the heuristics)

HTML validation   An automated inspection of HTML code to verify it meets the requirements of the HTML standard

Incident   An unplanned event occurring during testing that has a bearing on the success of the test; most commonly raised when a test result fails to meet expectations

Inspection   A group-review quality-improvement process for written material

Instrumentation   The insertion of additional code into the program in order to collect information about program behavior during its execution

Integration   The process of combining components into larger assemblies

Integration testing   Testing performed to expose faults in the interfaces and in the interaction between integrated components within a system (as distinct from large-scale integration testing, which is between systems)

Intranet   A private network using Internet technology contained within an enterprise to share information and computing resources between employees

JavaScript   An interpreted programming or scripting language used in server-based components or within the HTML of Web pages

Large-scale integration testing   Testing of the interfaces between systems and the consistency of use of data shared by or transferred between those systems and the business process that uses those systems

Link checking   Verification that the links in HTML Web pages reference the correct objects and those objects can be loaded

Load balancing   Software features that distribute the load between servers according to predefined rules

Load generation   The use of automated tools to simulate a user community executing transactions

Load profile   The specification of a load that a system might experience in production

Localization (testing)   Verification that a system's user interface and functionality has been successfully translated to another region's language

Master test plan   A document describing the overall approach, process, and policies for the testing in a project

Nonfunctional testing   Testing of those requirements that do not relate to functionality (e.g., performance, usability, and reliability)

Object load and timing   Tests that measure the time taken to load an object on a Web page

Object life cycle   The series of transformations of data that describes a real-world entity across systems

Penetration test   An attempt to subvert the security countermeasures of a system to demonstrate that they are effective

Perl   A programming language often used to write CGI programs most often on Unix- or Linux-based Web servers

Performance testing   Testing conducted to evaluate the compliance of a system or component with specified performance requirements

Ping   A basic Internet program that lets you verify that a particular IP address exists and can accept requests

Postdeployment monitoring   Automated monitoring of a Web service to detect failures in production

Process risk   Risks relating to the internal management of a project

Product (work product, deliverable)   A deliverable from any stage or activity of a project

Product risk   Risks that relate to shortcomings in the work products of a project

Project risk   Risks that relate to the external dependencies and influences of a project

Regression testing   Retesting of a previously tested program following modification to ensure that faults have not been introduced or uncovered as a result of the changes made

Reliability testing   Tests that verify that a product or system can deliver its service for an extended period without failure

Resource monitoring   The use of software tools to monitor the usage of resources in a system

Response time   The time it takes a system to return control to users after they have initiated some activity on the system

Retesting   Repeating previously run tests, usually to test that faults have been implemented correctly; sometimes used to include regression testing, which has a more specific meaning

Risk   A threat to one or more of the cardinal objectives of a project that has an uncertain probability

Risk analysis   The process of assessing the relevance, consequence, and probability of a risk

Risk-based testing   Testing oriented towards providing information about product risks

Risk consequence (loss, impact)   The potential loss or impact if a risk materializes

Risk identification   The process of identifying the risks of concern to a project

Risk management   The process of identification, assessment, response, monitoring, and control of risk

Risk probability (likelihood)   The probability that a risk will materialize

Risk register   The document or database that records all the risks of concern

Risk response   The planned activity intended to address a risk

Root cause   The ultimate cause of a failure traced back through the series of events that lead to the failure

Scalability   The measure of a system's ability to be upgraded to accommodate increased loads

Scripting language   In the context of test tools, the programming language used by a test tool in its test scripts

Script kiddie   An immature but dangerous exploiter of security holes on the Internet

Security assessment   A review of a site's hardware and software configuration to identify security vulnerabilities

Security audit   Typically, an audit of corporate security policies and how well a site or organization adheres to them

Security testing   Testing whether a system meets its specified security objectives

Security vulnerability   A bug in a software product or shortcoming in a system's configuration that could be exploited by a security attacker

Sensitization   Choosing a set of input values to force the execution of software to take a given path

Server-based component testing   Testing of the components that reside on (typically Web) servers

Service testing   Testing of a system's performance, reliability, failover capabilities, and management procedures

Shareware   Software distributed free on a trial basis with the understanding that the user may need or want to pay for it later

Soak test   Tests of a system for an extended period to find (what are usually) obscure problems

Static analysis Analysis of a program carried out without executing the program

Static testing Tests of products that are human readable, such as requirements, specifications, designs, or code using inspection and review techniques or automated tools

Stress testing Testing conducted to evaluate a system or component at or beyond the limits of its specified requirements

Structural testing (white-box, glass-box testing) Test case selection based on an analysis of the internal structure of software

Subsystem testing Dynamic testing of components and subsystems prior to system testing (normally performed by developers)

Systems integration testing Testing of the interfaces between systems and the consistency of use of data shared by or transferred between those systems

System testing See application system testing

Test A controlled exercise having (potentially) several objectives, including detection of faults, risk measurement, and confidence building

Test case A set of inputs, execution preconditions, and expected outcomes developed for a particular objective, such as to exercise a particular program path or to verify compliance with a specific requirement

Test case design technique A method used to derive or select test cases

Test design Activity following test planning, but before test scripts are produced; also, a deliverable comprising a set of test cases

Test effectiveness An assessment of the potential ease by which a failure mode (risk) can be thoroughly tested

Test execution tool (test running, capture-replay tool) A test tool that records test input as it is sent to the software under test; input cases stored can then be used to reproduce the test at a later time

Test harness A testing tool that comprises a test driver and a test comparator

Test objective A high-level definition of the purpose of some tests (usually to address a specified risk or failure mode)

Test priority number The product of three risk scores (consequence × probability × test effectiveness)

Test script (procedure) A document providing detailed instructions for the execution of one or more test cases

Test stage A set of test activities collected into a manageable phase of a project

Thin client A low-cost, centrally managed computer with limited capabilities used to access server-based applications

Tool host The host machine upon which a test tool is installed

Transaction analysis An analysis of the transactions that trigger flows of data through integrated systems for the purpose of designing large-scale integration tests

Transaction flow testing The use of transaction flowgraphs to structure tests through a system or collection of systems

Transaction flowgraph A diagram representing the flow of control and data through integrated systems

Transaction link testing Tests that aim to verify the integration of the complete end-to-end functionality of a browser interface through to back-end systems

Transaction verification Tests that aim to ensure that the correct server-based component is invoked and that the parameters passed to the component are correct for a forms-based transaction

Unit testing See component testing

Usability testing   Testing the ease with which users can learn and use a product

V-model   Diagrammatic layout showing baselines and the stages of testing that test against them

Visual browser validation   Visual checks that the appearance and behavior of Web pages are consistent across different browsers

VBScript   An interpreted programming or scripting language used in server-based components, in particular, Active Server Pages

Web accessibility testing   Automated analysis of Web page HTML to ensure it meets defined accessibility guidelines

White-box testing   See structural testing

About the Authors

Paul Gerrard is the technical director and a principal consultant for Systeme Evolutif, Ltd, a specialized software testing services company based in London, United Kingdom. He has conducted consultancy and training assignments in all aspects of software testing and quality assurance. Previously, he worked as a developer, designer, project manager, and consultant for small and large developments. Mr. Gerrard has engineering degrees from the Universities of Oxford and London. He is currently the joint program chair for the British Computer Society Special Interest Group in Software Testing, a former member of the working party that created the *Component Test Standard BS 7925*, and a former chair of the BCS Information Systems Examination Board (ISEB) Certificate Board for Software Testing. He is a regular speaker at seminars and conferences in Europe and the United States, and he has won the award for best presentation at EuroSTAR '95. He is also Web master for several Web sites, including http://www.evolutif.co.uk.

Neil Thompson is an independent testing consultant and manager, serving blue-chip clients through http://www.TiSCL.com, either directly or in association with other consultancies. He has worked for 25 years in information systems, initially with a hardware manufacturer and two of the United Kingdom's leading software houses, then with an international user organization. He also has gained 10 years' experience as a management consultant with global firms.

Mr. Thompson has a wide perspective on the information systems business through his roles as a programmer, systems analyst, and project manager. He has shared the frustrations of users and the sleep deprivation of operators, and as a scientist with artistic tendencies, he now feels fulfilled as a testing expert.

He is a graduate of Cambridge University, United Kingdom, and a member of the British Computer Society (and its special interest groups in software testing and configuration management), as well as of the Institute of Management Consultancy (London, United Kingdom). He has spoken at testing conferences since 1993.

Index

Recent Titles in the Artech House Computing Library

Metadata Management for Information Control and Business Success, Guy Tozer

Multimedia Database Management Systems, Guojun Lu

Practical Guide to Software Quality Management, John W. Horch

Practical Process Simulation Using Object-Oriented Techniques and C++, José Garrido

Risk-Based E-Business Testing, Paul Gerrard and Neil Thompson

Secure Messaging with PGP and S/MIME, Rolf Oppliger

Software Fault Tolerance Techniques and Implementation, Laura L. Pullum

Software Verification and Validation for Practitioners and Managers, Second Edition, Steven R. Rakitin

Strategic Software Production with Domain-Oriented Reuse, Paolo Predonzani, Giancarlo Succi, and Tullio Vernazza

Systems Modeling for Business Process Improvement, David Bustard, Peter Kawalek, and Mark Norris, editors

User-Centered Information Design for Improved Software Usability, Pradeep Henry

Workflow Modeling: Tools for Process Improvement and Application Development, Alec Sharp and Patrick McDermott

For further information on these and other Artech House titles, including previously considered out-of-print books now available through our In-Print-Forever® (IPF®) program, contact:

Artech House	Artech House
685 Canton Street	46 Gillingham Street
Norwood, MA 02062	London SW1V 1AH UK
Phone: 781-769-9750	Phone: +44 (0)20 7596-8750
Fax: 781-769-6334	Fax: +44 (0)20 7630-0166
e-mail: artech@artechhouse.com	e-mail: artech-uk@artechhouse.com

Find us on the World Wide Web at:
www.artechhouse.com